MANUMISSION

The Liberated Consciousness of a Prison(er) Abolitionist

Ralph C. Hamm III

SECOND EDITION

[Fully revised and edited]

Little Red Tree Publishing, LLC,
North Platte, Nebraska, 69101

Copyright © 2012 and 2016 Ralph C. Hamm III

All rights are reserved under International and Pan-American Copyright Conventions. Except for brief passages quoted in a newspaper, magazine, radio or television review, no part of this book may be reproduced in any form or by any means, electronic or mechanical, including photocopying and recording, or by any information storage and retrieval system, without permission in writing from the publisher.

Layout and Cover Design: Michael Linnard, MCSD
Text in Minion Pro, Times New Roman, Trajan Pro and Ariel.

Second Edition, 2016, manufactured in USA
1 2 3 4 5 6 7 8 9 10 LSI 20 19 18 17 15 16

Library of Congress Cataloging-in-Publication Data

Ralph C. Hamm III
  Manumission: The Liberated Consciousness of a Prison(er) Abolistionist / Ralph C. Hamm III. -- 1st ed.
    p. cm.
  Includes selected bibliography, and index.
  ISBN 978-1-935656-43-2 (pbk. : alk. paper)
  I. Title. II. Prisoners. III. Prison reform. VI Education in Prisons.
PS3612.A58565S77 2016
811'.6--dc23

Little Red Tree Publishing LLC
North Platte, Nebraska 69101
www.littleredtree.com

Honorarium

An honorable mention is separately paid to Askia Toure—an unsung hero in Amerik.k.k.a's black consciousness movement, the original "black scholar"—one who was either the mentor of, or left an indelible impression upon, the psyche of every black AmeriKlan-made writer of the principal era spoken of within this book. Without Askia's influence there may not have been such a prolific Sonia Sanchez . . . no formation of The Last Poets . . . no all-encompassing Sun-Ra . . . no Amiri Baraka . . . nor a host of other poets who lent their creative substance to the black consciousness movement in this country between the years 1960-1980.

Without the bards, the poets, the musicians, the storytellers, there would not have arisen significant black consciousness within the walls of Walpole State prison to found the black prisoner self-help organization called Black Africans Nation Toward Unity (BANTU): an organization that relied heavily upon every word and phrase uttered by Askia's poet/ess class, as they took up the rallying call for us to unite and take the forefront in the struggle for prisoner and human rights when our so-called black political leaders left us hanging in the air or simply fell short of the mark.

Dedications

This book is dedicated to my companion and best friend Maria "Dada" Johnson, without whose faith, courage, and love, I would, in all probability, have succumbed to the forces of oppression many years ago.

To her daughters, Stacey, Tamara, and Stephanie, who are like my own; as well as to their husbands, Brian and Edwin, all of whom have welcomed me as a part of their extended family.

To the grandchildren of Dada: John, Darius, Damaris, Bria, and Braedon; five good reasons why the struggle against racism, ignorance, and repression are important—to secure a slavery-free future.

Contents

Foreword by Michael J. Linnard   viii
Introduction by Ralph C. Hamm III   xvii

Prologue:
    Into the light of understanding . . . into the fresh air.   xxi

---

Lesson 1: From Plantation to Constitutional Sanction.   1

    a. The birthplace of institutional slavery.   1
    b. The Thirteenth Amendment: From plantation to prison.   4
    c. Black illusions.   5

Lesson 2: The Truth Regarding the Massissippi Abolitiists.   11

    a. Who were the real abolitionists?   11
    b. Media resistance (cf., 1850s to 1970s).   23
    c. Anti-abolitionism vs. abolitionism, in Walpole.   25

Lesson 3: Massissippi Liberalism and the Caste System.   33

    a. White supremacy and racism.   33
    b. Unconscionable denial.   41
    c. Keep them in their place (a psychological profile).   45

Lesson 4: "Free Your Mind And Your Ass Will Follow."   53

    a. Recognizing domination.   53
    b. Paolo Freire methodology/ABE in Walpole Prison.   57
    c. Experimentation and success.   59

Lesson 5: Unequal Justice under the Law.   69

    a. The implications of *Dred Scott v. John Sandford*.   69
    b. Duplicity.   72
    c. Disparate and exorbitant.   76

Lesson 6: The Prison-Industrial Complex.   83

    a. Same game different name.   83
    b. The economics of human bondage.   86
    b. Profit sharing and propaganda.   91

Lesson 7: Preferences and Percentages in Mississippi Parole.   97

    a. Attachment to the leash and lash.   97
    b. Quotas and the race factor.   102
    c. A design to failure.   107

Lesson 8: Rude Awakenings (The Recapitulation).   119

    a. Another peek under the cowl.   119
    b. Revelations.   121
    c. Fading back and forth to black.   126

Epilogue: On Becoming BANTU.   131

Appendix:

A   COINTELPRO Revisited .   147
B   Trail Transcript Testimonial.   153
C   Opening Statement (to 9/15/99 Parole Board).   165
D   Appeal for Reconsideration (Parole Board Decision).   173
E   The "Cooperating Witness."   181
F   "Mississippi"   187

Selected Bibliography   191
Index   195
About the Author   204

FOREWORD

Having published three other books by Ralph C. Hamm III, I was asked to consider publishing a new edition of his major work of 2012, *Manumission: The Liberated Consciousness of a Prison(er) Abolitionist*. I willingly took on the task but soon realized that it was a book of substantial depth and range, reflecting Ralph's personal journey of self discovery and his ascendancy into a leadership role in prison reform, and his didactic aspirations for comprehensive "black consciousness."

I decided that the original cover design did not do full justice to the magnitude of the subject. I was inspired to design a new cover that would capture the historical nature of the black experience and some of the major characters involved in the original struggle against oppression toward manumission in its fullest sense.

Considering that the book was written over a 5 or more year period stretching back to 2007/8 and the tortuous editing process, which had to be undertaken while Ralph was denied access to a computer and very limited contact, it is a remarkable achievement. Richard Gawel-Cambridge, a great friend and personal supporter of Ralph's for many years, worked tirelessly to manage the editing and production process between Ralph and the printer. A great labor of love.

As I began to read and study the entire manuscript I developed a feeling that it would benefit from structural adjustments to the layout and editing. One was to develop a Prologue separate from the individual lessons. I also decided, because of the density of the writing and content, to reposition the extensive notes and references from the back of the book to the bottom of the page, so as to increase understanding and access. Needless to say I assiduously checked all notes and quotes, updating as required. I modified various Appendix's and added more. Regrettably, in the editing process, it became apparent that two major references and supporting text needed to be omitted from this edition. I established irrefutable evidence that one was fraudulently created and the other was a work of fiction.

The first was the fraudulently produced "Willie Lynch Letter," written by Dr. Kwabena Faheem Ashanti," in 1976, which has been used and lauded as genuine in the black community—and in some places continuing today—for many years as representing the systematic and organized repression of black slaves in 18th century in the Southern States of America.

The other was the "King Alfred Plan," a fictional CIA plan, which made its first appearance in the John A. Williams 1967 novel, *The Man Who Cried I Am*. Shortly after it was first published Williams actually reproduced the plan separately and distributed it on the New York subway, where it was picked up by the black community and assumed to be genuine.

However, the omission of both these documents does not diminish, in any sense, the powerful impact or integrity of the message. In fact the reality of modern black history is replete with many other damning documents and evidence of institutional racism and oppression at all levels of American society.

This is a book that should become required reading in all prisons and places of education where black history is taught. Ralph's own life is not only the history of personal tragedy, criminal injustice, and prison brutality, but the true expression of the human spirit to obtain manumission in its fullest sense.

Michael Linnard
Nebraska, 2016

In Memoriam

To the loving memory of my sisters, Gladys Hamm and Verna Johnson, both of whom were victims of medical malevolence.

Finally, to the memory of Professor Dante Germanotta, one who truly understood the importance of the educational concepts of Paolo Freire and the vision of the NPRA, thereby adding his flavor to the sauce. For making abolition, through creative education, more interactive, and a reality for not only the men confined within Walpole Prison, but also for his students from Curry College, who undertook the journey with him inside of the prison walls.

>[Ralph]
>Aluta continuaa!
>Ralph C. Hamm III

Special Thanks

To Jamie Bissonette, who has become more than a sister to me and encouraged me to write the first edition of this book following the reception given to *When The Prisoners Ran Walpole: A True Story In The Movement For Prison Abolition*. For over the past six years, she has counseled, supported, and championed my cause for manumission.

To Richard Gawel-Cambridge, whose unselfish support in forwarding me the reference books and materials required to fulfill my work has been invaluable—in the sense that without his assistance, this book would not have been written.

The dialectic that introduces necessity as a support for my freedom expels me from myself. It shatters my impulsive position. [. . .] black consciousness is immanent in itself. I am not a potentiality of something; I am fully what I am. I do not have to look for the universal. There's no room for probability inside me. My black consciousness does not claim to be a loss. It is. It merges with itself.
—Frantz Fanon, *Black Skin, White Masks*, 1952

ACKNOWLEDGMENTS

"Blessed are those who struggle to survive,
oppression is worse than the grave—
it is better to die for a noble cause,
than to live and die a slave."
—The Last Poets

A special acknowledgment goes out to those men who have, as slaves of the State, shared this struggle with me in one form or another. The following names have either fallen in the direct cause of abolition, or in later years as a result thereof:

Jerry Funderberg	Larry Williams
Frank "Parky" Grace	William Royce
Richard Devlin	Fred "Red" Williams
Carmen Gagliardi	Joseph "The Pollack" Subilowski
Joseph Corriea	John Kerrigan
Donald "Kela" Robinson	Jerry Sousa
Curtis Johnson	Sam Hunt
Roosevelt Smith	James Preston
"Giggie" Washington	Albert De Salvo
James "The Whale" Connors	William "Whitey" Hearst
Joe Gleason	Herbert "Beaver" Jones
Richard Guppy	Benny Butler
Ronald Pelletier	Robert "Big Bob" Heard
Steve "John Doe" Jenkins	David Royster
Herman Hunt	Harry Ambers
Sebastian Pina	Ronald Casseso
Stanely Bond	Alvin Cambell
John Gray	James Gallo
Mr. Reddick	Marshall O'brien

Joseph "J.J." Josepatis
Richard Baptiste
Henry Tamileo
Arnold "Butch" Jackson
Bruce Rumer
Ronald Stokes
Thomas Royce
Arthur Gagne
David Thomas
Bradford Boyd
"Cocaine Smitty" Smith
Walter Nelson
"Tiny" Dirring
Joshua Gens
George Pinto
Kenny Star
Vincent "The Bear" Flemmi
Perry Hooks
Lenny "The Coahog" Pardiseo
Ed White
James Robuchaud,
Bo Burns
Leroy Manning
Robert "Gonk" Gonsalez
Lamont "Legs" Brewer
Paul King
Charles Hawkins
William "Broadway" Bradford
Frank Coleman
Lawrence "Buddy" Burnett
John Cochise
Jimmy White

Ray Rich
Al Little
Richard Duarte
Dean Lecain
Andy Pomerance
Luman Funderberg
Raymond Lebeau
Elmo Johnson
Charles Smith
Leo Greco
George Pimental
Charles Holley
Richard Washington
Wayne Montgomery
Eddie Diaz
Thomas Brown
Doug Banion
"Miami Lou" Alexander
Ronnie Coleman
"Big Bill" White
"C-Note"
Lucious Aaron
Peter Enos
Robert Bonds
Al King
Robert Thompson
Albert Blake
Arthur Gauthier
Roosevelt Pickett
Norman Longville
Lebeau Long

. . . and to those former slaves of the state, whom I only know in spirit, that are interred within the graves of the Pauper's cemeteries outside of the walls of several Mississippi prisons.

$150 REWARD

RANAWAY from the subscriber, on the night of the 2d instant, a negro man, who calls himself **Ralph Hamm**, about 61 years old 6 feet 7 inches high ordinary brown color, 260 pounds and rather muscular built; baldy, has been raised on the plantation these past 40 years as a field hand, but somehow obtained a Doctor's Degree in Metaphysics, and was last seen in the Boston Commons lecturing the truth of Being to the masses for the past 18 months. I expect that he is still now in the Boston area trying to secure his escape to **Freedom** (in all probability back to the west coast of **Africa**), perhaps he may try to get employment on the lecture circuit. He is a para-legal, and is also handy in the capacity of a law clerk. Had on when he left a chambray blue prison shirt, and blue denim jeans, new—he had other clothing. I will give 50 dollars reward if taken in **Boston**; 100 dollars if taken one hundred miles from Boston in this state, and 150 dollars if taken out of this state, and delivered to me, or secured in any jail so that I can get him.

Kevin Burke

Salem, Ma.,

Introduction

As I moved into my third year of service upon my court-ordered-1969-second-degree life sentence to the Massachusetts Correctional Institution (MCI) located in South Walpole, Massachusetts; I had the distinct honor and privilege to assist in the founding of Black African Nations Toward Unity (BANTU). I was not yet twenty-two years of age.

I, along with black prisoners, Jack Harris, Henry Cribbs, Donald Robinson, Ronald Penrose, James Hall, James McAllister, Raymond White, Charles (2X) McDonald, Alphonso Pinckney, Sam Nelson, and Solomon Brown, comprised the cofounding internal board of directors of BANTU.[1]

We had banded together to embark upon an historic mission: to disseminate the life-saving benefits of black consciousness to the African American prisoners held captive within the walls of Walpole prison. Our singular mission was soon to evolve into an effort to resuscitate the entire Walpole prisoner population (black, white, and Hispanic) through an infusion/transfusion of cultural history and innovative educational concepts, utilizing the flexible format of the National Prisoners Reform Association (NPRA)—effectively a union for prisoners—as our springboard.

Later in the year 1972, I was fortunate to become one of the first internal board of directors for the MCI-Walpole NPRA via an election held by the general prisoner population. As a result of that election, I became one of the organization's first co-vice presidents. At the outset, the NPRA was a prisoner-elected umbrella organization designed to channel human and other

---

1. Jamie Bissonette, *When the Prisoners Ran Walpole: A True Story in the Movement for Prison Abolition,* (Cambridge, MA: South End Press, 2008), p. 72-74.

valuable resources to the various, and diverse, prisoner self-help programs existing within the prison.[2]

The NPRA evolved into the recognized grievance negotiator for MCI-Walpole prisoners as well as their collective bargaining agency. The NPRA board of directors determined that the organization had to place itself upon equal footing with the prison guard's union in an effort to be taken seriously in our transition from merely slaves, to scale paid workers. So, toward that end, we moved to be certified as a worker's union with the State Labor Relations Commission. A full version of that story is in print.[3]

We of BANTU considered ourselves "abolitionists," but not in the traditionally recognized historical sense. Our definition of the work of a modern day abolitionist was to free those mentally enslaved through education and cultural awareness. To that extent we would embark upon a quest to deliver our brethren from the bonds of perpetual mental slavery. Prison abolition came later, by way of discussions with Reverend Edward Rodman,[4] and in pursuit of NPRA's ultimate ambition.

This, then, is a true account of the state's imprisoned black slaves and their search for their lost identity . . . for manhood and what my stance as a modern day abolitionist has taught me about my servitude.

To fully appreciate and understand the lessons that both BANTU and NPRA learned in Massachusetts as self-professed abolitionist organizations, and how I consciously evolved, in particular as a "runaway slave," I must return to the history lessons in the black history course mentored by David Dance[5] in Walpole prison between the years 1972 and 1973. I will return to 1638 in the

---

2. Bissonette, Ibid., pp. 70-71; begin specifically, "On March 17, prisoners at Walpole rebelled against guard manipulation."
3. Bissonette, Ibid., passim.
4. "He came to Boston a committed prison abolitionist dedicated to eradicating slavery in all its forms. He taught prisoners and allies crucial skills for engaging in the struggle." Bissonette, Ibid., p. 13.
5. "In the first week after Hamm's release from segregation, David Dance, a Harvard undergraduate active in the Black Panther support work in Boston, received the administration's permission to start a black history course inside Walpole." Bissonette, Ibid., p. 69.

Baystate, and to the origins of the slave trade in America, as well as return to the 1830s-1850s slavery abolition movement in this country. This is necessary to establish a backdrop for Massachusetts' role in creating, sustaining, and perpetuating that system of chattel slavery that has become the underpinnings of America's prevailing institutions. I must also draw parallels to today. For only by way of tracing the steps back to the past could I obtain a clear view of the present and secure a proper outlook for the future.

In American society, a number of factors hinder the evolution of consciousness, or insight, toward a clearer vision of the "self." The method by which children are educated, in many ways, restricts their capacity to truly learn and hinders their creativity. Consequently, young people often experience the struggle for material survival resulting in frustration and resentment. In adulthood, this frequently leads to a variety of compensatory, addictive, and compulsive behaviors. The result is the persistence of social and political oppression, cultural and ethnic intolerance, and crime. This hindrance to the evolution of consciousness is a critical aspect of the tracking system in place within American society, thereby those designated the underclass are corralled, controlled, and channeled into delinquency, prison, and political/social death. It reduces human beings from subjects to mere objects in history.

This book, presented in the form of lessons, speaks to a history of racial and ethnic domination in Massachusetts, that intrudes upon the collective psyche of its citizens. It exposes a self-righteous veneer of white supremacy and manifest destiny—a legacy of puritan values—as perceived through the jaundiced eyes of the European majority and inflicted upon the state's ethnic minorities in the name of explicit capital gain through domination. It is about the creation of an atmosphere of uncertainty and fear,[6] as the means by which to crush opposition and suppress change. It is about the history of America and what underlies her present day domestic and foreign policies. To emphasis this I chose, in places, to use the blended word

---

6. "The oppressed are afraid to embrace freedom; the oppressors are afraid of losing the freedom to oppress." Paolo Freire

"Mississippi," referring to Massachusetts and Mississippi. The combination of an overtly racist former "Jim Crow" State and the occlusive systemic institutional racism of a New England State, to my mind, accurately defines the experiences that countless numbers have suffered and continued to endure. I explain this more fully in Appendix F.

My becoming BANTU, in service to NPRA, was not a single or solitary lesson. Rather, it was a evolution—an awareness of self in history, even as history was unfolding around me.

Ralph C. Hamm III
2016

AMERIKlan JUST-US (MASSISSIPPI-STYLE)

If they came for me
before first light

                              on thanksgiving day morning,

with their christian hypocrisy
reflecting their might . . .

                              would you question
                              their means of injustice?
                              Would you care
                              who was wrong or right?

Or would you cower
behind closed doors,

                              and drawn curtains,

afraid to confront
their collective sight?

                              Allow those crosses to burn,
                              and then maybe, in turn,
                              they'll come for you next
                              in the night.

PROLOGUE

Into the Light of Understanding . . . Into Fresh Air.

Spring of 1972. What a year it turned out to be. I had recently been released from my first stint in two of the State penal system's infamous segregation units (i.e., Bridgewater Departmental Segregation Unit and Walpole Prison's Block 10), after having had my cell firebombed and my head split open by Walpole Prison Superintendent Robert "More Gas" Moore, accompanied by his twenty-guard "goon squad"[1] in 1970, only to find myself in the middle of a full-scale property-damage riot on March 17.[2] I thought, "What could happen next?"

The Massachusetts Department of Correction had a new Commissioner, John O. Boone, and amazingly, he was black. I actually met with him on a couple of occasions after the March riot, as a newly elected member of the Walpole Prison Inmate Advisory Council [PIAC], at those times, I felt like a fish out of water. I was truly out of my element (fire), not knowing what to logically ask for in the sense of grievances for the collective prisoner body. I had barely two years of prison life under my belt, and most of that time had not been spent pondering the gripes of the entire population. I found it more comfortable to allow Bobby Dellelo[3] to talk as

---

1. "... the 'goon squad,' a gang of guards who celebrated using excessive force to subdue prisoners." Bissonette, Ibid., p. 1.
2. "To stop property destruction, Donnelly brought in state police armed with shotguns and tear gas. Five prisoners were injured in either the rebellion or the state police takeover. After all the damage was tallied, it was estimated that repairs would cost $1.6 million." Bissonette, Ibid., p. 71.
3. "He knew how to survive and he knew how to escape . . . he understood the relationship between power and leadership. He was a shrewd politician who was able to negotiate the complex alliances within Walpole." Bissonette, Ibid., p. 13; also, pp. 30, 76, 78, 86-87, 115.

Council Chairman, while I sat back and observed everyone's interactions. Bobby instinctively knew what was required to quell the madness, due to his physical presence and forceful personality forged by his long experience of youth offenders schools and adult prison—I learnt a great deal from watching and listening to him.

As I observed the white prisoners airing their complaints to the prison administration and the Commissioner of Correction, John O. Boone, basing their grievances upon rights secured by way of the US Constitution, I came to the realization that a void existed within my conscious mind. The white prisoners presented their issues upon a foundation of culture rooted within their history here in Massachusetts and in the very founding documents of the United States of America. What did we—black people—have?

It became crystal clear to me that I did not know my true place in the history of this state, country, nor, in the world, which left me with no viable stake in the Massachusetts body politic. Not only was I viewing the evolution of my life through lenses fashioned from alabaster, but so too were all of the other black prisoners on the Council and within the general prisoner population.

I immediately took an impromptu poll and discovered that blacks, as a segment of the prison population, could only trace our ethnic history (with any degree of certainty) back to the neighborhoods and city streets where we grew up through adolescence. I was shocked into the realization that everything taught to me thus far in my life . . . everything that I retained as knowledge . . . was predicated upon European culture, and upon a Eurocentric perspective of the world. I knew nothing of myself, other than I appeared to be existing, and except the information my mother had passed to me concerning her own mother that left me ashamed, spiritually lost, and as a consequence, angry.

The Civil Rights Era of the 1960s, which I had just barely survived, had given me painful images of protesting black people marching with signs and prostrating themselves upon city streets—to be fire hosed, beaten by police, attacked by dogs, shot at, tear gassed, and arrested. I had grown through my formative years within a state of psychological trauma, harboring an intense distrust and hatred for white authority figures, without any answers to my questions concerning why people of color (non-whites) were being treated the way that they were in this country. I had no historical reference from which to draw a conclusion, nor any insight through which to filter what was personally happening to me—or what I was witnessing transpiring around me.

All this began to change when a black prisoner named Henry Cribbs asked me if I wanted to enroll in a black history course that was scheduled to begin that Spring. He told me that only twelve prisoners could attend at a time, and that he was seeking those who were serious about learning their heritage—who would not waste the instructor's time and energy. Due to the fact that I was one of the elected black prisoner leaders seated upon the Inmate Advisory Council, we agreed that it would be in all of our best interest for me to attend the classes.

Our course instructor was David Dance, an undergraduate student of Harvard University's Phillip Brooks House,[4] and he had recently obtained permission from the Commissioner of Correction John O. Boone[5] to bring a black history course to the Walpole Prison black prisoner population.[6] David had enlisted Robert "Big Bob" Heard, a leading official of Boston's Black Panther party,[7] as his co-instructor. Together, over the course of the ensuing year, they would bring the history of my people alive and tutor this twelve-prisoner class upon the struggle for existence of non-white people around the world.

History, literature, prose, drama, sociology, psychology, science, religion, philosophy, art, and poetry were all presented to me from an African perspective. I began to learn the truth underlying all that was, and all that will be—using a clear vision and strong fingers to pull myself up and out of the grave of ignorance in which I had, up to that point, been historically interred. I had broken through the thick veil of darkness into the light of understanding . . . into the fresh air.

---

4. ". . . David Dance persuaded the prison administration to allow him to teach a black history course to 12 black prisoners. The group was afforded space once a week in the prison general library." Bissonette, Ibid., p. 73.
5. Bissonette, Ibid., pp. 41-50.
6. Bissonette, Ibid., pp. 72- 74.
7. "Dance co-taught the program with Robert Heard, a high ranking Panther Party member who had recently arrived in Boston." Bissonette, Ibid., p. 69.

I found myself within the transformational stage of evolving into a sentient being of substance . . . a person to be reckoned with . . . possessor of a sound cultural and historical footing in the world. I was to realize years later, in retrospect, that this was the moment in my life when I began to break the psychological cycle of my perpetual slavery.

Therefore this book, presented in the form of eight lessons, each broken down into three parts, is essentially the story of my transformation. Each lesson contains elements of historical narrative and expository writing, regarding the specific knowledge. In addition I have added descriptive passages that contextualize the subject matter relating it to my experiences in prison, the prison reform movement within Massachusetts and MCI-Walpole specifically, and the cultural dynamics of America in the post civil rights era of the 1970/80s.

LESSON 1

From Plantation to Constitutional Sanction

a. The birthplace of institutional slavery.

One of the first historical myths that I was taught was in regard to the Plymouth Pilgrims. Essentially they were not the morally sound, pious, individuals depicted within elementary and secondary school textbooks, as secondary school (high school) was the last educational experience undertaken by the majority of the prisoners confined within MCI-Walpole.

Of the 102 passengers on the 1620 voyage of the *Mayflower*, only 37 could actually be regarded as "pilgrims." In truth, they considered themselves as separatists. These separatists did not land upon America's shores seeking religious freedom; rather, they came for conquest—using their religious belief of manifest destiny as the moral high ground upon which to maintain and sustain their barbarity. The separatists came to the new world with far more muskets than Bibles, which is a testimony to their intent.

When the mock pilgrims made landfall, the Native Americans shunned them by moving inland—leaving the separatists to fend for themselves on the coastline. Just as soon as the Europeans landed at Plymouth, and prior to even seeing the first native, they began to pillage and plunder Native American food stores, desecrate burial sites, and break into dwellings to steal the belongings of families when they were not at home.

These lower class Englishmen were not dressed in the white-and-black costumes of Hollywood fiction, but wore brightly colored clothing. They drank a lot of home brew and were recorded as consuming at least a half-gallon of beer a day, which they preferred over water. Governor William Bradford wrote in 1642, regarding the severity of punishment in his colony:

> "And yet this could not suppress the breaking out of sundry notorious sin, especially drunkenness and uncleanliness, not only incontinence between unmarried persons, for which many both men and women have been punished sharply, but some married persons, but that which is even worse, Sodomy."[1]

In America, *Mayflower* ancestry is still considered the pinnacle—especially in Massachusetts. However, the first whites to colonize Massachusetts' shores were in large part the dregs of Europe. They came from the poor houses, taverns, prisons, and were viewed by most Europeans as those who were too lazy to work.[2]

Although the first twenty Africans, captured and kidnapped arrived in 1619, at Jamestown, the Massachusetts slave trade saw its tentative start in 1638 when Captain William Pierce of Salem sailed his ship *Desire* to the Bahamas. Once docked, he traded captured Native Americans for cotton, tobacco, salt, and Africans.[3]

By 1641, less than twenty years after the first whites began to colonize this country in earnest, the institution of slavery found its roots in Massachusetts. The laws supporting the enslavement of human beings were drafted in this state as the model for New England's slavery system,[4] which in turn spread to the remaining American colonies. In 1700, New England, with its tall ships and accessible ports, became the slave trading center in America—with Boston at the hub of this evil trade.[5]

From the earliest days of slavery, prior to its wide spread use and institutionalization, Native Americans proved to be undesirable as useful slaves to the Europeans. They were too

---

1. "History of the Plymouth Plantation," 1898 ed., p. 459. James Dertz, *The Times of Their Lives: Life, Love, And Death in Plymouth Colony*, (New York: W. H. Freeman, 2000), pp. 1- 9, passim.
2. John Daniels, *In Freedom's Birthplace: A Story of the Boston Negroes*, (1914 reprint, New York: Arno Press, 1969), pp. 2-3.
3. Daniels, Ibid., p. 1, and note.
4. The Massachusetts Body of Liberties outlawed bond slavery, except in the case of "strangers."
5. William H. Whitmore (ed.), *The Colonial Laws Of Massachusetts, 1660-72*, (Boston, 1889), p. 53.

acquainted with the land and would run off into the woods and swamps never to be seen again. They also proved to be extremely vulnerable to European borne diseases and spiritually adverse to the type of perverse servitude that the whites had in mind.[6] Blacks that were kidnapped from Africa became the primary source of forced labor, as they were more resilient to European diseases and were the architects of the earliest civilizations.[7]

The trade in molasses was the foundation for the institution of chattel slavery and the reason why America rose to such prominence so quickly. Molasses was the base ingredient in the production of rum, and rum was bartered in exchange for kidnapped blacks from the West Coast of Africa. A pro-American bulletin of 1731 stated that "the molasses trade is the most (if not only) valuable one in New England."[8] John Adams, the second President of the United States was recorded as saying the following:

> "I know not why we should blush to confess that molasses was the essential ingredient in American Independence," molasses made rum, it traded for African lives . . . Africans thereby proved to be, "the most perfect agent of production known to commerce."[9]

In Massachusetts, it was determined, as early as 1646, that at the rate Africans were being kidnapped and transported to America, if the ten-year-indentured-servant status were to be extended to them, they would outnumber the colonists in a very short span of time. So, a more oppressive means of population control had to be implemented . . . the concept of perpetual slavery. By European standards, perpetual slavery also made for a good investment and sound economic sense. At its peak, Massachusetts merchant ships transported 50,000 Africans annually for sale to the southern states . . . a whopping 63 percent of New England's exports by 1772.

---

6. In Native American cultures the males were the hunters and gatherers, while the females performed the heavy work (i.e., building, farming, child rearing, etc.); so, the males were unaccustomed to the labor forced upon them by whites.
7. Chancellor Williams, III, *The Destruction of Black Civilization*, (Chicago: Third World Press, 1976), passim.
8. *Case of the Northern Colonies*, 1731, p. 3.
9. J. W Dubose, eminent authority on Confederate history.

As efficient commerce and economics was the driving force behind institutional slavery, I reasoned that those same factors drove it from private ownership to government usage after the Civil War ended in 1865, via the Thirteenth Amendment to the United States Constitution.

b. The Thirteenth Amendment: From plantation to prison.

> "Neither slavery nor involuntary servitude, except as a punishment for crime whereof the party shall have been duly convicted, shall exist within the United states, or any place subject to their jurisdiction."
> —Thirteenth Amendment, US Constitution

Prior to the passage of the Thirteenth Amendment, there was no mention of imprisonment in the United States Constitution. The Thirteenth Amendment, in abolishing slavery, gave way to the authorization of slavery as a punishment for a crime in this country, and thereby became a vehicle to control former slaves and their future generations—as opposed to being a method to deal with serious crime.

Southern plantation owners were thus afforded the means, sanctioned by the Constitution, to perpetuate the peculiar institution of slavery for economic gain. Their immediate response to the passage of the Thirteenth Amendment was the convict-lease system. The newly acquired status of emancipated slave was soon replaced with the status of criminal, with the issuance of the "black codes" in 1865 by the former Confederate States. Specific crimes such as vagrancy or quitting one's job were racialized, where black people could be "duly convicted" and compelled into forced labor, often cheaply leased out as farm hands to the very same plantation owners from whom they were allegedly emancipated. In this manner, the state government received income. Many convicted emancipated slaves were once again kidnapped, held beyond their sentences, or were actually innocent of the crimes for which they were imprisoned.

During the era of Reconstruction, black leaders failed to see the significance in fighting against the convict-lease system, because they believed that the fight for voter's rights and against lynching were more important. The convict-lease system, to my mind, was in and of itself a virulent form of legal-lynching . . . and the right to vote via the Fifteenth Amendment remains an issue that must be signed-off by the U.S. President on a regular basis. Nothing much has changed since 1865, as black people accept the rhetoric that they are not personally affected by the machinations of the penal system, as such propaganda spews forth from the mouth of the slave master's children: that criminals deserve what they receive, even if it amounts to racialized torture or murder.

Essentially the convict-lease system exploited the loopholes and federal policies that discouraged the prosecution of whites for continuing to hold slaves, from the aftermath of the Civil War in 1865 through to the dawn of World War II in 1933, propelling the economics of slavery into the twentieth century.

Black people once considered free by the terms of the Emancipation Proclamation in 1863 were soon to learn that the passage of the Constitutional Amendment abolishing slavery in the states was not worth the paper upon which it was written and only transferred their public recognition as animals to that of criminals—as noted above. By construing prisoners as human beings subject to slavery as punishment, the Thirteenth Amendment drew the elusive parallel between the plantation and the prison.

c. Black illusions.

Along with the signing of the Emancipation Proclamation came the promise of forty acres of land for the freed slaves. In 1865, General William T. Sherman issued Field Order 15 that set aside parts of South Carolina and Florida to be parceled out to blacks. Most freed slaves did not receive their promised land, because President Andrew Johnson reversed the policy that year.

My mother, Margaret Elizabeth Hamm, was from South Carolina, having been born on July 9, 1920, and she told me stories of how her mother and their relations cursed the terror that was unleashed upon them by the promise held within the Emancipation Proclamation. She spoke of how 1866 saw the rise of the Ku Klux Klan and how they utilized threats, terror, and murder to maintain their claim of "white rule" of the South.

With fire in her eyes, and tight jaws, she told me stories that her mother passed on to her concerning her grandparents being forced off their land in South Carolina by the night riders, and how her mother died still fighting the men and women[10] of the Klan in 1932.

President Andrew Johnson issued his own plan for Reconstruction in 1865, minus the parceling of land to former slaves. It is safe to say that millions of former slaves, and their children, went to their graves still waiting for their promised forty acres of land. The Klan carried out its cross burnings, as the principle method to strike fear into blacks, throughout the twentieth century . . . whenever a claim of property rights became a public issue.

Emancipation and the Thirteenth Amendment perversely made black people more vulnerable in so-called freedom than they were in chattel slavery. Serious threats came from both white mobs and the court system then, and in 1973—as nets of terror sanctioned by common law, regulated by legislative acts, and recognized under the federal Constitution. Slavery continues as an institution by way of the penal system, under cover of maintaining the order of society and public safety. It has been designed to perpetuate itself one way or another, but especially through the socially accepted practice of criminalizing black people—time tested to garner the optimal results, on into the twenty-first century.

Today, imprisonment is specifically utilized as a mechanism to disenfranchise blacks as property owners and to erode our potential political power. As more and more people of color are herded into prison, gerrymandering and election laws have been enacted within several States to strip ex-convicts of their right to vote. The Thirteenth Amendment has thereby become the effective means by which to marginalize the dictates of the Fourteenth, Fifteenth, and Nineteenth Amendments to the US Constitution; through the criminalization of black-and-brown skinned people.

The convict-lease system, the farming out of prisoners, continues today as blacks are arrested and convicted to serve

---

10. The female counterpart of the Ku Klux Klan, the Knights of the White Camelia, found a home in Radcliffe University in Cambridge, Massachusetts, in 1923.

exorbitant and disparate prison sentences, often upon the merest of criminal charges, in comparison to prison sentences ordered by the court for their white counterparts to serve upon similar offenses.[11] Their labor is then leased out to the highest corporate bidder. It should come as no surprise that the federal prison system is the leader in convict-leasing to corporations, under the guise of rehabilitation and vocational programs.

In 1973, Massachusetts slavery in the form of convict-leasing belonged to the state by way of license plate manufacturing; making street signs and forging sewer covers; government and privately contracted printing... later, silk screening; government and privately contracted furniture manufacturing and repair; eye glass manufacturing and repair; to name a few industries, all for a penny-a-day pay scale or nothing whatsoever for the prisoner laborers. The NPRA unionizing effort sought to strike at the heart of the lease system, seeking equal worker's compensation for equal work, which is why we were set upon by New England's version of the night riders (the state police) and terrorized and brutalized out of existence.

The racialization of crime created another alarming trend. Frederick Douglass once commented before a Convention of Colored Men in Louisville, Kentucky, that "taking advantage of the general disposition in this country to impute crime to color, white men color their faces to commit crime and wash off the hated color to escape punishment."[12]

The first white person whom I recall in my lifetime to actually blacken his face, don an afro-wig, and commit a crime was an ex-convict named John McGrath—the same person who was responsible for bringing the concept of the NPRA from the Adult Correctional Institution in Cranston, Rhode Island, to MCI-Walpole.[13] John was eventually caught and convicted of

---

11. The earliest example of this practice that I have found was recorded in Worchester, Massachusetts in 1768; when a black man was accused of raping a white woman and was sentenced and hung, while a white man accused of the same crime was sentenced to sit on the gallows. See; Sharon Harley, *The Timetable of African American History*, (New York: Touchstone, 1995), p. 38, c.
12. Phillip Foner, *The Life and Writings of Frederick Douglass*, (New York: International Publishers, 1955), vol. 4, p. 379; Address to the People of the United States, Louisville, Kentucky, September
13. Bissonette, Ibid., p. 86.

armed robbery in the 1970s. To me this incident highlighted the reality that the disposition of this country to racialize crime had not changed since 1883, and regrettably the very foundation of the Massachusetts chapter of the NPRA maybe less secure than we originally thought.

Charles Stuart would begin a new wave of blaming blacks to cover crimes committed by whites in this country, when in 1989, he shot and killed his pregnant wife, then attempted to cover up the crime through the assistance of his brother, and fingered a black man (Willie Bennett) for the crime, in an effort to collect upon the wife's insurance policy.[14]

Throughout the past four decades, or as far back as I can recall, black men, women, and children have been shot dead by white policemen under "suspicion while being black." Regrettably this continues today unabated. In every instance, grand juries of their peers have acquitted them by simply determining that they were doing their jobs or duty. Their duty, indeed! When suing for wrongful death damages under the US Constitution, surviving black family members often come to the painful realization that they have no Constitutional rights or protections that whites are bound by law to respect, and that the Thirteenth Amendment did not free them from the status of slave, because we have been criminalized by the slave master ideology of white America as a class.

> "We can think about the moral panic of black rapists,[15] particularly in the aftermath of slavery. The myth of the black rapist was a key component of an ideological strategy used against black people in the aftermath of slavery. And so the moral panic around crime is not related to a rise in crime in any material sense. Rather, it is related to the problem of managing large populations particularly people of color—who have been rendered dispensable by the system of global capitalism."[16]

---

14. See; Timeline, this book, in Lesson 3.
15. The moral panic of the black rapist was successfully utilized in ads by George Bush against Michael Dukakis during their Presidential run for the White House in 1988. In 2007 the same ploy was used unsuccessfully against Duval Patrick in his bid for Governor of Massachusetts.
16. Angela Y. Davis, *Abolition Democracy: Beyond Empire, Prison, and Torture*, (New York: Seven Stories Press, 2005), p. 43. Also, read: Calvin C. Hernton, "Dynamite Growing Out Of Their Skulls," an essay in, *Black Fire, An Anthology of Afro-American Writing*, ed. Leroi Jones and Larry Neal, (New York: William Morrow & Company, Inc., 1968), pp. 78-104.

I have come to learn through history that the more times have appeared to change, the more they have remained the same. I have seen that it is the moralistic surreality of a Eurocentric culture to blame people of color (its victims) as the ones solely responsible for society's ills. It is also the misbegotten illusion of blacks to believe that the Thirteenth Amendment has changed their status in society for the better. Frederick Douglass said that the old slaves sang a chorus:

"We raise de wheat . . .
    dey gib us corn,
we bake de bread . . .
    dey gib us huss,
we peal de meat . . .
    dey gib us skin—
          and dat's de way
          dey take us in.

We skin de pot . . .
    dey gib us likkuh,
          and say dat's good enuf
          for de nigguh."

Lesson 2

The Truth Regarding the Mississippi Abolitionists.

a. Who were the real abolitionists?

My high school history textbooks taught me in the 1960s that the struggle for the abolition of slavery, hence the underground railroad, was manned in Massachusetts by high-minded, morally righteous, white humanitarians... with a black person sprinkled here and there for the sake of appearance or color. I was led to believe that Africans, and ex-slaves, lacked the mental capacity to undertake such an endeavor as spearheading their own cause of freedom.

Names such as Ralph Waldo Emerson, Samuel Sewall, Harriet Beecher Stowe, William Lloyd Garrison, and Henry David Thoreau held prominence as those whites who led the crusade for the abolition of slavery in the North. Actually this is not entirely true! In my estimation, having evolved through David Dance's black history course in Walpole, only two of the aforementioned names were admirable: William Lloyd Garrison, with his *The Liberator* newspaper, and Henry David Thoreau. This was 1973.

I came to learn that such people as David Walker (author of *Appeal*, in 1829), Frederick Douglass, Lewis Hayden, Harriet Hayden, Robert Morris, Charles Lenox Remond, and William C. Nell were the true champions of the abolition movement in Massachusetts, as far as I was concerned.

Although white historians had placed Massachusetts white

abolitionists at the forefront of the underground railroad efforts in the North, more than two-thirds of all of the escaped slaves seeking passage upon the railroad through the Baystate were aided by Hayden and his associates.[1]

Many of the safe houses or stops along the heralded underground railroad, that were owned by Massachusetts whites, were facilitated by them in an effort to engage in moneymaking contracts with the fugitive slaves for labor, in exchange for food and lodging. It served many of these so-called abolitionists' economic purpose to be affiliated with the movement.

As I read my lessons in history, my ever-awakening black consciousness asked several questions, such as:

- If the North was actually "free," as the white historians often stated, then why was there a need for the underground railroad in Massachusetts?
- Why weren't the escapees from the South allowed to walk freely in the streets of Massachusetts, even after the "Fugitive Slave Law" was passed in the 1850s?
- Why was Canada the determined "promised land" of Harriet Tubman, Sojourner Truth, Frederick Douglass, and others?

Ralph Waldo Emerson wrote, concerning white abolitionists:

"The abolitionist wishes to abolish slavery, but because he wants to abolish the black man. He considers that it is violence, brute force, [not] intellectual rule, [that] holds property in Man; but he thinks the Negro himself the very representative and exponent of the brute force base; and that it is the Negro in the white man which holds slaves."[2]

Emerson went on to say that the Negro,

"[stands] in nature below the series of thought, and in the plane of vegetable and animal . . ."

---

1. Benjamin Quarles, *Black Abolitionists*, (New York: Oxford University Press, 1969), passim.
2. A. W. Plumstead and William H. Gilman, eds., *The Journals and Miscellaneous Notebooks of Ralph Waldo Emerson*, vol. 13 (Cambridge, MA: Harvard University Press, 1977), p. 35.

Harriet Beecher Stowe, who authored *Uncle Tom's Cabin* (1849)—based upon a composite portrayal of ex-slave Josiah Henson—was not concerned about how slavery effected Africans, held in bondage, but rather worried about how it *impacted the souls of white men.*

Henry David Thoreau recalled a reaction amongst a New Bedford audience when a white abolitionist spoke about his intention to help fugitive slaves; he wrote:

> "The murmur ran around the room, and was anxiously whispered by the Sons of the Pilgrims, 'He had better not!' and it was echoed under the shadow of the Concord Monument, 'He had better not!'"[3]

Contrary to the popular historical myth, only a small minority of whites spoke up in favor of the humanity of the African captives held on this continent. Those that did were labeled "nigger lovers," and were often objects of violence in Massachusetts. Today, this same white minority are the called "wiggers" (white niggers) and subject to be ostracized, and violently set upon, by members of their ethnic group.

So-called white abolitionist Samuel Sewall may have written a pamphlet condemning slavery, but he still professed blacks to be inferior to whites. He believed that blacks, according to Jewish Tradition, were descendants from Ham, the alleged cursed son of Noah, and therefore were not fit to hold a position in white society. In fact, Sewall himself owned a slave named "Scipio." Over 760 prominent Massachusetts citizens, some of whom called themselves abolitionists, owned slaves by 1830.

Other so-called abolitionists in Massachusetts wanted an end to slavery because they hated black people and wanted them all shipped back to Africa, to make America "lily white" by their standards. People like Benjamin Franklin remarked about the economic inefficiencies of the system but never reached its immorality. Then you had those who were terrified by the perceived notion that there would be a mass exodus of

---

3. Lawrence Wilson, *Another view of the Pilgrims*, New England Quarterly, (June 1961), p. 174.

white women to the big, brawny, "bucks," if Africans remained in North America—which was evident in almost every lynching of a black male by a white mob, where the mob members paid special attention to the murdered black man's genitalia by always cutting it off. Frantz Fanon expressed within his book, *Black Skin, White Masks* (p. 137) that:

> "Still on the genital level, isn't the white man who hates blacks prompted by a feeling of impotence or sexual inferiority? Since virility is taken to be the absolute ideal, doesn't he have a feeling of inadequacy in relation to the black man, who is viewed as a penis symbol? Isn't lynching the black man a sexual revenge? We know how sexualized torture, abuse, and ill-treatment can be."

As the months progressed, and my understanding increased, I paralleled my newfound insight to the condition of my own circumstance—the aspects of my imprisonment. I was recently sentenced to life imprisonment for the "intent" to rape a white woman. My sentence was egregiously excessive and comparable to the lynching of black men in the South for "reckless eyeballing" of white women. However, Mississippi was more civilized than the Southern States and took into consideration torture and the economic advantage entailed in imprisoning blacks for life as opposed to simply killing them at a profit loss.

The full magnitude of this scheme became clear to me in the 1980s, with the unveiling of the prison-industrial complex (PIC). Essentially, I was sentenced to life in prison as a symbolic castration, after the public display of the legal lynching. I was the only person in Massachusetts jurisprudence to ever be sentenced to life in prison for intending to commit a crime; and no judge in the state or federal court would descend to that level of immorality to impose a similar sentence on a first time adult offender, because of the color of my skin.[4] I was thereby adjudged "unfit" to hold a position in white society, by Sewall's standard,

---

4. Trial counsel performed no pretrial discovery into the case, to include lack of discovery upon the forensic evidence (i.e., blood, hand, and fingerprints) testified to at trial by police Detective Lt. Tylus to have been found throughout the interior of the 1965 Ford Mustang Fastback automobile where the charged assault with intent to rape was testified to have occurred; thereby leaving the owner of the inculpatory evidence

because I was even by name a descendant of Ham(m)—an inference not lost upon white Mississippians,[5] as they silently acquiesced to their attraction to myths, and a perverse love of torture.

In 1973, I took great pride in being an abolitionist and BANTU as an abolitionist movement (program). The struggle that we undertook was one to abolish ignorance and the mental bondage perpetuated by the institution of education, thereby removing the silken web that had cocooned our minds. The cause for the abolition of prisons—the physical kind—came later, and has always been of secondary importance to me, as aptly demonstrated in Lesson 4.

BANTU's "underground railroad" did not shuttle contraband fugitive slaves from the United States to Canada; rather, we transported black history books[6] (the knowledge of self) on our underground library from one end of Walpole Prison to the other.

Of all the notable names that made up the underground railroad of the 1800s—that included heroes such as Harriet Tubman, Sojourner Truth, and Frederick Douglass—the abolitionists that I admired most were Lewis Hayden of Boston, and William Parker of Pennsylvania. Both men were fugitive slaves. Hayden escaped from Kentucky to Boston in 1845 and was an entrepreneur who, since his arrival in Boston at the age

---

unidentified. Trial counsel also coerced an "unknowing" and "unintelligent" waiver of trial by jury, by threatening me with an all white jury incapable of affording me a fair trial if I did not heed his advice. The Massachusetts Appeals Court held that "counsel's advice was based upon the fact that Hamm is black and his victims white ... [w]e think counsel's advice was reasonable and not the result of incompetence." Commonwealth v. Ralph Hamm, 471 N. E. 2d 416, 421 (1984) Trial counsel was held not to have to be accountable to the "Canon of Ethics," by way of its first directive for trial counsel to investigate the material facts of the case, because the Appeals court found that his defense strategy was "of a legal and not factual nature" and that he had "access to the prosecutor's case file," Id.; thereby allowing trial counsel to fulfill his true role of coprosecutor in my trial.

5. See; Appendix D - Transcript Testimonial Statement Of The Case.

6. The purpose of the 1830 "Slave Codes" in this country was to prevent insurrections and other dangerous forms of servile resistance. Laws or "Codes" were enacted forbidding slaves to read or write, which was carried over in principal to 1960s-1970s Walpole Prison. This also meant that disciplinary sanctions were in place for uttering abolitionist doctrines and circulating abolitionist propaganda, as: "threats to the orderly running of the institution"—an extension of the "Slave Codes."

of forty, had established a clothing business—making him one of the wealthiest black men in the city. He was also the leader of the abolitionist organization hailed The Vigilance Committee.[7] Most of the fugitive slaves who made their way to Boston were initially given food and lodging in his three-story house on Southac Street. As women had performed most of the work on the Underground Railroad, Lewis's wife Harriet was no exception as she fed, sheltered, and nursed ill fugitive slaves back to health en route to their final destination of Canada.

In my estimation, the most noteworthy act that Lewis Hayden performed as leader of The Vigilance Committee in Boston was the rescue of Shadrach Minkins. 120 years later, the heroics of these black men and women during the 1850s inspired me in my work as a board member of both BANTU and the NPRA in the 1970s. I was both moved and motivated by their passion and commitment to struggle for the liberation of Africans kidnapped and enslaved in America—in the face of what must have seemed insurmountable odds—at severe risk to their own lives.

When the prison authorities locked me up in segregation, on trumped up disciplinary charges so that I would remain in punitive isolation, and threatened me with physical violence and death for my militancy, I always took into consideration the struggle of my ancestors, which afforded me great strength and fortitude in all of my endeavors.

For instance, I would bring to mind the Shadrach Minkins episode. On February 15, 1851, Minkins—a fugitive slave from Norfolk, Virginia, where he had escaped months earlier in May 1850—was arrested by federal deputy marshals at the Taft's Cornhill Coffee House[8] in Boston. At about two o'clock that afternoon, a group of twenty or so black men, with collars turned up high and sou'westers shielding their faces, forced their way into Boston's Doric Courthouse. They pushed aside federal

---

7. Joel Strangis, *Lewis Hayden and the War against Slavery*, (New Haven, Conn: Linnet Books, 1999), p. 86; Gary Collison, *Shaddrack Minkins: From Fugitive Slave to Citizen*, (Cambridge, MA: Harvard University Press, 1997), pp. 151-153.
8. A few doors away from William Lloyd Garrison's office at *The Liberator*. William Hayden had mobilized the Vigilance Committee with remarkable swiftness. For, in less than two hours after his arrest, Minkins's rescue had been successfully pulled off.

deputy marshals and constables, then took Minkins from their custody, and carried him out into the rain soaked city street to the cheers of what was then estimated to be the largest gathering of African Americans in Boston's history. One of Minkins's rescuers brandished the city's official Sword of Justice over his head,[9] which he had snatched from the wall of the courtroom. The rescuers moved in a shouting procession north along Court Street, picking up more supporters as they went—past Paul Revere's house, whose significance and symbolism to the American Revolution was not lost upon the crowd—onto Cambridge Street and into the black neighborhood situated on the back end of Beacon Hill (soon to be surnamed, "Nigger Hill"), on toward the Charles River. It was there that Minkins disappeared.[10]

The federal government, as well as the local government of Massachusetts, was serious about enforcing the Fugitive Slave Law. However, the lawmen were not prepared for Minkins's daring rescue by the Vigilance Committee. An enraged President Fillmore called for a special cabinet meeting, after which he declared Minkins's rescue "a scandalous outrage," and then ordered federal and civil authorities to recapture him. By the time Fillmore had issued his order, Hayden had driven Minkins to Concord, and in four days after his rescue, Minkins was in Canada.

Hayden's exploits and life were an inspiration to the members of BANTU, and to me in particular, as we embarked upon business ventures inside of Walpole Prison. With the entrepreneur's spirit, we purchased and operated leather craft businesses (making hand bags, wallets, and belts), plaster molding (making coin banks, lamps, wall plaques, and African statues and figurines), and wood working businesses (making foot lockers, toy chests, doll houses, furniture), whose items were sold in the prison lobby, as well as within a storefront that we rented in the Boston area. The proceeds from the sales went toward purchasing a

---

9. The symbolism of the raised Sword of Justice was not lost upon me, as I was to mimic the posture in Walpole Prison on the morning of May 18, 1973, when the state police took over the prison. Bissonette, *When the Prisoners Ran Walpole*, p. 180.
10. Strangis, Ibid., pp. 74- 79. Leonard Levy, "The Sims Case: The Fugitive Slave Law in Boston 1851," *Journal of Negro History* 35 (1950), pp. 39-74.

bus that drove visitors to the prisons and the bus driver's salary, sometimes paying BANTU members' bail, family support issues (i.e., overwhelming bills, emergency food, overdue rents, and hospital bills). We even bought an ambulance for a needy black community in Alabama.

When a new Brother arrived at Walpole Prison and had no funds, we paid for his first prison canteen (store) order for personal hygiene products. We purchased additional books and educational materials. Lewis Hayden had spent his life, after freeing himself from the yoke of slavery in Kentucky, utilizing his funds and acquired resources aiding his fellow kidnapped Africans in America. He was, for all intent and purpose, the patron of BANTU, and I worked and strove to achieve in his memory.

In 1873, Lewis Hayden became one of the first Africans in America to be elected to a northern state Legislature, in Massachusetts. Exactly one hundred years later, another first, State Senator William Owens, took the forefront in the cause for reform and the abolition of the State's prison system to the floor of the State Senate. Both men maintained their roles as staunch community leaders and as role models for the extended BANTU family.

Then there was William Parker. He was twenty-nine years old in 1851, born a slave in Anne Arudel County, Maryland, and had escaped to Pennsylvania in 1842. He was the leader of a secret black militia, which could mobilize on short notice to fight off slave-hunters and recover their kidnapped victims utilizing any means necessary. At twenty-two years of age in 1973, with the heart of a militant, I was captivated and drawn to the exploits of William Parker. His calling to free his fellow Africans from the hands of kidnappers who wanted to re-enslave them, became my calling to free my Brothers from twentieth century slave-hunters who set upon Africans to re-enslave their minds. My secret militia? The board of directors of BANTU initially, then later the "hard core" element of the prison population, members of the NPRA, who could be cajoled at times by my friend Larry Rooney—who himself had adopted the role of abolitionist, much like John Brown (1858) of Harper's Ferry fame.

On the night of November 6, 1849, four slaves escaped from the plantation of Edward Gorsuch in Maryland.[11] Gorsuch was sixty-four years of age at the time. By September 1851, he had still not found the four runaways, which embarrassed him in front of his fellow Maryland slave owners and, by his estimation, set a bad example for his remaining slaves. But it was at this time that he received some encouraging news—two of his runaways had been spotted in a town called Christiana in Pennsylvania, the heart of the underground railroad route, fifteen miles north of the Maryland border.

Gorsuch gathered up his son, two nephews, and a few sympathetic Marylanders; heavily arming themselves, they set out for Pennsylvania. Once in Pennsylvania, he appealed for government assistance under the terms of the Fugitive Slave Law and acquired the additional services of a US Deputy Marshal and two constables.

Unbeknownst to them, their party was being tracked by Philadelphia abolitionists. An underground railroad spy named Samuel Williams gained Gorsuch's confidence by offering advice about his fellow blacks in Lancaster County; thereby, learning the slave-owner's plans. Williams sped ahead of the slave-hunters to Christiana, where he notified the underground that Gorsuch's party was on the way.[12]

Parker, his warrior wife Eliza, at least two of Gorsuch's runaways, and a number of Parker's armed militiamen, secured themselves upon the second floor of Parker's fortified house by the time that the Marylanders and their posse arrived outside of the dwelling before dawn on September eleventh. The US Deputy Marshal read arrest warrants aloud to the occupants and told them to surrender themselves. Parker told him that he could not care less about him, the warrant, or the United States government.

As dawn broke, and heated arguments with some gunfire was exchanged between the two opposing parties, Eliza blew the

---

11. Thomas P. Slaughter, *Bloody Dawn: The Christiana Riot and Racial Violence in the Antebellum North*, (New York: Oxford University Press, 1991), pp. 4-6, 11, 14, 17-19, 44.
12. Slaughter, Ibid., pp. 51-74.

emergency horn kept in the house. Within minutes several dozen armed black men arrived upon the scene and pointed their guns at Gorsuch's now surrounded posse. Someone from the crowd yelled at Gorsuch to take his old ass back to Maryland before he got hurt. Gorsuch's son loudly queried of his father if he was going to take that "from a nigger;" whereupon Parker threatened to knock the son's teeth down his throat. The son ran forward and fired a shot at Parker, but missed. One of Parker's men shot Gorsuch's son at point blank range with a shotgun.

All of the white men fired their guns at the crowd, and three blacks were shot but not killed. Edward Gorsuch was struck in the head by a rifle butt and knocked to the ground. He fought back but was eventually killed by a torrent of blows from clubs and corn cutters. The deputy marshal and two constables ran for their lives. Edward Gorsuch was the only fatality.

Gorsuch's death sent shock waves through Washington, and across the South. William Parker vowed not to be taken alive[13] and set out with two other fugitives for Rochester, New York, where he was to meet up with his old friend Frederick Douglass. Douglass had moved to New York from Boston in 1847 to establish his newspaper, *The Morning Star*. A one-thousand-dollar reward was placed upon Parker's head. Frederick Douglass considered Parker, and his men, the black men that he had dreamed of: fearless, self-confident, and "heroic, defenders of the just rights of man against man stealers and murderers." At 8:00 p.m., on the night of their arrival in New York, Parker and his two companions were escorted to a ship bound for Montreal by Frederick Douglass. Douglass shook each man's hand, and Parker gave him Edward Gorsuch's pistol as memento.[14] Both men realized that the pistol was a symbol that the war against slavery had taken a new, deadlier, turn. The Christiana incident has been considered by historians, as well as myself, as one of the greatest moments in the history of the

---

13. Robert C. Smedley, *History of the Underground Railroad in Chester and the Neighboring Counties of Pennsylvania*, Lancaster: The Journal, 1883, pp.223-24, 247-53, 260-68.

14. Frederick Douglass, "Life and Times of Frederick Douglass," in *Douglass Autobiographies*, (New York: Library of America, 1994), pp. 724-726.

Underground Railroad.

In 1852, during a speech given at the National Free Soil Party Convention in Pittsburgh, Frederick Douglass was to state that "the only way to make the Fugitive Slave Law a dead letter is to make a dozen or more dead kidnappers;"[15] referring to the Christiana resistance.

Although my struggle as an abolitionist in Walpole Prison during the 1970s was not undertaken as an overtly violent struggle, when compared to the 1850s in this country, Walpole was marred by many deaths. I was at war against intolerance and ignorance, in an effort to strike a deathblow to the rote brainwashing system of education that kept black people in perpetual bondage.

The education of the oppressed had to take into account the tragic dilemma between speaking out and remaining silent; of being wholly oneself or being divided; between rejecting the oppressor, or accepting him as the model of freedom; between prisoner solidarity, or alienation; between following the prescribed rules of action, or having choices; between being a spectator, or a man of action-castrated in our power to create and recreate, in our ability and power to change our world; so I was taught by Paolo Freire.

The innovative entrepreneurship of Lewis Hayden and the righteous militancy of William Parker, which was passed on through BANTU and the NPRA self-help format to the entire Walpole Prison population, had a lasting and profound impact upon these associations' peripheral and subsequent members. The effected board members went on to create subsidiary self-help programs in Walpole Prison and MCI-Norfolk during the 1970s.

By the close of the year 1973, prisoner abolitionists and Vietnam combat veterans (Bob Lee, Larry Rooney, William Johnson, Efrid Brown, Bob Hayes, and Hugh Johnson) would co-found the American Veterans In Prison (AVIP), in an effort to assist veterans in their attempt to receive their just benefits from the Veterans Administration and the federal government, as well

---

15. Slaughter, Ibid., pp. 132-37; Smedley, Ibid., pp. 129-130; Stanley W Cambell, *The Slave Catchers*, (Chapel Hill: University of North Carolina Press, 1970), p. 53.

as to assist them in dealing with the overwhelmingly oppressive nature of post-traumatic stress disorder (PTSD) incurred by way of their participation in the war and exacerbated by the ongoing battle for survival inside of Walpole Prison.

They secured therapeutic assistance from the Department of Legal Medicine (DLM), through the volunteer work offered by Ms. Pamela Brighton. Ms. Brighton was a pioneer in the field of PTSD in Massachusetts, long before anyone else would take up the cause for imprisoned veterans. AVIP went on to receive two citations from Governor Dukakis in the 1980s at its chapter in the North Central Correctional Institution, Gardner, for its work with PTSD, the "Last Wish Foundation," and "Toys for Tots." The AVIP chapter at MCI-Norfolk still exists today, although its charitable work for the community has been stifled and muted by the Department of Correction.

Walpole Prison of 1973 groomed other such self-help advocates and abolitionists as Fred Williams, Hector Rodriguez, John Clinkscales, Frank Arujo, James Haley, Floyd Hamilton, and Louis Ladetto, who are a few of the names that I recall being associated with the founding of Inside/Out, Incorporated. Inside/Out, Inc., was a self-help drug abuse program designed to assist in the abolition of severe drug dependency existing within the prison during the 1970s, which boasted paid community therapists and prisoner counselors/facilitators via a Law Enforcement Assistance Administration (LEAA) grant. Inside/Out was the first drug rehabilitation program in the Mississippi penal system, which was mimicked by numerous community-based programs and duplicated by government-controlled (i.e., DOC-controlled) so-called treatment programs in existence within the system today.

These flagship programs were birthed into existence while I was confined within punitive segregation (Walpole's Block 10), and Robert Dellelo was on escape, which is a testament to BANTU's adult basic education tutorship and NPRA's formatting that specified the necessity to shed the dominating mind-set of the oppressor/oppressed—to take control of our own destiny and to fulfill our own needs.

b. Media resistance. (cf., 1850s to 1970s)

> The press is almost, without exception, completely corrupt. I believe that in this country, the press exerts a greater and more pernicious influence than the church did in its worst period . . . the people who read their newspapers are in the condition of the dog that returns to his vomit.[16]
> —Henry David Thoreau

One-hundred and fifty years ago the overwhelming majority of Massachusetts newspapers were pro-slavery, anti-abolitionist, and anti-black. *The Morning Post, The Boston Transcript, New Bedford Mercury, North American Review, Newburyport Daily Herald, Merchantile Journal, Yarmouth Register,* and *Columbian Sentinel* are remembered in history as the most prominent. Yet, the most virulent of them all were T*he Boston Pilot, The Courier,* and *The Boston Herald.*

The Boston Pilot had a reputation for defending the Constitutional rights of southern plantation owners to possess Africans, while it promoted the "natural inferiority" of black slaves. The editors of the paper opined that the black race was more happier in slavery than they were in freedom and further opined that blacks "loved there masters as do dogs . . ."[17] The newspaper catered to Boston's Irish population, who were often encouraged by the paper toward anti-black violence.

A quote from Henry David Thoreau's "Slavery In Massachusetts" essay berated the 1850s media:

> "Could slavery suggest a more complete servility than some of these journals exhibit? Is there any dust which their conduct does not lick, and make fouler still with its slime? I do not know whether the *Boston Herald* is still in existence, but I remember to have seen it about the street when Sims[18] was carried off. Did it not act its part well—serve its master faithfully? How can a man stoop lower than he is low? do more than put his

---

16. Henry David Thoreau, "Slavery in Massachusetts," in *The Reform Papers* (ed.), Wendell Glick, (Princeton, NJ: Princeton University Press, 1973), p. 99.
17. *The Boston Pilot,* May 3, 1862; May 10, 1862; May 31, 1862.
18. Thomas Sims, a fugitive slave, was arrested in Boston in March 1851 (six weeks after Minkins was rescued), and marched to the port surrounded by an armed guard of 300 policeman and white citizen volunteers.

extremities in place of the head he has? than make his head his lower extremity? When I have taken up this paper with my cuffs turned up, I have heard the gurgling of the sewer through every column. I have felt that I was handling a paper picked out of the public gutters, a leaf from the gospel of the gambling-house, the groggery and the brothel, harmonizing with the gospel of the Merchant's Exchange."[19]

Thoreau wondered in the 1850s if the *Boston Herald* still existed. In the 1970s through to the 1980s, there was a resounding "Yes!" And it was still crawling on its belly ... still stooped lower than low, with its extremities where the head should have been ... and it was just as racist and despicable a rag in the 1970s as it was during Thoreau's time. *The Boston Herald* had kept true to its incitable tradition and true to the times. As a gutter paper, it still catered to the master—from the slave traders of the Merchant's Exchange in the 1850s, to the neo-slavers of the twentieth century: the embryonic prison-industrial complex that, like Frankenstein's monster, was in the primary stages of being pieced together with human parts.

Boston's Irish population claimed to have come into this country as abused immigrants and indentured servants. It is ironic that being considered as oppressed people themselves, as they were depicted within the Massachusetts news media, they were historically and traditionally the severest opponents to the abolition of slavery on this continent. Violence was not only condoned amongst themselves as against blacks, it was culturally expected. This was truth that had to be revealed to Walpole's predominantly Irish population, in the hope of maintaining peace.

In the 1840s, there was the racially vicious *Boston Pilot* newspaper. For years it conducted its venomous campaign against "nigger loving" abolitionists, to the point of inciting mob violence against them. Its campaigns were similar to those of the *Boston Herald* American newspaper in the 1970s, with its racist assaults upon the Commissioner of Corrections John O. Boone (whom they dubbed "Boone the coon"), and the prisoner

---

19. Thoreau, Ibid, pp. 101-02.

abolitionists of the NPRA,[20] as well as its fascist pogrom against school desegregation in the 1970s—often encouraging, through its reporting and editorials, Boston's Irish communities and their regional politicians to violence . . .[21] then sympathizing with those political leaders, and the so called plight of their Irish constituents.

William Lloyd Garrison remarked in 1845 that the Irish of Boston were a "mighty obstacle . . . in the way of Negro emancipation on our soil."[22] His sentiment held true 129 years later in Walpole Prison, as racism was the single greatest obstacle on the path of unity that the NPRA had to confront. The Irish of Mississippi controlled the State Senate, police forces of the State, the County District Attorney offices, the courts (i.e., judges, clerks, and bailiffs positions), the Department of Correction and its staff, the Parole Board, the State's news media outlets, and the governor's office. They were the leading cause controlling the violence permeating Walpole Prison's population, during the ascendancy of BANTU and the NPRA as prison abolition movements. For well over one hundred years, the Irish controlled the political pulse of Boston, hence Mississippi, and that type of control historically breeds arrogance, which, in turn, translated into white supremacy.

BANTU had decided that it was time for a reality check . . . for a lifesaving transfusion of consciousness.

> "In terms of consciousness, black consciousness claims to be an absolute density, full of itself, a stage pre-existent to any opening, to any abolition of the self by desire."[23]

c. Anti-abolitionism VS. abolitionism, in Walpole.

The rise of black consciousness in Walpole Prison during the early 1970s was not a black power play, as some might be inclined

---

20. Bissonette, Ibid., pp. 14,88, 130, 131, 236 n.256.
21. Dennis P. Ryan, *Beyond the Ballot Box: A Social History of the Boston Irish, 1845-1917*, (East Brunswick, NJ: Associated University Presses, 1983), p. 137.
22. Oscar Handlin, *Boston's Immigrants: A Study in Acculturation,* (Cambridge, MA: Harvard University Press, 1959), pp. 132-33.
23. Frantz Fanon, *Black Skin, White Masks*, (New York: Grove Press, 2008), p. 113.

to assume. It was a time of emancipation from the oppression caused by a century of post-slavery brainwashing perpetuated by the dominant European culture, thereby, making it an exciting period of great creativity and experimentation.

The chains of repression had begun to fall from my mind, but with an active movement to abolish mental slavery came a new round of anti-abolitionism. This media event was not caused by the enlightenment of the black captives held within the prisons of Mississippi,[24] but rather by what the local media and pro-slavery advocates perceived as the tearing down of the walls of the prison plantation by Commissioner John O. Boone and an active/vocal prison reform movement.[25] Abolitionism was once again perceived as a threat to European economic stability.

Inside of Walpole Prison, BANTU had embarked upon a mission to reeducate and empower its members to the reality of self and to the responsibilities that self-awareness imposed upon us as black men in relation to our respective families and communities. However, I did not stop there. As a result of numerous discussions with Robert "Bobby" Dellelo, I came to understand that it was our collective responsibility to attempt to infuse the entire prison population of Walpole with the self-enhancing transfusion of a liberated consciousness.

In the years 1972-73, the BANTU board of directors, almost to a man, had awakened to the fact that there was only one consciousness in the universe . . . and that metaphysical force bound us all together on the physical plane of existence. Our differing skin tones or pigmentations were the result of hemispheric conditions exacted over a millennium of climate. So, nature itself was the agent of our differing surface characteristics. As much as we human beings love to harp about our differences, we have far more aspects of ourselves in common. One crucial trait of our commonality in Walpole was that we were all sharing the unfolding prison experience together—being the objects of Constitutionally-sanctioned slavery, together.

---

24. For instance, MCI-Concord boasted a prisoner facilitated program called "Peaceful Movement," but it was praised by the media because it did not advocate for the abolition of prisons.
25. Bissonette, Ibid., pp 99-131, 200, 240, 385, 244, 534.

This experience was not an "I" situation—it was a "we" dilemma, that as one body we had to resolve. But we had to possess the unifying principle of a single consciousness, motivated by the same fundamental purpose. We had to invoke a collective creative force.

To BANTU, and thus to the NPRA, the single conscious force had to arise from partaking in, and understanding, the common ground upon which all of the ethnic groups in the prison stood. The creative collective had to be rooted within our common history. Be it benign or volatile, the truth had to be shared.

Connection ... communication ... consciousness.

It may have been true that the Irish were the single-most obstacle in the way of peace and unity in the prison, as they were during the cause of the abolition of slavery in the 1800s in this country and state, but it was the purpose of the collective "we" to reveal to them who was pulling their historical strings ... the true anti-abolitionists (i.e., the institution of education, of justice, of government, and the media).

We had to pull ourselves away from the inhuman voices of our ancestors, so that we could have a new and constructive dialogue. This dialogue could not be about retribution, revenge, or reparations, because none of us were responsible. This effort had to be one of conscious reconciliation, and the recognition that whether we liked it or not, our futures were tied together. We were reclaiming our lives from those who claimed to possess us ... exploiting us by perpetuating our ancestral pasts against our present and future.

I spent a lot of time during the course of my day speaking with (educating) NPRA block representatives. I questioned them on the perception of the racial barometer (tension) in their respective cellblocks: Were the prisoners talking to one another more, as opposed to alienating and isolating themselves based upon their ethnicity? How often did the reps notice prisoners reading and/or discussing our political situation—could they give a number, or gauge a percentage? What was the reps' opinion on the impact of the race-relations seminars? Were there any prisoners whom they thought Larry and I should speak with on the matter of race and the importance of NPRA unity?

I also made it a point to frequent the prison visiting room, not simply to troubleshoot (as was every board member's responsibility) but to answer any questions posed by visitors regarding the NPRA political struggle. I saw these impromptu appearances in the visiting room as an opportunity to subtly ask the visitors if they noticed any changes in the demeanor of the prisoner they had come to visit, especially in regard to his impressions on politics, knowledge of history, and concern about race relations in the prison.

The NPRA garnered invaluable information about the awareness of our constituency (and what may need to be improved upon in the way of communication with the prisoner body) utilizing the aforementioned approach—making our jobs as negotiators and instructors much easier, as well as affording us the first-impression ability to spread the abolitionist agenda and ideology to the outside community (bypassing garbled media accounts of the struggle).

Being a hands-on person, I always liked to follow the adage, "If you want something done right, then do it yourself." In this manner, I knew that the job was accomplished to the best of ability, and the results were not being interpreted and relayed to me through a third or fourth party—having lost much in the translation, due to modification of the message and personal impression in the retelling. One of the tactics that I used to employ, when I determined to venture out into the visiting room as a board member and executive committee overseer, was to tote particular books with me whose contents I hoped visitors would question me about. This practice was designed to encourage the visitor, and the prisoner whom they visited, in a healthy dialogue regarding history, politics, and race. If a child was present, there arose the possibility that the child would be inquisitive (as is their nature), which lent to my ability to tutor on the primary level . . . raising important topics that I knew were not being addressed within the child's school curriculum.

I found myself reaching into the future—the next generation of possible abolitionists. In many cases, visitors would approach me on subsequent visits to inform me that they had purchased a particular book and desired to discuss with me what they

Lesson 2: The Truth Regarding the Mississippi Abolitionists.

had come to understand from reading it. There were occasions when a visitor or two, sitting adjacent to the person that I was speaking with, would also chime in with questions or opinions. I remember making telephone calls to the prison kitchen, where Fred Williams was the chief prisoner-cook, and asking for food to be sent out to the visiting room.[26] Once the food arrived, I would gather people around me for my rendition of the BANTU in-house seminars. It came to pass that several visitors, and often their children, would look forward to these seminars.

On the days when I could not make it out to the visiting room before they arrived, the visitors would have me summoned. I would walk through the door to the screaming glee of the children, who would rush me and jump upon me. The delight of the visitors and their children was not lost upon the agent provocateurs (the die hard racist anti-abolitionists in our ranks) that viewed my interaction with these predominately white young women and their children as a threat to white supremacy and their manhood.

I symbolized the myth of the "big black buck" (being six foot six inches in height, muscular, and weighing 230 pounds) whom it was foreseen that white women would abandon their men for, and so complaints were lodged with the NPRA president, Robert Dellelo. We agreed that I should curtail my visiting room seminar practice, for the sake of NPRA unity, regardless of the inroads these seminars had created, unless I was summoned there for an actual emergency.

According to some of the prisoners, their children seemed to miss my excursions to the visiting room the most—often becoming sulky, moody, and unmanageable, as they watched the door and realized that I was not going to walk through it.

I had come to realize through the visiting room experience that there were several prisoners, both black and white, who were solidly aligned with the prison administration and did not appreciate the fact that we (the prisoners) had learned to talk *with*, as opposed to *to*, each other upon a higher level of consciousness. Being con men and manipulators themselves, the

---

26. This is a time prior to the advent of vending machines in Walpole.

level of consciousness that BANTU and the NPRA inspired was a threat to their power, as that power could only be wielded in an atmosphere of ignorance and intolerance much like the control our oppressors maintained.

The anti-abolitionists witnessed firsthand how consciousness demanded a higher frequency of communication, which had enabled me to utilize the varied and often subtle strands of connection that bound us all to each other . . . and, unfortunately, to our prison/plantation reality. We were not black . . . we were not white . . . we were blue, together.[27] Our individual beings may have expressed our "being" as consciousness/self passing through translucent panes of different colors (modified energy/matter) and manifesting as different and separate lives of varying hues, perhaps; but, most importantly . . . significantly, we are but one light. Cultural synthesis was the only way.[28]

BANTU was educating each ethnic group in Walpole Prison to its true role in history, and their aiding and abetting the cause of our common foe[29]—the system—through arrogance and acts of violence toward one another. Armed with this knowledge and understanding, future acts of violence could not be attributed to ignorance. We expressed through our seminars that we, as prisoner-slaves . . . a collective whole, could all be counted within the ranks of the anti-abolitionists via subliminal seduction of the system, or by choice—based upon our actions and inactions. Another old adage held true: if you were not a part of the solution, then you were a part of the problem. If you brought into being, through your consciousness, the concept of being an "inmate" or a "resident," then the prison system totally controlled your

---

27. Bissonette, Ibid., Opening the Door to Blue Unity, p. 78.
28. Cultural synthesis is a mode of action for confronting Culture itself as the preserver of the very structures by which it is formed. Paolo Freire, *Pedagogy of the Oppressed*, (New York: Continuum International, 2007), p. 180.
29. Our Race Relations Seminars afforded instructed readings and lectures from such books as: *Before the Mayflower*, by Lerone Bennett Jr.; *The Wretched of the Earth*, and *Black Skin, White Masks*, by Frantz Fanon; *To Be Free*, by Herbert Aptheker; *The Glass House Tapes*, by Louis Tackwood; *The Reform Papers*, by Henry David Thoreau; *Africa's Gift to America*, by J. A. Rogers; *The Mass Psychology of Fascism*, by Wilhelm Reich; *Boston's Immigrants: A Study In Acculturation*, by Oscar Handlin; and *Black Abolitionists*, by Benjamin Quarles; to name a selected few.

thoughts and influenced your behavior for the system's benefit. However, you still had a choice to exercise at your option.

Most of the race relations seminars were held in the school area twice a week, on Tuesday and Thursday nights. They were required attendance for those prisoners who were strongly recommended by NPRA cellblock representatives to partake of them but were also open to anyone in the general prisoner population. On average, close to thirty prisoners regularly attended each seminar session, often with more white prisoners in attendance than black.

As a result of these sessions, racial confrontations took a dramatic drop in occurrence; and upon any given time of the day prisoners could be seen in their respective cellblocks, or even in the main corridor and prison yard, energetically debating the contents of the books and reading material handed out at the seminars. When our instructions came to include a number of Hispanic prisoners, as their numbers had rapidly increased within the prison population since the inception of the NPRA, Hector Rodriquez and Miguel Trinidad facilitated the session. Both Hector and Miguel were regulars at all of the seminars.

In those days we could not always afford books for everyone.[30] Books, therefore, had to be shared by prisoners living in the same cellblock. Also, during the weekdays when the seminars were not in session, one of the facilitators would have chapters extracted from the books and typed up on mimeograph paper—to have 150 or more copies run-off on the NPRA office mimeograph machine. Every board member received a copy of these mimeographed chapters, to keep them abreast of the seminar's progress.

These seminar sessions consisted of lectures from the chapters in the given books, question and answer segments, and reference/dissection of any potential racial disturbance that may have occurred in the prison or within the outside community.

After educating interested segments of the prisoner population to the true history of chattel slavery and indentured servitude in this country, no one desired to be identified or

---

30. Red Book Store, Cambridge, MA, "Prison Book Program" supplied us with books.

categorized as a slave, nor one who aids-and-abets the enslavers. Everyone wanted to be recognized as an abolitionist, which meant that they were compelled to shed their anti-abolitionist mentality, relinquish their previously accepted identification as an inmate or resident, and sever the puppeteer-slavemaster strings that bound them.

> "I used to dream militant
> dreams of taking
> over America to show
> these white folks how it should be
> done,
> I used to dream radical dreams
> of blowing everyone away with my perceptive powers
> of correct analysis"[31]

---

31. Nikki Giovanni, excerpted from her poem, "Revolutionary Dreams," 1973. She is world renowned for her 1973 popular music recording of her poem "Ego Tripping."

Lesson 3

Mississippi Liberalism and the Caste System

a. White Supremacy and Racism.

I began to witness, yet not understand, the depths and breadth of racism when I was a child in Mississippi back in 1959—when I was still eight years old.

My father was an avid baseball fan, and after several futile attempts to encourage me to share in his enthusiasm and embrace the game, he decided that he should take me to Fenway Park for a Boston Red Sox game. I do not recall any anticipatory feelings toward seeing an actual live baseball game, but I do recall being overjoyed at the prospect of spending a day with my father. He brought a baseball glove home with him from work one day—handed it to me with a smile on his face, and told me that the glove would allow me to catch flyballs that came my way as we sat in the stands of Fenway the next afternoon.

No baseballs came my way that afternoon in Fenway Park, but what did fly in my direction was spit, popcorn, beer, empty bottles, and racial epithets of "nigger!" "little tar baby!" "spook," and "coon!", hurled at me by white adults and their children attending the game. Initially, my father was spared the insults because he was so light-skinned (with straight hair) that they must have assumed him to be white like them. But when he took me in his arms and proceeded to rush with me up the aisle to the exit, he received the jeers of "nigger lover" and objects of refuse and food thrown in our direction.

I received similar treatment twice more, between the years 1962 and 1965, while attending a game at Fenway with white adult chaperones. When I complained to these chaperones (who were counselors from the Essex County Training School), they blamed me for the incidents . . . and I was punished by having to perform two hours of push-ups once we returned to the training school from the outing. To this day, at age fifty-eight, I despise the game of baseball and the Boston Red Sox in particular. I equate the Red Sox insignia as a symbol for racism, similar to the cross of the Ku Klux Klan. Although I was not yet born to remember what happened to baseball legend Jackie Robinson in 1945, when he tried out to play for the Red Sox, my father and mother were, and they related to me their recollections of the incident after my father and I returned from the ball park in 1959. They told me that when Jackie Robinson came to Massachusetts in 1945, owner Tom Yawkey was said to have shouted from the stands, "Get those niggers off the field!" In 1959, team manager Mike Higgins was reported to have said, "There will never be any niggers on this team as long as I have anything to say about it!" These same sentiments existed in 1949, when the Sox passed on signing Willie Mays to the team roster. People talk about the curse of the "Bambino" (Babe Ruth) as the reason why it took so long for the Red Sox to win the World Series of Baseball; while I grew up to believe that it was the curse of Jackie Robinson and Willie Mays, as for many decades after the 1940s black players have refused to play for the Red Sox . . . narrowing their chances of winning anything.

I recall several outstanding incidents of white supremacy and racism that occurred within Mississippi between 1959 to 1997 that not only shaped my consciousness and aided me in helping to develop BANTU and the NPRA during the 1970s, but also helped to prevent me from drowning in the cesspool of Mississippi politricks—submitting to be relegated in a caste system that is perpetuated by this State's mass media, school system, and various other institutions designed to suppress people of color.

The following is my recalled Timeline[1] of Overt Racism:

---

1. (TIMELINE): Daniel Golden and Donald Lowry, "Boston and the Post War Racial Strain; Black and Whites in Boston: 1945-1982," *Boston Globe*, 27 September 1982; Dan Shaugnessy, "Red Sox Pained By Their Past, Team Has Taken Positive Steps,"

Lesson 3: Mississippi Liberalism and the Cast System.

- In 1965, Reverend Martin Luther King Jr. led a march from Roxbury to the Boston Common in protest of school segregation in Boston. Ironically, two of the events coordinators—Reverend Edward Rodman and Phyllis Ryan—were to play an integral and critical role in the prison abolition/reform efforts in Massachusetts in the 1970s, as well as become the community voices of both BANTU and the NPRA seven years later. Reverend Vernon Carter protested outside of the Boston School Committee's office for 114 days, until Governor John Volpe signed the Racial Imbalance Bill. Around the same period of time, Boston School Committee member Joseph Lee gave a speech defending white supremacy and school segregation, wherein he stated that white children did not want to be transported into schools with a large proportion of backward pupils from unprospering Negro families who will slow down their education. I also recall that a white public school teacher named Jonathan Kozol was terminated because he allowed his black students to read Langston Hughes's poetry; and school committee member Thomas Eisenstadt confirming the firing of Kozol as being justified, comparing the reading of Langston Hughes's poetry to reading the history of Adolf Hitler.

- There was a four-day rebellion in the Grove Hall section of Boston, sparked off after Boston Police savagely beat, kicked, and dragged women protesters from the welfare office—all the while calling them "niggers." The

---

Boston Globe, 28 March 1997; Bill Russell, *Go Up for Glory*, (New York: Berkley Publishing, Coward-McCann, 1966); Howard Bryant, *Shut Out: A Story of Race and Baseball in Boston*, (New York: Rutledge, 2002); "Blacks in a Changing America: The Challenge of Being Black in Boston," *Boston Globe*, 28 June 1982; Jonathan Kaufman, "2 Claim Police Assaults During Anti-Klan Clash," *Boston Globe*, 19 October 1982; Lonnie Isabel and Timothy Dwyer, "Tales Of Deer Island," *Boston Globe*, 18 May 1980; Jonathan Kozol, *Death at an Early Age: The Destruction of the Heart and Minds of Negro Children in the Boston Public Schools*, (1967 reprint, New York: Penguin Books, 1985); William E. Alberts, *Mainstream Media as Guardian of Racial Hierarchy*, (Boston: William Munroe Trotter Institute, 1996); Jack Tager, *Boston Riots: Three Centuries of Social Violence*, (Boston: Northeastern University Press, 2001).

patty-rollers also clubbed National Association for the Advancement of Colored People (NAACP) officials, and arrested the then Council of Churches official Byron Rushing twice in one night. Byron Rushing was elected to the Massachusetts House of Representatives a few years later and was encouraged to assist BANTU and the NPRA in our efforts to secure meaningful vocational and educational programs for State prisoners during the 1970s. *The Boston Herald*, when reporting the Grove Hall rebellion, lived up to its racist heritage by labeling the incident as "communist inspired," thereby attempting to dissuade any possible broader community support and further alienate black peoples' struggle for dignity and human rights, as was the newspaper's wont in the 1850s through the 1860s.

- In 1968, the Administration Building on the Boston University campus was taken over by two hundred black students demanding African American studies programs and a change in the school's admission policies.

- 1970 is remembered as the year a study was released which concluded that even in the 350-year history of slavery and racism in Boston, no ethnic group was ever as segregated as blacks still were in the 1970s. The study spoke to the fact that black males earned less than three-fourths of what whites earned, making it a worse income gap than the prevailing decade. It is also remembered as the year white officials refused to allow their invited guest speaker at the 350th Anniversary of the Pilgrim's landing, Native American Frank James, president of the Federated Eastern Indian League, to speak because they didn't like the truth of content contained within his speech.

- During 1971, the Boston Celtics basketball team held festivities honoring Bill Russell, and as the event was unfolding, white vandals broke into his Reading home. They smashed his trophies, defecated upon his bed, and smeared feces upon his walls. His teammate, Tom Heinsohn, was reported as saying that two local white sports reporters confessed to him that they would never have voted for Russell, because they refused to vote for a black as MVP of the basketball league.

- During 1973, Bill Russell describes Boston as the capitol of US bigotry. When he tries to move out of his Reading neighborhood, his neighbors file a petition trying to block him from moving. When that failed, the neighbors attempted to purchase the home that he was trying to obtain ahead of him. Russell's teammate K.C. Jones has a cross burned upon the lawn of his new house in Framingham by the Ku Klux Klan.

- 1973 is also recalled as the year that sixty black prisoners in Deer Island House of Correction were subjects of heroin addiction experiments funded by the federal government.

- In 1974, federal court Judge Walter A. Garrity cites the Boston School Committee for being evasive, procrastinators, intransigent, and displaying bad faith in desegregating Boston's all-white public schools; and he orders the forced busing of black children to attend school in the most overtly racist communities in Massachusetts Irish dominated Charlestown and South Boston. Boston Police had to escort black children through rabid crowds of rock throwing and bottle tossing whites, who shouted, "Bus them back to Africa!" "Everyone should own a nigger," "Kill niggers!" "Klan Kountry!" and "French-fried niggers for sale!" The irony was that, prior to busing in 1974, South Boston High School was ranked as one of the worst public schools, academically, in the nation-boasting, on average, only two to three graduates for college per year. City Council members Louise Day Hicks, James Kelly, Thomas "Dapper" O'Neil, and school committee member Pixie Paladino led white protest marches spewing their hatred of black school children. Daily racial violence against blacks escalated in Boston, spurred on by local printed news media, as it did against the abolitionists in the 1850s. The violence included beatings, brawls, fire-bombings, dynamitings, arson, lootings, shootings, and murder. Forty-two classified mini riots occurred between 1974 and 1976.

- In 1975, while sunning themselves and resting upon Carson Beach in South Boston, several black Bible salesmen from down South were attacked by hundreds of whites wielding pipes, rocks, and sticks. Their car was destroyed, and two were severely beaten and hospitalized, for trying to spread the "Good Word" in liberal . . . Christian . . . Mississippi.

- The year 1976 is remembered around the world as the year when black businessman Theodore Landsmark was speared with a poled American flag by a mob of anti-black Bostonians on City Hall plaza. The United Press International photo of the incident earns a Pulitzer Prize.

- 1979 is notorious as the year when Darryl Williams, a black student football player from Jamaica Plain High School, is shot in the neck and permanently paralyzed while he stood upon the sidelines of a high school football game at Charlestown High School. Two Charlestown white males are arrested for the shooting and released from jail on a $100 bail.

- In 1982, thirty people are injured by Boston patty-rollers on motorcycles and horses, who attacked one thousand anti Ku Klux Klan protesters with billy clubs and mace.

- William Atkins is murdered by five white males, after being chased while rocks and bottles are being thrown at him, in the Savin Hill subway station in 1982.

- In 1982, another black family is firebombed in their home, and eight whites are arrested. This is significant because they are simply ordered by the court to refrain from taunting, beating, and fire-bombing black people, as their punishment.

- Also, in 1982, a sixteen-year-old black girl is raped by a gang of Boston Police at a private club in Roxbury called the Silver Shield Athletic Association. She is found dead weeks later in Franklin Park. The case is covered up by both State and federal courts and remains unsolved.

- 1985 is hallmarked by *Boston Globe* columnist Mike Barnicle, who seeks a more acceptable term for "nigger" and coins the word "yummies" (young urban maggots). The *Globe* utilizes the new word to continue in its criminalization of Africans who are descendants of those kidnapped and enslaved by the Baystate. Barnicle asked, "What do you do with a yummie?" Then answers himself "Lower the eligibility requirements for the electric chair to age nine." He is fired from the *Globe* in 1998 for fabricating his columns, only to be hired by the most historically racist rag in Mississippi—*The Boston Herald*.

- In 1986, Boston's white media released a study admitting that their stories concerning the predominantly black neighborhoods of Roxbury and Mattapan overwhelmingly portray blacks as drug dealers, thieves, rapists, murderers, and as victims of perpetrators of crime.

- In 1989, Charles Stuart murders his pregnant wife Carol and blames a black man, William Bennett, after picking his photo out of a photo array in the Boston Police station. *The Boston Globe*, led by their Negro editor, arouse racist fears concerning the Boston black community, thereby acquiescing to random strip-searching of young black males on the streets by Police Commissioner Frank

Roache and his infamous patty-rollers. Mayor Raymond Flynn and ascot wearing Nation of Islam Minister Donald Muhammad appear on television press conferences beside Commissioner Roache, condoning the unconstitutional strip searches, which leads to random raids upon black homes and the destruction of the home of William Bennett's mother by the police, as they are presumably searching for the black killer of a pregnant white woman. Politicians call for the reinstatement of the death penalty, while media commentators refer to black people in Boston as "animals." The court rules that the random strip-searching of black males is unconstitutional, and Minister Donald Muhammad refrains from appearing in future press conferences regarding the Stuart case.

- In 1990, Charles Stuart jumps off a bridge to his death, as the truth surfaces that he killed his wife Carol for insurance money, aided by his accomplice brother Matthew. Boston patty-rollers are aired on television, politely wiping their feet on mats, and removing their hats, as they respectfully enter the Stuart home—in stark contrast to the televised smashing in of doors with battering rams and ransacking of William Bennett's mother's home. William Bennett, who is the innocent victim, is railroaded to prison on unrelated trumped-up charges and is forced to serve seven years; as the media publishes claims that although he may not have committed the murder, he had to be guilty of something else he went unpunished for in his lifetime. Matthew Stuart serves less than five years in Concord prison due to some obscure law from the Magna Carta concerning sibling accomplices.

- South African freedom fighter Nelson Mandela was released from prison after having served twenty-seven years and visits Boston in 1990. Blacks are kept away from the official celebration, with the minor exception of a few local black politicians. His motorcade speeds through the black community without stopping, at 50 miles per hour.

Whites who barely sneezed during his internment are televised welcoming him like a long lost brother.

- In 1990, Boston Celtic's rookie Dee Brown and his white fiance, who are out house hunting, are forced out of their car at gun point by the Wellesley police who claim that Brown looks like a bank robber. He is handcuffed and forced to lie face down in the street, as a spectacle for white passersby, an example of driving while black, especially in the company of a white woman.

- In 1994, Harvard University Klansmen strike again with the release of Harvard professor Richard Hermstein's none peer reviewed, technically flawed, and racist book *The Bell Curve*, co-authored by Charles Murray, another example of white supremacist pseudo-science.

- Thanksgiving Day, 1997: The Day of Mourning, the United American Indians of New England march through the center of Plymouth during the Thanksgiving celebration. Over fifty local police block their path and tear gas them.

There are, of course, hundreds of other incidents of liberally applied racism in Mississippi that have occurred over the course of my lifetime, but the aforementioned list contains incidents that left an indelible impression upon my psyche. They all stand as catalysts that awakened my consciousness, as they keep me ever vigilant.

b. Unconscionable Denial.

Liberal Massachusetts, for the most part, harbors the same racial bias and intolerance as their brother/sister Klansmen in Mississippi (circa 1865-1969). In 1865, after this country's Civil War was over, the Sons of Liberty (formerly known as the Knights of the Golden Circle) reemerged from underground, where they had been forced to go by US President Abraham

Lincoln for their violent acts of sedition. They resurfaced in 1865 as the Ku Klux Klan, ending in 1871. It started again in 1921, by 1923 Knights of the Ku Klux Klan[2] had set up a chapter in Harvard University in Cambridge, Massachusetts,[3] and by 1925, the Klan boasted a statewide membership of 130,780 Klansmen. These Massachusetts Klansmen and their spawn became the State's school principals and teachers, university/college presidents and professors, lawyers, judges, doctors, politicians, and various other State professionals during the Civil Rights Era of the 1960s.

My experiences dictate that the similarities, which bind the Mississippi Klansmen with the Massachusetts Klan, are as follows:

1. In Mississippi, the Klansmen shield their faces under pointed hoods, whereas in liberal Massachusetts, they may hide their pointed faces behind law books and patty-roller shields, as well as under scully caps or Boston Red Sox hats;

2. In Mississippi, the Klan cloak themselves under the mantle of the blazing cross, and cross emblazoned robes, while in liberal Massachusetts, they often cloak themselves under the mantle of the double-cross, a self-righteous veneer of white supremacy and manifest destiny, utilizing mainstream media outlets, and hell-fire-emblazoned judicial robes;

3. A Mississippi Klansmen will call a black person a "nigger" to his or her face without the necessity of crowd support and outwardly demonstrate his racial hatred toward that black individual, whereas in liberal Massachusetts, he will smile in a black person's face when alone, then call him or her a "nigger" behind their back, and surreptitiously demonstrate his racial

---

2. The Knights of the Ku Klux Klan was founded in 1915.
3. See; Lauren E. Baer, "The Ku Klux Klan at Harvard," *Harvard Crimson* Online, posted at: http://www.thecrimson.com/article/1999/2/18/the-ku-klux-Klan-at-harvard/

hatred through support of racially biased regulations, public policies, and practices;

4. In Mississippi, Klansmen will openly lynch a black person from a tree with a braided rope, then evade prosecution for the act from the judiciary altogether, whereas in liberal Massachusetts, a black person is legally lynched in a courthouse by entwined state and federal judicial robes forming the noose, and thereby sentenced to a lifetime of prolonged and agonizing death-through-torture in the penal system, by way of disparate and obscenely exorbitant prison sentences.[4]

For me, the aforementioned similarities in character and custom create the amalgamation: Mississippi.

In Mississippi, one is victimized due to the color of one's skin,[5] then unconscionably blamed for the victimization.

The Black Consciousness Movement of the 1970s acted as a life preserver would for a passenger leaping for safety from a sinking ship. Without it, there was a distinct possibility that I would have remained adrift in the proverbial sea of chaos—tempered and retarded by localized caste alienation, and unconscionable denial of existent racialized politricks. The movement taught me the all-important lesson to view liberal Mississippi as if it were a Trojan Horse full of unpleasant and deadly surprises, which I had harvested from the history of slavery and the abolition movement in this State.

To me, in the 1970s, liberals appeared to be like sharks that circled their mortally wounded prey . . . searching for

---

[4]. I was arrested in Lawrence, Massachusetts on November 28, 1968, and sentenced to life in prison for "intent to commit rape' upon a white woman by allegedly saying "not yet" in June 1969.

[5]. In 1984 the Massachusetts Appeals Court utilized the color of my skin as the means by which to deny my 1980 motion for a new trial. In 1999 and 2004 the Mississippi Parole Board questioned me about, and then penalized me for, the skin color of the victims of the crime-thereby fulfilling their KKK legacy by denying relief in both instances, due to race.

The Harvard Crimson

VOL. LXXXIV. No. 26   CAMBRIDGE, MASS.   OCTOBER 22, 1923   PRICE 5 CENTS

KU KLUX KLAN AT HARVARD AWAITS MOMENT TO STRIKE

"We May Be Inactive but Our Influence is Felt" are Leader's Ominous Words

SEEKING MORE MEMBERS

Indications Point to Good Deal of Activity in Increasing Numbers Before Action

Started two years ago and ever since, month by month, growing more powerful, the Harvard Ku Klux Klan has only been waiting for the favorable moment to show its strength.

And now there are indications that the next few weeks will see the largest drive yet for Klan membership. As yet the branch has worked under considerable secrecy but coupled with this drive the Harvard public may expect to see the Klan pursue a more open policy, leading probably to a formal statement of its aims and platform.

The shadow of the Klan lies from West to East across the country. Only recently the Fiery Cross has been seen in Boston. And now Harvard, considered the stronghold of culture and conservatism, is about to try its strength with the boasted omnipotence of the Invisible Empire.

TRADITIONAL POLICY

Following its traditional policy the Crimson refrains from publishing the names of known members of the Harvard branch of the Klan. They will, however, if necessary, be given to authorized persons.

The Harvard Klan was started some two years ago and made its influence felt with a membership drive. At that time a Mr. W—, the organizer of the Chicago chapter and an imperial officer of the Klan, and a Mr. T— were most active in furthering the organization. But the greatest strength and size of the Klan has come only in the past six months.

Klan Opposes Open Door Policy

Whether or not the action of the University last year in decreeing the policy of non-discrimination tended to increase Klan membership is an open question. The plank in the Klan's national platform bearing on the subject is well known, and what part of it the Harvard branch stands for may be only a question of degree. But it is certain that the decision of last spring was a signal for violent demonstrations in meetings of the Harvard Klan. Yet in the final test, the decision was reached to attempt no active participation in the domestic issues of the University.

Such policy has apparently been pursued during the first few weeks of College. The Klan as such has not interfered with social or religious organizations, and the Harvard public, lulled possibly into a false sense of security, has wondered at the apparent inactivity.

Questioned the other day concerning the plans of the organization, a prominent member hesitated to admit this inactivity. "The Harvard Klan," he said, "is inactive. But it is very far from being disorganized, nor can I say that even now its influence is unfelt." And the remarks and actions of associate members fully bear out his statement.

KU KLUX KLAN WILL STRIKE WHEN READY

Like all organizations the Klan has sought for a representative Harvard membership. While few prominent undergraduates have openly declared their allegiance, yet from the very nature of the organization it is impossible to tell what man's friends or acquaintances may belong or may be aspiring to membership. The national platform, to which the Harvard branch subscribes, appeals at once to men of the most advanced and most conservative political opinions. Nor can the type be defined until the Klan chooses to abandon its present temporary inactivity.

What the reasons are for the present apparent stagnation is more difficult to ascertain. The Klan's activities in Oklahoma have raised adverse criticism from the public, criticism which, as some have suggested, a relatively small chapter might be unwilling to encounter in the year's first demonstration. Others interested in the Klan have suggested that there may be division in the Harvard branch itself. To many Harvard may appear so much 100 per cent American that education by the Klan is futile. While more despairing members may see so little Americanism in the University, so much unpatriotism, such a mass of political, racial, religious, and intellectual filth, that the task of making it pure would be too Herculean for even the "white wings" of the Invisible Empire.

Coeducation may not appear as a plank of the platform to be published by the Klan, yet it has lately looked with no aversion on the scheme of founding a branch of the Kamelia (the female of the Klan) at Radcliffe. This latter plan holds innumerable possibilities for furthering the principles of the Klan.

But what the definite policy of the Harvard Klan may be can only be ascertained from their more open appeal for members, which the University can expectantly await within the next few weeks.

the opportune moment to safely rush in and take a bite, then frantically swim off to a safe distance in search for another vantage point from which to strike. It was my opinion then that these opportunists were at Walpole only until the "next thing" came along to peak their interest, like a stone-ruptured and blood-spattered school bus. I probably felt similar to what most of my ancestors who had ventured North on their way to Canada, via the underground railroad, must have felt-cautious of the handshake that might hide a snake.

Through my interaction with liberals, I found that most enjoyed the status quo as it was, with the possibility of a little tweak here and there-as long as they maintained control. They were good at placing Band-Aids upon open wounds but lacked the wherewithal to stem the actual bleeding or to truly accept an opinion on the matter that was contrary to their own. They shunned militancy, because we were radical, and radicals believed in change now (or yesterday)-consciously and continuously engaging ourselves without much compromise and working toward the prospective end result. Liberals enjoyed meetings and social functions by which to talk-to brag and solicit monetary contributions-and discuss how many black friends that they might have. Radicals preferred less talk and more action.

So, we of BANTU gravitated toward and communicated mainly with our external board of directors and their political allies, who also appeared to be radical, leaving most discussions with the outside community liberals to the white members of the NPRA board of directors. The South Boston based Citizens And Relatives Concerned About Prisons (CARCAP) suffered the same alienation from BANTU, as its South Boston office location fueled the air of distrust and the appearance of racism.

c. Keep them in their place (a psychological profile).

There have been periods in America's past when the country was consumed with the issue of crime out of an unwarranted fear that blacks were somehow propelling society to the brink of collapse. Such an exaggerated fear of crime existed during the antebellum period, following the Civil War, in the midst of prohibition, during the Great Depression, and in the politically tumultuous 1960s. In such times, during each of these periods, society was definitely in a state of disconcerting flux.

However, there is an advantage in viewing these eras retrospectively, because one can discern that the media-hyped clamor about crime was merely a ruse—a scapegoat for other political and economic forces that were the real culprits, the real criminals, behind the social turmoil.

For instance, during the antebellum period which began around 1830, the real roots of societal turmoil were probably twofold:

1   A general anxiety contributed to the growing understanding that the slavery issue was going to lead to war; and,

2   The abolitionist movement had divided society into three opposing camps:

   a) Those who desired a multicultural society,
   b) Those who wanted free blacks but not black citizens, and
   c) Those who wanted to maintain the system of slavery.

The 1960s had brought forth similar fears of blacks and crime. White social pundits who accepted Martin Luther King Jr. and civil rights could not fully appreciate and understand the call for human rights. The media charged that the upheavals throughout the country's inner cities was the result of criminality gone unchecked, and "communist" sleeper cells riling up "their Negroes" in an attempt to destroy America from within. Black Panthers were toting guns in the streets. Black combat-trained Vietnam War veterans were returning home to smoldering ghettoes, without jobs or a vision for a meaningful future.

The cauldron of "Chocolate City" was boiling over into the suburban home through television, and white America refused to accept responsibility for turning up the heat via centuries of perpetual social, economic, and political repression upon the under-class of the black populace. White America was being subliminally fed night terrors by the news at eleven, envisioning hordes of angry ex-slaves roaming the countryside in search of prey like twentieth century Nat Turners. The federal government refused to ease the pressure and applied more oppressive measures to the situation. They knew that white America always felt better of itself when it blamed its victims for their discomfort.

> "... the punishment we deserve can be diverted only by denying responsibility for the wrong and throwing the blame on the victim: by proving—at least in our own eyes—that striking the first and only blow we are simply acting in legitimate defense." (Frantz Fanon, *Black Skin, White Masks*, page 125, citing G. Legman, *Psychopathologie des Comics* Temps Modernes, No. 43, pp. 916ff.)

And the government took full advantage of this knowledge—it prepared itself for the worse.

In the early 1970s, the Black Panther Party gave me something else to be concerned about. Their newspaper published what appeared to be a comprehensive plan by the US Government for urban warfare that involved rounding up the entire minority population, in a similar manner to the detention centres of Japanese and Germany Americans in the early months of Americas entry into World War II. At the same time highways in and around Boston's predominately black neighborhoods were being widened and reinforced, a new police stations was also being constructed—reinforced with steel—that contained subterranean levels of detention cells, war rooms, and heavy weapons armories.[6]

If the beatings at night by the "goon squad,"[7] the killings, and the close proximity of the electric chair were all part of my reality now, I could only imagine what was in store for us minority group prisoners already confined within the nightmarish conditions of the state's prisons. I sat in my cell anxiously watching television news accounts, and "Big Bob" Heard afforded me weekly reports

---

6. Station No. 2 was being constructed along these lines in the heart of Boston's largest black community.
7. See Bissonette, Ibid. pp. I, 95, 101-102.

on the construction of Police Station No. 2 across the street from his Black Panther headquarters in Boston.

My main concern, at the time, however, was focused upon my family and friends in the outside community slated for extinction under the "plan." It became my romantic/idealistic notion to step up the completion of our self-help programs to place functional able bodies out in the community as a vanguard of an envisioned People's Army. They might eventually kill us all, but I hoped not without a fight. Chattel slavery was in the past, and I prayed that black people had not become so psychologically disenfranchised and passive in the twentieth century as not to resist.

The Panther's publication and distribution of the plan appeared to have an almost instantaneous effect upon civil rights leaders of the country. People like Jesse Jackson, Andrew Young, and Maynard Jackson were transformed overnight. They seemed to us to have devolved further back in time to that of the court jester and minstrel of medieval Europe, or so it appeared to many.

In response we began to rely more upon the spoken words of our poets and musicians, regarding the direction our struggle should embark upon. The change in the demeanor of our venerated leaders was an altering of black consciousness, or an attempt to redirect the movement of the masses toward a media-prescribed solution, of working within the system. The majority white culture appeared to view this shifting of consciousness as a more palatable initiative, because it basically meant business as usual. The Negro leaders were under control. In the most favorable light, to us, the change was viewed retrospectively as an effort to stem the full effects of the plan. But that may be affording those individuals too much insight and credit for self-sacrifice. Yet, the overall struggle for human rights had been altered.

Meanwhile . . . back on the plantation. The struggle for prison reform and the abolition of mental slavery was also under pressure, and a change of focus was inevitable. It was "adapt, or die in the prison system!" Scores of NPRA members and self-help prison program leaders were being rounded up in nightly raids by the "goon squad" for shipment to the federal prison system—thousands of miles from families and friends. Some were murdered in federal custody, while others were planned to be murdered. Prisoners from Walpole Prison were slated for transfer to Bridgewater State Hospital for chemical lobotomies, while the death toll began to mount once again within the walls of the maximum security prison. There was also the threat of perpetual punitive isolation and segregation, as rumors that a sensory deprivation unit was on the drawing board to be constructed in the State.[8] I had reached a crossroads: remain true to the disappearing cause of abolition and reform, or become mute and thereby express the appearance of adaptation on the hope of effecting change through a protracted struggle. I opted to bide my time on the belief that I could learn more valuable lessons, reach more students, which afforded the opportunity for this book to be written.

When I received my life sentence from the Essex County Superior Court, I couldn't fathom how I could receive such a disparate and exorbitant sentence to prison for "intent" to commit a felony in liberal Massachusetts. My mother was born and raised in South Carolina during the 1920s; and through her experience with white people who desired her to "psychologically train" me "to be mentally weak and dependent but physically strong,"[9] she stymied the psychology and made me strong in both areas. She informed me that I was sentenced so severely because of the development of my mind. In 1969, at the age of eighteen, I could not wrap my head around the concept of imprisoning someone who had no adult criminal history, without having actually killed someone, for the rest of their life because of what they believed that someone to be thinking or was capable of thinking . . .

> "But the black man is attacked in his corporeality. It is his tangible personality that is lynched. It is his actual being that is dangerous."
> Fanon, Ibid., page 142.

Several years after my mother had made her observations known to me, and I had undergone years of intense study and growth regarding the history of my people kidnapped and held

---

8. The Departmental Disciplinary Unit (DDU) was built adjacent to MCI-Walpole, and accessed through a steel gate cut/built into the wall surrounding Walpole prison.
9. See Bissonette, Ibid., pp. 2, 69, 73, 92.

captive in this country, I came to fully appreciate what she had meant about the development of a black person's mind being a threat. BANTU and the NPRA had come and gone as viable conduits for prisoner unity and social change, and I had openly exposed myself (my self) to my oppressors.

Throughout AmeriKlan his-story, with regard to my people, the stronger and more educated black male was killed outright in front of the rest as an example of what happens to a "nigger" slave boy when he decides to become human again. The example then, as today, became a part of a tracking system of checks and balances by which to instill a mentality of fear in Africans, thereby retarding the efforts of an entire race from becoming human again.[10] Fear is the mind killer!

So it should be understandable why my first reaction was to say, "No!" and also understandable that my first action was a reaction to being assimilated.[11] Sun-Ra, intoned:

> "Resist me
> Make me strong.
> Resist me
> For since I cannot be what you will
> I shall always be that much more so
> What I will.
> Resist me
> Repulse my dreams.
> Thus is a spark brought from nothing . . .
> Stone rubbed against stone

---

10. ". . . it is because the white man feels frustrated by the black man that he in turn seeks to frustrate the black man, hemming him in with taboos of all sorts." Fanon, Ibid., pp. 152, 154 n.38.

11. Fanon, Ibid., p. 19. Also, see; "Whether he likes it or not, the black man has to wear the livery the white man fabricated for him." Fanon, Ibid., p. 19. Read: "The oppressed, having internalized the image of the oppressor and adopted his guidelines, are fearful of freedom. Freedom would require them to eject this image and replace it with autonomy and responsibility. Freedom is acquired by conquest, not by gift. It must be pursued constantly and responsibly. Freedom is not an ideal located outside of man; nor is it an idea, which becomes myth. It is rather the indispensable condition for the quest for human completion." Paolo Freire, *Pedagogy of the Oppressed*, (New York: continuum International, 2007), p. 47.

Upon the thirsty grass,
Dried and baked by a burning son . . .
Then suddenly: flame
Flame feeding flame.
. . . now, nothing is the same:
The stones are blackened
The grass is ashes
The burning sun is no less itself
But all else is changed
Nor ever shall be as it was before."[12]

---

12. Sun-Ra, poem: "Saga Of Resistance," 1960s; he made his mark as a musician-philosopher, and leader of one of the most important bands in the Black Consciousness Era-The Myth Science Arkestra. Albums to his credit are: "The Magic City," "Heliocentric Worlds," "Planet Earth," "When Sun Comes Out," and, "When Angels Speak of Love."

LESSON 4

"Free Your Mind And Your Ass Will Follow."[1]

a. Recognizing domination.

I was born in Boston, Massachusetts, on November 28, 1950, to Margaret Elizabeth Hamm and Ralph Conrad Hamm Jr. My formative (mis)education from kindergarten through to the end of the third grade was undergone in the Boston public school system. I completed the fourth, fifth, and sixth grades, dropping out of school in the seventh, in Lynn, Massachusetts, where my family (mother, father, and five sisters) moved to from Boston in 1961.

As a result of my rebellion toward junior high school, and my delinquent behavior at home, when my mother and father separated in 1963, the juvenile court of Lynn ordered that I be sent to the Essex County Training School located in Lawrence, Massachusetts, to remain therein until I reached "sixteen" years of age. The judge determined that if my mother could not sufficiently *break me*, then it was in the hands of the State to do so. I had to be "trained." So, I remained in the training school for three years, or until 1966.

During the 1950s, while I was being "broken" in the elementary schools of Boston, it was their method to cram the history and beliefs of the Eurocentric dominant society into my skull, and to track me toward the labor force as a menial—custodial and factory—laborer, in service to the white majority. White students, on the other hand, were encouraged

---

1. A phrase coined by the funk band "Parliament Funkadelic" in the 1970s, declared their manifesto by band leader George Clinton.

toward careers as doctors, lawyers, teachers, politicians, and even the United States presidency. I was thereby infused with a fabricated consciousness where past centuries of chattel slavery had permanently deleted, destroyed, and thoroughly trashed my ancestral history of past accomplishments and my personal understanding of African tribal morals and disciplines. As a kidnapped people held in bondage for over three hundred years, we had been stripped of human developmental sciences, which are the basis of the knowledge of self.

The Boston public school teachers, as well as those in Lynn, were not permitted to mention slavery to black pupils, even at the expense of explaining the growth and importance of the cotton industry in this country.[2] I was forbidden from learning anything regarding my true history in the world, to the point where my parents had been trained not to educate their children; and I was thoroughly deprived of my historical base, because my education was mandated by law to be left up to my oppressors.

In substitution of my history, I was taught in school that being called African was something to be ashamed of . . . that it meant someone who was lowly and ignorant, having descended from the "dark continent" whose inhabitants were cowards . . . that the savages were unjustifiably fearful of the white men who had come to their continent only to civilize them and bring enlightenment. These savages ran away from enlightenment and hid in the dense jungle, where they would shoot poisonous darts from blowguns at their white benefactors. Frantz Fanon further explains the process in his work, *Black Skin, White Masks*, page 126, that:

> ". . . the black schoolboy who is constantly asked to recite [history] identifies himself with the explorer, the civilizing colonizer, the white man who brings truth to the savages, a lily-white truth. The identification process means that the black child subjectively adopts a white man's attitude. He invests the Hero, who is white, with all his aggressiveness—which at this age closely resembles self-sacrifice: a self sacrifice loaded with sadism . . . [G]radually an attitude, a way of thinking and seeing that is basically white, forms and crystallizes." (See, also, Fanon, Ibid, page 127.)

---

2. Rogers, Ibid. p. 122.

African religious beliefs were portrayed to me as being steeped in superstition, devil worship, voodoo, and raising the dead as zombies.

What I wasn't taught in public schools was that Africans who were kidnapped and brought to this country in chains, as farm animals and laborers, were denuded of any background knowledge that would allow them to connect with their natural divinity, or claimed kinship with being created in the image and likeness of God. I was programmed to believe that God, and his only begotten Son, were white-that it was in my best interest to worship them, hence, to worship the image of white people.[3] I was taught that anything black symbolized bad and was evil, ugly, and unseemly, while everything white was good, wholesome, beautiful, handsome, and Godlike. Africans, not Europeans, were so depraved and animalistic that they practiced cannibalism whenever they were hungry.[4]

Essex County Training School exposed me to another method of (mis) education having been sent to the training school under the label of "stubborn child." If the lessons in formal education were not met with the satisfaction of the school "master," corporeal punishment was meted out. I was forced to perform calisthenics (push-ups) until complete exhaustion, then kicked and punched when I collapsed on my face, by adult men who were called "counselors." I was spat upon and called "nigger," "coon," and "spade," in front of the entire school, which held only three black children—as a spectacle to promote fear and subservience in the minds of the two remaining black children, and to instill a warped sense of white superiority in the minds of the white children who were the majority. If one ran away from

---

3. "The black man wants to be like the white man. For the black man, there is but one destiny. And it is white. A long time ago the black man recognized the undeniable superiority of the white man, and all his endeavors aim at achieving a white existence." Fanon, Ibid., p.202.

4. Captain John Smith (born 1580-1631) wrote, "So great was our famine that a savage we slew and buried, the poorer sort took him up again and ate him; and so did divers ones another boiled and stewed with herbs. And one amongst the rest did kill his wife, powdered her, and had eaten part of her." *The General Historie Of Virginia, The Fourth Booke*, p. 294 (1606-1625); Rogers, Ibid., p. 45 n.3. Also, see; "Confronted with the black man, today's white man feels a need to recall the age of cannibalism." Fanon, Ibid., p. 200.

the school, as I often did, the return to school custody was met by the same exemplary punishment with the entire school as the audience.

Due to the fact that history is written by the winners, it is difficult to gauge or to judge the battles fought or those that continue to be waged against the oppressor without painstaking research and study. The winners control the means of discourse, and thereby tend to distort, misrepresent, and usurp the history of the vanquished—ignoring all that does not support their "official version." It is this official version that is disseminated within the schools, and the mainstream media, as the truth. As a result, the public is trained, and accepts at face value, the pabulum that has been force-fed to them through the system of rote education. The unquestioning of the winner's yarn, however, carries serious adverse consequences: a populace alive, yet in the dark, with minds unilluminated by the light of understanding.

It was not until the year 1972—having somehow survived formal education, training school, a year in the military, and two years in prison—that I was to begin to lift the veils of darkness covering my eyes. As a member of David Dance's black history class, in Walpole prison,[5] I was to relearn my true ancestry and history, and thereby begin to reverse the damage that the deprivation of my historical base had caused me. I was twenty-two years of age then, having suffered through the over ten years of Eurocentric rote (mis)education/brainwashing "orbiting" within my mind, distorting my thought process, and suppressing my true knowledge of self, which is the system's intent. I learned that I had been purposely denominated from birth, divided from my people of origin for centuries, and debased from my original nature.

Through the assistance of Paolo Freire, and his book *Pedagogy of the Oppressed*, I came to realize that the core of the rote system of (mis)education is domination. It does not embrace the concept of freedom through knowledge; rather, it enslaves the individual and manipulates him with misinformation to not act as a subject in history, thereby relegating him to an object and preventing him from becoming an authentic human being. Freire titled this

---

5. Bissonette, Ibid., p. 69.

the "banking concept of education."[6]

At this stage, it became less of a question on how to teach black prisoners, and more of a determination to develop a method by which to dissolve our slavery to archetypes.

b. Paolo Freire methodology/Adult Basic Eduction (ABE) in Walpole Prison.

In late Summer/Fall of 1972, the twelve board members of BANTU were encouraged by Chairman Jack Harris and Secretary Solomon Brown to conduct an experiment in basic education, based upon Paolo Freire's concepts and methods. We were to endeavor to assist two elderly and functionally illiterate black prisoners in primary math, writing, history, and their reading/comprehension skills without the sanction of the Department of Correction nor the Department of Education.

At the board of directors meeting in 1972, we all discussed, and related to, how the mainstream Eurocentric method of rote education had failed to instill within any of us a true sense of accomplishment, self-worth, or trustworthy historical knowledge. Instead, the system actually suppressed our ambition and creativity.

Freire had informed us that "knowing" was not an act through which someone is changed into an object and passively accepts

---

6. Paolo Freire explained to me why not to adopt a teacher's attitude: "(a) the teacher teaches and the students are taught; (b) the teacher knows everything and the students know nothing; (c) the teacher thinks and the students are thought about; (d) the teacher talks and the students listen—meekly; (e) the teacher disciplines and the students are disciplined; (f) the teacher chooses and enforces his choice, and the students comply; (g) the teacher acts and the students have the illusion of acting through the action of the teacher; (h) the teacher chooses the program content, and the students (who are not consulted) adapt to it; (i) the teacher confuses the authority of knowledge with his or her own professional authority, which she and he sets in opposition to the freedom of the students; (j) the teacher is the subject of the learning process, while the pupils are mere objects. It is not surprising that the banking concept of education regards men as adaptable, manageable beings. The more students work at storing the deposits entrusted to them, the less they develop the critical consciousness which would result from their intervention in the world as transformers of that world. The more completely they accept the passive role imposed on them, the more they tend simply to adapt to the world as it is and to the fragmented view of reality deposited in them.," Freire, Ibid., p. 73.

what "others" attempt to force-feed them as actual knowledge; that is the European rote system of education in America. In the contrary, true knowledge necessitates curiosity of the world that the student confronts on a daily basis, transformation of action upon reality, intervention, and rejuvenation, which became the core belief of both BANTU and the NPRA, as we interacted with our membership body, thereby instructing the entire Walpole Prison population in 1973. We understood that the student must consequently apprehend and reinvent their learning and be able to apply it to concrete situations. This is the reason why there were so many committees in both organizations.

We further acknowledged that the person who fills up with another's contents, in contradiction to his "being" in the world, cannot learn because he is not challenged.

BANTU thereby developed a six-point template to follow:

1. Encourage the student to help design, and fully participate in, his own educational process;
2. Utilize the student's vocational and life experience as the basic foundation;
3. Identify any of the subliminal damage caused by the rote system of (mis)education;
4. Emphasize Paolo Freire's methodology;
5. Encourage the student's creativity; and,
6. Make the educational experience open-ended, ever-evolving, and enjoyable.

We determined that ABE should evolve in an effort to allow the student to participate in his own educational process, rather than to cram our existing knowledge and experience into his head. The student, therefore, was encouraged to have a voice in what he desired to learn and was afforded the opportunity to critique the process through which he was learning—if the process was indeed an enjoyable one, and if the process was progressing at a desirable speed while affording the optimal results for the student.

We encouraged the student to pick his own subject matter. This was principally accomplished through observation, with focus and reliance upon the student's past "vocational and/or social" experiences. Whatever held substance and meaning in the student's world experience determined the avenue or direction his basic education was steered into traversing. In the course of time, the lynchpin of our instructional dynamic was to impart our learned knowledge when the student asked the appropriate question, thereby not imposing our will upon the creative process. In this manner, for learning to progress between the student and the tutor, it became the job of the student to ask the next question.

c. Experimentation and success.

One of my first students was Ed White. At the time of this first ABE experiment, Ed was close to seventy years of age. He could not read nor write, knew nothing of his ethnic history short of the final years of chattel slavery-memories related to him by his mother when he was a child. But he enjoyed tinkering about with the lights and basic plumbing needs as the MCI-Walpole handyman designee. I came to learn from him that being a handyman, a jack of all trades, was his vocation and employment prior to his incarceration. The prison administration had afforded Ed a brown tool belt, with a sundry of small tools-a leather belt that he wore everyday, and took great pride in possessing—as he moved about the prison looking for a light bulb to change, or a minor something to repair.

I capitalized upon Ed's tool belt to initiate the process of showing him the basic English alphabet, through word association with the items that he carried upon the belt. For example, *A* was for adhesive, *B* was for belt, *C* was for cord, etc. I helped Ed to modify a system that interacted with his world experience—what he did on a daily basis, and associated his daily experience upon. Letters within the alphabet that exceeded the number of items on his belt had to be associated with the things and places that he encountered, as I accompanied him upon his daily rounds throughout the prison.

Almost immediately, Ed took enjoyment from the number of words that he had learned to spell by way of the word association process. MCI-Walpole was a relatively small prison in the 1970s, originally designed to house five hundred prisoners. All facilities—that is, cellblocks, dining hall, gymnasium, library, auditorium, chapel, school area, yard, and visiting room—were all accessed through a central corridor. So Ed was consistently being monitored by all twelve members of BANTU's board of directors throughout the course of the day, as he performed his job. We all participated in assisting Ed to associate commonalities in his personal life with his learning process.

An unforeseen, yet welcomed, dynamic arose in our instructional methodology, where some of the literate guards and prisoners were observed taking time to listen to Ed spell words that were associated with his immediate surroundings. They would actually coach him through any difficulties that he might be having (obviously taking their cue from watching BANTU members coach him) and introduce him to new words in his immediate vicinity.

Another welcomed development that arose from the joy and pride Ed took in his reading and spelling progress was that he was always open to nightly one-on-one tutoring from BANTU board members other than myself. These tutorial sessions often took place within his cell, after the final meal of the day was served in the dining hall.

There were other residual effects, aside from the fact that we had unwittingly enlisted a number of prison guards, and inmates, in Ed's basic education instruction. It had also trickled down, across, and over, to a number of prisoners and guards who were themselves functionally illiterate; but were either too ashamed to openly admit it, or to seek help. Ed's experience was allowing them to learn peripherally.

Often, I would watch from an unnoticed vantage point as unlearned guards and prisoners would struggle to mouth the words that Ed was seen and heard spelling aloud, and walk up to the bulletin board after Ed had left and strain in an effort to discern what he had just read. These same individuals would also move within earshot whenever Ed was being instructed by someone. It was during this time that I recalled Paolo Friere's words:

"Liberation is thus a childbirth, and a painful one. The man or woman who emerges as a new person, viable only as the oppressor-oppressed contradiction is superseded by the humanization of all people. Or to put it another way, the solution of this contradiction is born in the labor which brings into the world this new being: no longer oppressor nor longer oppressed, but human in the process of achieving freedom."[7]

We had taken Ed, his brother, a host of his peers, ranks of the oppressor class, as well as ourselves, to the depot—to board one of the cars marked "literacy" upon our modern day underground railroad, as we set out for the promised land of humanity. This new approach to adult basic education, which diminished and offset rote, encouraged a substantial amount of creativity on the part of the ones being liberated, as we were, in reality, mutually emancipating each other.

Thus encouraged, we introduced our third method in creative adult basic education, which entailed story telling—a modified version of African oral tradition. We began this method with two students. We had Ed White, of course, but had now involved his younger brother Bill, who was in his middle to late sixties, and on the same basic educational level as Ed.

Each of the twelve BANTU board members, at almost any time of the day requested of them, would avail themselves to sit and read to the White brothers. We also listened to stories that they had memorized and wanted to share with us, and we asked them questions.

In the course of a few weeks, after an impromptu meeting of the board to evaluate progress in our instructional method, we had determined which specific stories that Ed and Bill individually gravitated toward. It came to pass that each brother would request a particular short story, or chapter from a novel, to be read to them repeatedly. Usually, these stories came from Langston Hughes's "Selected Black Writer's Collection," or a chapter excerpted from one of James Baldwin's books (for example, *The Fire Next Time* or *If Beale Street Could Talk*). Ed's overall favorite, however, over the course of a couple of months

---

7. Freire, Ibid., p. 49.

came to be Ralph Ellison's *Invisible Man*. I believed that something resonated in the story line with him personally, striking chords of familiarity paralleling his own life. He never spoke on it, and I never questioned him on the topic, but there was a look in his eyes and an awareness. Armed with the information concerning the reading interests of the two brothers, we encouraged each of them to read and spell words from the story being narrated to them. Eventually, over the course of several weeks, we had encouraged them to read the entire story or chapter to us.

Ed, in particular, came to carry a copy of "his" story with him to work everyday—in his tool belt or pants' back pocket, and could often be seen in the main corridor of the prison, or in a cellblock, reading the story aloud to anyone patient enough to listen to him. Many prisoners and staff did listen to him and would encourage him to read more. Such was the dynamic in the prison these days, when the culture of BANTU and the NPRA had taken hold of the collective prisoner consciousness.

My greatest joy and recollection was the first day in 1975 that I witnessed Ed White carrying a copy of *Invisible Man* in his tool belt. He had learned to read the entire book, one chapter at a time.

Basic mathematics, short of algebra, was another challenge undertaken by BANTU and the adult basic education experiment.

Based upon our viewed success in the reading and writing aspect of the project, I now consciously sought out the aid of the prisoner population and sympathetic line staff.

Once the prisoner population consciously accepted a shared responsibility in the education of the White brothers, adult basic education self-evolved from simply being a BANTU program experiment into becoming an NPRA joint effort. Paolo Freire's education of the oppressed had transcended the pages of his book and had manifested itself as reality within Walpole Prison . . . as critical consciousness.

In the instance of basic math being tutored, I will utilize the example of Ed's younger brother Bill. Bill White appeared to enjoy physical labor, or it was a force of habit instilled within him from childhood and possibly the public school's rote education system tracking methodology. He preferred to work alone and did not engage in sharing company with anyone. Much like Ed, Bill was a "hands on" type of person, who learned life's lessons through practical application, rather than through a text book and a teacher. Bill was instructed in math before reading.

Ed was more outgoing, and Bill was more introverted. Bill White stood about six feet in height, and weighed close to 280 pounds. He rarely spoke to anyone, and he spent most of the time during his week days working in the prison foundry, shoveling coal into the massive blast furnace that liquefied the metals utilized in the molding or casting of the state's sewer covers. On the weekends, he mainly sat alone in his cell upon his bed, often muttering to himself. Occasionally, his mutterings turned into loud, angry, outbursts, which precluded both guards and prisoners alike from bothering him. It was then rumored that Bill had killed a man with his bare hands, but that was eventually proven to be untrue.

Bill and I were housed within the same cellblock. One evening, while Bill sat upon the floor in the far corner of the first tier of the block, I decided to give him my undivided attention. I noticed him gathering debris from off the floor (i.e., discarded cardboard cracker boxes, candy and gum wrappers, string, bread ties, lint), place it all in front of him, and begin to manipulate it. His back was to me, so I approached him, sat down near him, and watched what he was doing.

Up until this time, everyone had just assumed that he was crazy and simply enjoyed playing in the trash and dirt upon the floor. I was amazed to observe that Bill was not idly playing with the trash, but that he had skillfully molded people out of the lint and string, and had crafted small buildings and vehicles out of the cardboard boxes and candy wrappers. There were also the makings of a train and a bridge. Bill always wore a thin denim prison coat that had big inside and outside pockets.

Obviously, he must have brought some of his creations with him in his coat pockets, because I knew that he did not have the time to make all that was on the floor that night—he had not been sitting there that long. Neither of us said a word to one another. Cell count was called. Bill picked up his creations, placed them within his coat pockets, and we went to our separate cells for the evening lock-in count.

The following evening Bill went through the same routine as the night before. This time, however, I actually observed him removing his previously constructed structures from his coat pockets and arrange them upon the floor. To my surprise, after Bill made his first lint and string person of the night, he actually turned and showed it to me. He mumbled something inaudible to me, then turned back to his arranged structures, placing the molded figure upon the floor with the rest.

In the course of a couple of hours, as I patiently sat quietly and watched, Bill had constructed a miniature town or city. In my cell that night, I pondered why Bill had actually spoken to me; he never talked to anyone. I believed that it possibly had something to do with him watching me work with the NPRA and BANTU (we often held emergency meetings of the board in the cellblock), or that he knew that I was working with his brother Ed. He never talked to Ed either, so this evolved through his own observations and desire to trust me. I was flattered.

The third evening when Bill sat upon the floor to construct, I walked over to him with two large marshmallow fluff/grape jelly/peanut butter sandwiches in a plastic bread bag, along with two cleaned out and emptied marshmallow fluff containers full of "Tang" orange drink. I offered a sandwich and a container of "Tang" to him, and he readily accepted, offering me his thanks, in a clear deep voice.

After a couple of bites of the sandwich, and a sip of drink, Bill began to point out and explain to me what he was making. It was a town that he remembered working in before his imprisonment. I discovered through this verbal exchange that he could count to ten. If he had to count to twenty, for instance, he would count to ten twice and refer to it as "two ten."

This revealed to me that Bill had a basic, albeit limited, understanding of mathematics. I encouraged him to pick his work up off the floor, once we had finished eating, and together we carried his constructions over to one of the neighboring game tables (similar to a large wooden picnic table), in the center of the cellblock first floor.

There were two other prisoners (Curtis Johnson and Lebeau

Lesson 4: "Free Your Mind and Your Ass Will Follow."

Long) seated at the table playing a game of dominoes when Bill and I sat down. They opted to leave, but I signaled them to stay. As we watched Bill arrange his little cardboard buildings upon the table, I noticed for the first time that they were constructed with uneven sides, which gave the assembled town a nightmarish quality. I pointed this out to him, and he simply shrugged his shoulders.

Lebeau got up from his seat and hurriedly walked into his nearby cell. When he reemerged, he did so with a red plastic ruler in his hand, which he placed upon the table in front of Bill. He then sat down beside Bill and began to explain to him how to use the ruler by measuring the walls of one of the cardboard buildings situated upon the table.

By early 1973, Lebeau had actually taught Bill how to use the ruler in the construction of his buildings for his miniature model town. As time went by, I would watch them from my perch on the second tier, where my cell was located. Lebeau and Bill would measure cardboard squares and rectangles together at the game table and reconstruct Bill's town.

Eventually, the two of them painted the models with water-based acrylic paint with the assistance of Curtis Johnson, Frank Arujo-Wells, and Mike Ralph,[8] who were all members of the prison art class. The ensemble actually encouraged Bill to venture to the art class with them, where he learned about triangles, T-squares, and the proper use of the compass to make accurate circles.

Within two to three months, Bill had learned to accurately count to one hundred, and how to effectively use and apply measuring instruments in his creative pastime. It was through this experience, I believe, that he willfully accepted tutoring in how to read and write—as all of this was taking place around the same time—and he came to be assisted by nearly every prisoner housed with him in the cellblock, both black and white.

No longer could he be heard mumbling aloud in his cell in anger; rather, I often heard him laughing with his newfound friends in those days. I smile now as I write down this recollection, hearing his booming voice, and seeing the big grin on his face.

---

8. Michael Ralph was the former chairman of MCI-Concord's "Peaceful Movement," who was punitively transferred to Walpole for his attempt to align PM with the NPRA.

Adult basic education had grown to include race relations seminars, as the BANTU and the NPRA board members were encouraged to proceed upon this course based upon the assistance given to both Ed and Bill by the general prisoner population. We believed that the prisoners were receptive, and they were. Any prisoner in Walpole could attend a seminar, or be recommended to attend, as an encouragement to learn about the various cultures subsisting within the confines of the prison.

BANTU and the NPRA looked upon the seminars as a joint effort to stem the tide of violence that surrounded us, through enlightenment and understanding. It was my belief then, as well as the belief of the NPRA president Robert Dellelo and most of the NPRA's board of directors, that it was important for us as an organization/union to learn as much as humanly possible about our diversity and collective cultures, in an effort to facilitate the means toward presenting a unified front to our adversaries. We knew that violence was often the result of ignorance and fear of what is unknown, as one aspect of the equation was always utilized as fuel for the other.

A recommendation for a prisoner to attend a race relations seminar was often given by Larry Rooney, Robert Dellelo, Floyd Hamilton, Jerry Sousa, Richard Devlin, or myself as a result of having to intervene in a potentially violent racially motivated incident amongst a group of prisoners. For our part, we exercised this option regularly, and it garnered the desired results—it brokered peace.

In the years following the demise of BANTU and the NPRA, the ex-NPRA (i.e., Robert Dellelo, Richard Devlin, Al Blake, Frank "Parky" Grace,[9] and Floyd Hamilton) would take the ever-evolving concept of adult basic education to a new level. They were to actually receive Law Enforcement Assistance Administration funding to introduce an enhanced and expanded

---

9. Frank "Parky" Grace was the leading official of the Black Panther Party in New Bedford, Massachusetts; as well as a Cape Verdean Vietnam combat veteran. In the 1970s "Parky" was framed for a murder in New Bedford, and thereby sentenced to prison for life without parole. In 1983 he overturned his conviction, and ultimately was released from prison. His imprisonment on trumped-up murder charges is viewed as a result of the FBI COINTELPRO attack upon black leadership in this country.

version of Adult Basic Education to the entire Walpole Prison prisoner population in the mid-late 1970s. However, once the DOC learned that the funding was being made available for the project, through the assistance and oversight of MacLean's Hospital,[10] they sabotaged the effort by instituting a major prison lockdown.

> "if they took our insides out would we be still
> black people or would we become play toys
> for master players
> there's a reason we lose a lot it's not our game
> and we don't know how to score."[11]

Community volunteer Mel Springer (Fellowship Program) and BANTU/NPRA member Arnie King attempted to resuscitate ABE after the lockdown, and had a modicum of success for a few years thereafter.

The elementary aspect of ABE died during its birth but was reconceived and implemented upon a higher educational level through Professor Dante Germanotta and Curry College months later . . . on into the 1980s.

Afterthoughts

1. As prisoner self-help organizations, both BANTU and the NPRA were a genuine development in adult basic education in and of themselves—as a previously unschooled attempt to organize MCI-Walpole's entire prisoner population. Our pursuit of unity collectively generated responses from our historic oppressor, which allowed our individual creativity to have full range. We treated our neighbors as ourselves and shared in the growing pangs of liberty together. Every cause of momentum was both a joy and a revelation . . . every common task undertaken culminating as a first step for a newborn—a recantation of Ed

---

10. Doctor Wesley Profitt had successfully convinced the LEAA to fund the adult basic education project with a million dollar grant, but the DOC wanted the credit for the project and the grant money.
11. Nikki Giovanni, excerpted from her poem: "Toy Poem," 1973.

White's euphoria in his learning progress. The experiences of Ed and Bill, then, can be envisioned as a parable—a mystery revealing the objective of an entire prison population's mutual, yet basic, education within the practice of freedom.

2. The way of the Beast is mis-education through repression determined to stifle creativity and to mute the true expression of nature within human life; determined to distract from the spiritual in order to overemphasize the physical and material; determined to impede progress upon the Quest for Life—the most basic of human motivations; determined to drive a stake through the heart of nature-love, the creative center from which human kind, and everything else, emanates.

3. In 1973, ABE revealed to me, and to the NPRA, that the obsession of European rote education is of "being in control" based upon the dream of eliminating uncertainty through the control of nature—be that environmental or human/social nature, always working against the grain. This abrasive way of thinking had to give way to the reality of moving creatively with the flow of events, as this is the nature and true reality of the universe, as well as the indigenous principle underlying the founding of BANTU. Mikhail Bakunin called it "anarchy." Western physicists call it "chaos theory."[12]

---

12. Chaos theory offered me insight into human creativity. I learned that chaos is embodied within the human mind and body, which afforded both BANTU and the NPRA the ability to creatively respond to the constant changes in our prison environment. Self-organization, also known as "creativity," out of chaos occurs everywhere in nature, and advances the concept that everything is related.

Lesson 5

Unequal Justice under the Law.

a. The implications of *Dred Scott v. John Sandford*.

One evening in June 1972, the twelve prisoner-members of the Black History course sat down in the prison library and faced our instructor, David Dance, for our weekly tutorial session. Upon walking into the room, everyone had glanced at the table that served as his desk. Once we had all settled in our chairs behind a row of additional tables and greetings were exchanged between the tutor and his students, David asked us why we were all here. Some of us answered that we were here to learn about our history, to which David shook his head and replied that it was not the question. He spread his arms to suggest the entire environment, and asked again, "Why are you here?"

Henry Cribbs intoned, "I'm here for murder!" Charles (2X) McDonald said that he was in prison for allegedly violating the law. Other answers were thrown into the open discussion, and David patiently waited for the clamor to subside.

David looked around the room to ensure that he had everyone's attention, then pointed to the stack of papers on his desk, and said, "Directly, or indirectly, you are where you are today because of this." The stack of papers turned out to be stapled individual copies of the 1857 United States Supreme Court decision on *Dred Scott v. John Sandford*, as we were to learn once Ronald Penrose passed out a copy to each of us. We spent the remainder of the evening (two hours) reviewing the case.

Our given assignment for the week was to finish reading

the decision, and then be prepared to discuss how we believed the implications of the court decision had impacted upon our individual lives, and the lives of black people as a collective whole in this country, which would be the class topic for several weeks to come.

On this day, we had attempted to dissect Chief Justice Roger B. Taney's fifty-five-page decision. I can truly say that twelve angry black men left that history class for their cells that evening. As was my routine, just prior to going to sleep that night, I followed my ritual of reading a poem. As my weary eyes began to droop, I recall Sonia Sanchez whispering to me before I dozed off:

> "in the night
> in my half hour
> negro dreams
> I hear voices knocking at the door
> I see walls dripping screams up
> and down the halls . . ."

Dred Scott v. Sandford had the distinction of being one of the longest US Supreme Court opinions in history. Due to the fact that all nine justices of the Court had individually reported statements on the case, it encompassed 254 pages from the beginning to the end. Its most compelling aspect, however, was that the Supreme Court had written two new rules into the fundamental law of the nation: first, that no negro could be a United States citizen or even a State citizen "within the meaning of the Constitution"; and second, that "Congress had no power to prohibit slavery in the territories, and that accordingly all legislation embodying prohibition, including the Missouri Compromise, was unconstitutional."[1]

This was also my interpretation of the case in 1972, which was given credence by the 1979 Pulitzer Prize winner in history, Don Fehrenbacher, six years later. The remaining question then was, "How did this 1857 court opinion impact upon the lives of black people in the 1970s, and upon me in particular?"[2]

---

1. Don E. Fehrenbacher, *Slavery, Law, and Politics: The Dred Scott Case in Historical Perspective*, (New York: Oxford University Press, 1981), p. 4.
2. Fehrenbacher, Ibid., p. 59.

If, as *Dred Scott v. Sandford* implied, black people were only considered three-fifths of a human being, had no Constitutional rights that whites were bound by law to respect, could be "justly and lawfully reduced to slavery" for our benefit upon the whim of any white man, then the US Constitution meant nothing to us as an ethnic group, as the transference of institutional slavery from private plantations to government prisons via the Thirteenth Amendment was all too clear to me.

Black people in 1972 (as today) were in many ways still regarded as the property of the white man (the slavemaster's children), under the same logic utilized by Sam Houston in 1844 associated with territorial expansion—"manifest destiny" fueled by a warped sense of white supremacy. These property "rights" that kept black people in bondage in the 1850s were handed down through generations to 1972 as a seemingly impenetrable maze of semantics and sleight of hand—a psychological imposition upon my ancestors.

My reading of the United States Supreme Court Decision, along beside the US Constitution, gave me clarity of thought and vision pertaining to why and how black people could be fire hosed by local fire departments, bitten by police dogs, and beaten by police, tear gassed and shot by National Guardsmen for peacefully marching and protesting for human rights. I was coming into focus with an understanding of how local police and federal agents could lawfully murder and imprison black leaders with impunity.

This fact had been popping its ugly head up before me most of my life, but until recently I had refused to accept it. I also began to understand and respect the philosophy of Dr. Martin Luther King, and his concept of peaceful confrontation, because it took extreme courage to stand up to barbarity (your fear) with only faith as a shield and the concept of universal justice as your sword. Africans in America were in the throes of a centuries old protracted war, with a sworn enemy capable of committing the most atrocious acts known to man upon us—all in the name of their God.

Due to the fact that the US government had bullied and brainwashed the world into believing that people of color here, and abroad, had no inalienable rights respected by law or treaty, our cries for humanity would not even be heard in a petition before the Hague court for justice under the Geneva Convention. The laws and commandments of the Christian God were not recognized as being applicable to our cause. The United States Supreme Court had decided in 1857 that black people were nonentities, and that sentiment still prevailed in 1973. Ralph Ellison's novel, *Invisible Man*, took on new significance for me.

One lesson that I learned from being considered a proverbial specter is that therein resides the power to haunt, with the potential of a poltergeist. I believed that since my newfound education had taught me that most of "AmeriKlan his-story" was based upon a lie and the fiction of the conqueror over the conquered, that in my study of European folklore I had come to view their majority as a superstitious lot, who were easily motivated into action through their fears, more so than upon reality, black people could haunt them for our human rights to the ends of the earth, if need be. History had afforded us no other choice as chattel slaves and had left us with no viable alternative as captives held within Walpole Prison. So, by implication, the haunting had to continue.

Several years later, I would engage myself in courses of study in Old Colony Correctional Center, upon a journey to become a paralegal. But nothing regarding my work in the field of law affected me more, nor shed a brighter light of understanding AmeriKlan and Mississippi jurisprudence, than what I learned in 1972 regarding the case of *Dred Scott v. John Sandford*.

> "The passion for destruction" of the system of perpetual institutionalized slavery "is a creative passion";[3] it is a commitment to construct a "third" world free of oppression, repression, racism, sexism, violence, and fear.

b. Duplicity.

In 1972, the impact of *Dred Scott v. John Sandford* upon

---

3. Partial quote of Mikhail Bakunin (1814-1876), the Russian architect of the Anarchist Movement, in 1842.

my criminal conviction was not yet apparent to me. But, in 1984, the Mississippi Appeals Court rendered a Decision in *Commonwealth v. Ralph C. Hamm*, 19 Mass. App. Ct. 72, that made the implications of the *Dred Scott v. John Sandford* decision vividly clear.

Just as Chief Justice Taney shifted focus away from the diverse-citizenship clause, where the focus belonged, to the privileges-and-immunities clause—a shifting that was irrelevant to the case, as noted by Don Fehrenbacher,[4]—so too did Justice Peratta of the Mississippi Appeals Court shift the focus away from an unconstitutional jury waiver to counsel's advice to waive the jury in *Commonwealth v. Hamm*, Ibid.

In both cases, semantics and focus shifting was utilized in the opinion of the writing justice on the bench to justify an adverse decision, and thereby deny any claimed Constitutional protection sought by a black person.

What the Mississippi Appeals Court effectively accomplished in 1984 was to invalidate the Constitutional right to trial by jury, the federal right to effective assistance of counsel, as well as the Constitutional right to exculpatory evidence, with an argument that was "weak in its law, logic, history, and factual accuracy,"[5] based upon the color of my skin and the skin color of the victims of my charged crimes.[6]

It was the view of the US Supreme Court in 1857, as well as the Mississippi Appeals Court in 1984, that black people could be punished with the law but not protected by it.

The passage of the Fourteenth Amendment to the US Constitution did not eradicate all that Chief Justice Taney had opined on the question of blacks and citizenship:

> "But no example, we think, can be found of his admission to all the privileges of citizenship in any state of the Union after these Articles [of Confederation] were formed . . . and, not withstanding the generality of the words 'free inhabitants,' is it clear that, according to their accepted meaning in that day, they did not include the African race, whether free or not."[7]

---

4. Fehrenbacher, Ibid., p. 194.
5. Fehrenbacher, Ibid., p. 209.
6. *Commonwealth v. Hamm*, Ibid. 471 N.E.2d at 421.
7. Fehrenbacher, Ibid., p. 195.

The Chief Justice stated with his decision that the language of the Declaration of Independence did not mean what it said. He went on to say that Thomas Jefferson's self-evident truths "would seem to embrace the whole human family," but it was "too clear for dispute that the enslaved African race were not intended to be included."[8] So we, as African slaves defined by the soon to be enacted Thirteenth Amendment, and black people descended from slaves in general abiding in Mississippi, were not truly lawful citizens and thereby deemed to be on the same footing as domestic animals.

This is a legal truism that I keep in mind to this day, whenever I sue for just-us in a Mississippi court. The characterization of black people as animals also remains as a standing media theme in this State,[9] no doubt finding its historic and lawful justification in *Dred Scott v. John Sandford*.

However, back in 1972, I came to learn that everything related to the *Dred Scott v. John Sandford* case was not unsalvageable. Sure, the decision further alienated blacks in this country from the mainstream, but it also had the redeeming aspect of having galvanized the abolition movement to greater heights of activity. As a result of Chief Justice Taney's ruling against citizenship for Africans, some considered the passage of the Civil Rights Act in 1866, and the declaration contained within the first paragraph of the Fourteenth Amendment ("All persons born or naturalized in the Unites states, and subject to the jurisdiction thereof, are citizens of the United states and the state wherein they reside."), to be a reversal of the Scott Decision.

Although the reconstruction effort in American history did not prevail as well as expected due to the racial climate in the country, I believed that we (as black prisoners) could take some of the gains of the period, and ideally reconstruct Walpole Prison into an example of self-help prison reform—or abolish it altogether, in the long run. So, with reconstruction foremost in

---

8. Fehrenbacher, Ibid., p. 192.
9. For example, in the Lesson 3 Timeline, "animal" is used as a word to describe Black people in the Boston media during the investigation of the Carol Stuart murder.

our minds, and weeks of distributing mimeographed readings excerpted from Herbert Aptheker's book, *To Be Free*, we of the black history class began to talk in earnest with black prisoners in the general prison population about founding a black prisoner self-help organization designed to educate and assist blacks in their transition back to the community.

I took the opportunity to speak in the history class on how such a dehumanizing and rabid court decision was eventually turned by the antislavery movement in the country with the passage of the Civil Rights Acts of 1866 and 1875, as well as with the passage of the Fourteenth and Fifteenth Amendments to the US Constitution. I focused upon the perseverance of the few to turn the tide of politricks for the many. I did not speak about the failures of the era, only about its brief moments of success. Armed with these successes, and utilizing the United Nation's Declaration of Human Rights as a format, I discussed Bobby Dellelo's concept of our own Prisoner's Bill of Rights[10]—as Bobby had explained it to me.

Just as *Dred Scott v. John Sandford* was a wake-up call and a rallying call for both antislavery proponents and abolitionists alike, and the passage of the Civil Rights Acts and Constitutional Amendments momentarily bandaged the wounds caused by judicial politricks in this country during the 1850s-60s, the same fate that befell radical reconstruction during that era befell the radical changes to be demanded by the NPRA and its supporters to reform Mississippi prisons. History came to prove that on at least two occasions the institution of slavery was a hard nut to crack, and racism remained a firm bedrock upon which it was constructed—a principal that underscores all of America's institutions, and sociopolitical agenda, to this very day.

This understanding is one of the major influences on how I have come to survive over forty years of imprisonment. And I had to remain faithful and loyal to my work, not because of some result that I might have desired, but because it was my work . . . it was the expression of my life while I was doing it, as I could not live in history—only in the present tense. The measure of a

---

10. See; Bissonette, Ibid., pp. 215-216.

man's achievement is a correct estimate of his consciousness, or what he really is in spiritual reality, because he can do only to the extent that he is, and what he is depends upon his dominant mental attitude. I remained true to the best that there was in me.

c. Disparate and exorbitant.

When I first arrived in Walpole prison, in June 1969, one of the first things about the prison that was noticeable to me in regard to my environment was the small population of minority group prisoners, in comparison to the number of whites confined therein. Out of the estimated 465 prisoners, there were only forty-eight blacks, two Hispanics, and one Asian. There were no Native Americans imprisoned there as I recall, or at least no European was claiming Native American ancestry.[11]

The racial dynamic of the prison had changed by the time that I was released from segregation in March 1972. It appeared to me that the black and Hispanic prisoner population had doubled, possibly magnifying itself ten-fold in the Hispanic population (from two prisoners to close to twenty), while the white prisoner population, consisting of now younger men, had somewhat decreased (probably due to paroles and transfers to lower security prisons).

The racial minorities were still greatly outnumbered by the white prisoners, but we had a significant increase by the summer of 1972. It appeared to me that the swelling of minority group numbers in the prison population translated into a recognizable power base, but it also signified that more racial minorities were being imprisoned at a noticeable rate. I compared the escalating number of black and Hispanic prisoners to the social unrest occurring in communities of color, due to economic and political strangulation of these neighborhoods by those in power in the government—none of whom were black or Hispanic in Mississippi. Another dynamic was the increased number of

---

11. Today, being called a Native American appears to have become a fad in Mississippi prisons, as many white prisoners now claim to have Native ancestry as the means to circumvent the state's cigarette smoking ban, and the means by which to infringe upon a sacred rite through a claim of spirituality.

black Vietnam combat veterans returning home from war and the escalating number of these veterans being cleared through Walpole, which at that time was the system's reception and diagnostic center. So there was growing strength in numbers but at a cost to the outside communities. One thing was certain to me in 1972: the expanding black prisoner population and the social unrest in the poor neighborhoods of the State were linked, evidenced by J. Edgar Hoover's planning, illustrated by the "Black Messiah" memo.[12]

In May 1973, prior to the State Police invasion of Walpole Prison of May 18,[13] I was afforded the opportunity through BANTU and the NPRA to poll the prisoner population in reference to the nature of the offenses for which the men were imprisoned, and the lengths of the court-mandated prison terms. I accomplished the task by informing both boards of directors that we needed such a census to best fulfill our obligation as community oriented organizations, i.e., to facilitate the needs of our constituencies while they were imprisoned within the system, as well as cushion their transition back to the real world.

I spent a day or two typing up a simple inquiry upon mimeograph paper that asked the following questions:

(1) What is your race or ethnicity?
(2) How old are you?
(3) What is the nature of your conviction?
(4) How long is your prison sentence?
(5) What was your occupation prior to arrest?
(6) What was your completed grade in school prior to arrest?
(7) What is your desired occupational goal upon release? and,
(8) In what city or town did you live when your crime was committed?

The above questions assisted me in the screening of the primary reason for the poll, to discern the race, community of

---

12. See; COINTELPRO Revisited, in the Appendix A. Also see; Glen C. Loury, "*Race, Incarceration, and American Values*," (Cambridge, MA: The MIT Press, 2008), pp. 60-61.
13. Bissonette, Ibid. pp. 164-165.

origin, crime, and length of prison sentence of those presently confined within the prison.

BANTU understood the significance of the poll, although I cannot be sure that the NPRA board understood fully what the questionnaire was designed to reveal.

Six hundred questionnaires were run-off on the NPRA office mimeograph machine and distributed to the prisoner population by NPRA cellblock representatives one night in early May while the prisoners were confined within their cells for the evening (until the following morning). The block reps then went around and collected the forms prior to the cell doors being open for breakfast. No one was required to put their name on the questionnaire—it was strictly an anonymous poll. Once the block reps completed their collections, the forms were deposited in the NPRA office for "Tiny" Dirring and Sam Nelson to compute. As the co-vice president of the NPRA, and the author of the poll, I was on hand to oversee the project, which gave me a first-hand accounting of the sought after information.

It has been over thirty years since the results of the poll were made, and I cannot remember the exact tabulated percentages. I do, however, recall the overall results minus numerical equations. Of the 470 prisoners then housed within Walpole, we had received 418 returned and correctly answered questionnaires. Black and Hispanic prisoners more often than not arrived in maximum security from the mercy of the just-us system with less than three years of high school completion rate, and they came from the ethnic neighborhoods of Roxbury, Dorchester, Mattapan, New Bedford, Springfield, Brockton, and Worcester. The nature of their charged offenses were predominately drug related, i.e., assaults, armed and unarmed robbery, possession, possession with intent to distribute, breaking and entering of a dwelling, and a small number of sex offenses. Their sentences ranged from seven years to thirty years on the average, which turned out to be at least three times higher than their white counterparts. Most of the white prisoners were on an equal educational level as the blacks, but with a higher percentage of high school graduates. They came predominantly from the ethnic neighborhoods of Dorchester, Charlestown, South Boston, Cambridge, the North

End, and Fall River. Their sentences averaged out to be between two years to ten years. Their crimes were proportionately the same as the black and Hispanic prisoners. I discounted the 160 or so lifer's statistics in Walpole.

I, along with both the internal and external board members of BANTU, agreed that what we were witnessing in the exorbitant rates of imprisonment of racial minorities in Mississippi was part of a national trend and directly related to our overall struggle for human rights, as well as the extraction of the potential socioeconomic wealth of the represented black and Hispanic communities. With this realization came the conclusion that it was not the purpose of prison to reform or transform the individual; rather, it is designed to centrally concentrate and eliminate politically dissident and radicalized segments of the populace.[14] These results were also placed in context with the effects garnered by COINTELPRO-agent provocateurs, and Hoover's "Black Messiah" memorandum. Everything was tied together.

My focus thereby began to change from simply abolishing ignorance and the residual effects of chattel slavery (and its prevailing institutions) from the bound minds of black prisoners to the abolition of prisons altogether. What Reverend Rodman had been attempting to afford me insight into for months had finally sunk in.

As the years rapidly progressed into decades, over the past forty years, I witnessed racial minority communities implode due to the economical and social disenfranchisement caused by the stigma of prison. I watched as the sons of ex-prisoners followed in the footsteps of their fathers—entering the system with young children in their wake, to be raised for ten to fifteen years or longer by independent young black women. Just like their fathers before them, the children were brought up in a household where the male family figure was absent from the

---

14. From the white community came a small number of Weathermen. From the Black community came an increasing number of Black Panthers, De Mau Mau, and members of the Republic of New Africa; all of whom were housed within the walls of MCI-Walpole. The members of all of the aforementioned groups were serving life sentences via convictions obtained under dubious circumstances—all exemplifying radical organizational service to their communities of origin.

family unit—throwing it out of balance, leaving the adolescent boys to mature without an immediate male role model from which to pattern himself. No male role model at home often resulted in a search for male bonding in street gangs, that more likely than not utilized criminal activity like a rite of passage, which invariably creates drug addiction, perpetration of violence or victimization by violence, leading to prison, or an early grave.

If the black man survives his stint in prison, and is released therefrom, he finds upon his return to the world that he has been branded to the degree that he cannot find a place back in society, as is afforded his white counterpart. The wealth of the human resource thereby has been successfully depleted from the black community through institutionalization—i.e., legalized slavery and lawful lynching.

Over the years, BANTU, and former BANTU members who were unfortunately serving life sentences, have attempted to counter the destruction of the black community via the disparity inherent within the prison system, by introducing self-help programs into various prison environments in the state designed to support the family unit.

In Walpole, there was the "Big Brother" counseling program spearheaded by Jerome Miller and the Department of Youth Services, where once a week, juvenile offenders, from Single parent households, would be escorted into Walpole Prison by Youth Services chaperones to share their growing-up experiences with selected volunteers of BANTU. We did not expect to reach all of the youth in the program, but we did accomplish turning many away from the prison gates as adult offenders.

The "Big Brother" program found its way to Norfolk Prison, when many of BANTU's cofounding members transferred there between 1973-74. "Big Brother" would later evolve into "Young Fathers" and "Family Awareness" programs, in an effort to bring entire family units of the imprisoned black men together every other week to hash out family problems as one whole body.

As to be expected, with the success of these programs came repression from the DOC in the form of harassment and barring of volunteers from the community on a whim, locking up prisoner self-help organizers on trumped up charges in isolation for extended periods of time, or transferring the group leaders out of the prison in question, and finally suspending the program indefinitely pending illusive internal investigations.

Few, if any, meaningful prisoner self-help programs currently exist within the Mississippi penal system, primarily because they were successful. Those that do exist are under constant interference and curtailment by the DOC; so they are essentially just a name on the DOC website that the administration can point to as being operational without actually having to demonstrate their effectiveness.

The recycling statistics of recidivism from prisoners who have completed their prison terms and parolees that are being released from prison on an annual rate, which are computated for public consumption, attest to the glaring failure of DOC-controlled programs upon the offender on the one hand, and the success of recycling prisoners like commodities on the other hand—as recidivism fuels service-related jobs, security of corporate interests, and is sound economics.

The prevailing implications of *Dred Scott v. John Sandford* is that from the nineteenth century on into the twentieth century, the courts and the supporting institutions of criminal justice in this country "virtually stripped the Negro of federal protection against private acts of oppression and against public discrimination indirectly imposed . . . [i]t upheld laws and procedures that effectively disenfranchised him . . ."[15]

Yet, history was only a tool. I was not a prisoner of it, nor was it ever my destiny. It was the unspoken decision of both BANTU and the NPRA to risk our lives for freedom, using history as our tool of choice.

Enter the subtle physics (metaphysics) of the dream world: history superimposed upon the waking world to create a conscious dreaming body as a vehicle to higher consciousness. Once the dreaming energies were fully awakened, unbounded conscious perception came alive. And there we were, children playing the world-powerless, defenseless, besieged, and disenfranchised—lost within the intestinal tract of the beast. Therein came the

---

15. Fehrenbacher, Ibid., pp. 300, 1.

appearance of a golden light, and we ventured toward it, as if by instinct. I saw the countenance of black poets, bards, and historians. I recognized the voice of Nikki Giovanni, having been impressed upon my conscience by "Ego Tripping," and in that familiar voice she spoke to us, saying:

> "Where are your heroes, my little black ones?
>
> You are the Indian you so disdainfully shoot
> Not the big bad sheriff on his faggoty white horse
> You should play run-away slave
> Or mau mau
> These are more in line with your history,"

as my history appeared to be unfolding around me;

> "And you will understand all too soon
> That you, my children of battle, are your heroes
> You must invent your own games and teach us old ones
> How to play."[16]

But, unlike the others, I never emerged from the bowels of the digesting beast. And, within the illusory/timeless void, I saw my reflection upon bile-coated membrane walls and realized that I was now assembled within the ranks of the "old ones" Nikki spoke of . . . waiting to be taught the newest game to play by the children of the dream.

---

16. Nikki Giovanni, excerpted from her poem: "Poem For Black Boys," 1968.

Lesson 6

The Prison-Industrial Complex

a. Same game different name.

> "Turning the other cheek
> is a blessing
> over and over again
> it has been said;
> so, keep turning and twisting
> being spun
> until you're dead."
> —Extract from the poem, "Corporate Directives"
> Ralph C. Hamm III, 1979

Although the Prison Industrial Complex [PIC] did not come into being until around 1989, and the premise for this book is to detail how the black consciousness movement impacted upon my life and the lives of the prisoners confined within the walls of Walpole Prison during the 1970s, I would be remiss not to give the topic some mention. It is part of the evolution of my consciousness.

It comes as no coincidence that of the 2,220,300 languishing within American jails and prisons, as of 2013, most are poor and people of color—that is, they are mainly African Americans, Latinos, and Native Americans, as well as immigrants from the global south.[1] Included within these numbers are over 200,000 women, with 60 percent being women from the aforementioned ethnic groups.

Within the preceding pages I mused upon the following

---

1. U.S. Bureau of Justice Statistics. December 2014, NCJ 248479

point: as the economic situation worsens for the poor in this country, the strategy devised to maintain social control has evolved from annihilation to locking down people before they pose a serious threat to the status quo. Prior to the emergence of the PIC, the Black Panther Party newspaper, in the late 1960s-early 1970s, highlighted the thought that the federal government was considering utilizing the pre-existing prisoner of war camps in Amerik.k.k.a once used to inter Japanese-American citizens during World War II, as possible places to hold African Americans in response to widespread unrest. The goal of the 1970s has become the vision of today: to immobilize and inter people oppressed by their prevailing social condition (i.e., the hopeless and helpless who marginally sub-exist upon the bottom stratum of the social order), before they resolve to organize and demand meaningful change.

Blacks and Hispanics comprise close to 70 percent of those imprisoned today, even though they do not commit 70 percent of the crime.[2] Although blacks make up only 13 percent of this country's drug users, they are arrested five times more than whites on average, and twice as likely to serve a prison term; and the prison sentence will in all likelihood be 20 percent longer than their white counterpart. This aspect of AmeriKlan just-us is vividly, and painstakingly, clear in Mississippi—the birth place of institutional slavery.

These statistics are the result of race-based law enforcement practices and court procedures, and if the trend continues, it has been estimated by some that over six million ethnic minority group members will be imprisoned by the year 2020.[3] The reason for this alarming growth will lie in the fact that corrections funding has come at the expense of social programs proven to deter crime. The more minorities that are imprisoned due to diverted funds, the more future prisons will be constructed.

Essentially we have the reinstitutionalization of perpetual,

---

2. Jerome G. Miller, *Hobbling A Generation: Young African American Males in the Criminal Justice System of American Cities*, (Baltimore: National Center of Institutions and Alternatives, 1992).

3. Steven R. Denziger, *The Real War on Crime: The Report of the National Criminaljustice Commission*, (New York: Harper Perennial, 1996), p. 106.

chattel, slavery in the twentieth and twenty-first centuries, acquiesced by the Thirteenth Amendment to the US Constitution, and finding legal resolve within the US Supreme Court's 1857 Decision on *Dred Scott v. John Sandford*. Therefore, I find it safe for me to opine that Amerik.k.k.a's growing prison population is the new cash crop being planted and harvested from the urban, innercity poor. This country has entered into a bizarre world view where crime is good for the economy, recidivism is a business plan, and prisoners are a viable commodity. Poverty has replaced molasses, and drugs have replaced rum, in the exchange for slaves/prisoners.

> After the passage of the Thirteenth Amendment in 1865, the southern states enacted the "Black Codes." These new codes of conduct for black people were set into law to replace the "Slave Codes" that were in effect prior to the Civil War. Embodied within the "Black Codes" was a declaration stating that "anyone who was guilty of theft, had runaway, was drunk, was wanton in conduct and speech, had neglected job or family, handled money carelessly, and . . . all other idle and disorderly persons . . ."[4]

was guilty of a crime punishable by incarceration and forced labor. Vagrancy was thereby coded a "black crime." The use of the "Codes" was to force blacks into prison, and thereby lease out their labor to plantations and mills. In later years, convict leasing would be defended under a guise to make prisoners pay back to society, or for them to pay room-and-board for their imprisonment—that is, to monetarily pay for incarceration.

In Mississippi, a similar form of "leasing" has been in place since the 1970s, where prisoners housed within minimum security and prerelease facilities must find work in places of employment within the outside community, then turn over a percentage of their weekly earnings to the DOC for their upkeep (much like the ploy utilized by white abolitionists in the 1800s in this state who took in fugitive slaves aboard the underground railroad). In the county jail system, the sheriff of Bristol County has taken the

---

4. Mildred Fierce, *Slavery Revisited· Blacks and the Southern Convict Lease System, 1865-1933*, (New York: Brooklyn College, CUNY, African Studies Research Center, 1994), pp. 85-86.

nineteenth century of imprisonment into the twenty-first century with the reintroduction of chain gangs . . . making his charges pay $5 per day for their imprisonment, as well as pay for their own health care needs (or, one must assume, suffer, and die without treatment like so many other citizens do in this country).

Turning crime and prisoners into profit has become a big business in America, estimated to be raking in hundreds of billions of dollars a year, and it is the fastest growing enterprise in this country. Corrections has surpassed the capital outlay for education, the greatest escalating cost in the State budget, and every year more of this taxpayer money is finding its way into the bank accounts of private sector businesses profiteering from incarceration.

More than any other aspect of the prison industry, the brokerage of human beings has made it crystal clear that at the turn of the twenty-first century, and its first decade, Amerik.k.k.a has made chattel of its prison population, as human bondage is alive, and well, as an economic force generating immense profit.

b. The economics of human bondage.

> "There is, I believe, a clear relationship between the rise of the prison-industrial-complex in the era of global capitalism and the persistence of structures in the punishment system that originated in slavery."[5]
>
> —Angela Davis

Breaking the will of the black man by taking "the most restless nigger" and murdering him in front of other black males, females, and children has a long tradition in the US. For the most part, the US government kept pace with this practice in the 1960s, by the murders of twenty-eight Black Panther Party leaders throughout the country via the FBI and its COINTELPRO pogrom, as well as with the murder of Dr. Martin Luther King Jr. The motherland of Africa witnessed similar murders of its leaders by the Central Intelligence Agency (CIA) during this period of time, as Amerik.k.k.a, the World Bank, and the European Economic

---

5. Davis, Angela, *Abolition Democracy*, Ibid., p. 35; also, see, pp. 77-103.

Commission feared the possibility of Pan Africanism loosening their exploitative stranglehold from around the economic throats of African states. In the 1970s, during the period in Mississippi history heretofore detailed within the preceding lessons, the PIC had not yet been created. I was contending then with what we simply called "the system" (or, "the shitstem"[8]). But like everything else in the 1970s, the "shitstem" was evolving. It was in 1971 that The Last Poets gave us this dire forecast, when they intoned:

> "Automatic . . . pushbutton
> remote control,
> synthetics . . . genetics,
> command your soul.
> All products of the mean machine,
> the devil disguised as a human being."[9]

The proverbial dominoes had been set into place prior to 1641, through the industrial age and the exploitation of child labor in the United States. By the end of 1979, several dominoes had effectively fallen. These felled tiles passed me by at the beginning of the 1980s, with the expansion of the prison-warehouses in this country.

I surmised then that the growth in prison construction was spurred on by several reasons:

1. The rise of black liberation organizations in the inner city that were actively seeking socioeconomic change;
2. Grassroots community groups amongst the poor demanding better schools and educational opportunities, better jobs, and the end of police brutality and repression;
3. Women's rights advocacy vocally seeking equal opportunity, pay, and a partnership in the American Dream;
4. Another generation of urban minorities coming of age, with more rage and less hope than the previous generation;

---

8. Peter Tosh, a 1960s reggae singer from Jamaica, coined the phrase.
9. Excerpted from The Last Poets recording, "Mean Machine."

5. The politicians and media-induced hysteria pertaining to a rise in crime, which gave the suburban white populace the misplaced fear that blacks were committing violent crimes next door and would soon overwhelm them and all of society;
6. Politicos seeing an opportunity to capitalize upon the media-induced hype and trauma pertaining to crime, by which they were selling news for market shares, as the means to secure an election bid depending upon who could wring their hands the most and pound the pulpit the loudest, spouting "war on crime"; and,
7. Corporate America envisioned the opportunity to secure the promise afforded by the Thirteenth Amendment to the US Constitution, and thereby latched onto it with sharpened talons.

In 1973, BANTU and the NPRA forewarned the prison population that something ominous was coming down the proverbial pike toward us all. We knew that the final domino was about to fall and would unleash the beast that had the ability to adapt and counter our moves quickly. It was during these final days of the movement that I felt like a rhesus monkey caged within the social laboratory of prison, subject to experimentation by the State police and their mob-control techniques,[10] being shuttled in and out of segregation to undergo sensory deprivation tests-staged to gauge prisoner reaction to drastic environmental changes.

During my periods of segregation, the Walpole Prison population kept being turned over by the DOC, until most self-help program leaders were either transferred to the federal prison system or housed in the State's segregation/isolation units, and the unifying concepts of BANTU and the NPRA were just a memory by a controllable few. I witnessed how the DOC took

---

10. "Ed Rodman linked the events that night with the brewing school desegregation controversy outside the walls. The state police had just completed its training in riot control. They came in after the prisoners were already locked into their cells. Many were asleep. This action was in preparation for riots when the schools were desegregated . . ."; Bissonette, *When the Prisoners Ran Walpole*, Ibid., p. 184.

control of all of our efficient prisoner-run programs,[11] banned all outside community supporters who were an integral part of the NPRA era, vilified prisoner leaders to the general public and their supporters via the scandal-hungry news media, and then dramatically modified our usurped programs to tout them as their own creations, thereby receiving both government and corporate grants. We had shown them the way.

By 1984, the death knell had truly sounded in Mississippi regarding any realistic concept of community corrections. The death rattle was heard for many years emitting from the black community. It was during the decade of the '80s that two separate, and initially unrelated, events occurred: (1) the consolidation of the news media industry through corporate buyouts; and, (2) the rise in the use, and influence, of political consultants.

The birth of the PIC monster was parented by political and news media hype on the "war on crime," and the lack of money in the public tithe (nor the desire of taxpayers to direct necessary funds from elsewhere) for the construction of new prisons. Most of the taxpaying public began to express their concern over the escalating costs of incarceration and voted down many of the bond issues required for new prison construction. Also, many states were under court order to reduce their prison populations due to overcrowding.

Coupled together, these events spelled doom for the "war on crime." Private corporations and savvy politicians, both of whom had a vested interest in prison expansion, devised an effective strategy. If local state governments could not cajole their populaces to vote for the general obligation bonds needed for new prison construction, then companies such as American Express, Merrill Lynch, Allstate, Shearson Lehman, General Electric, Corrections Corporation of America, Wackenhunt Corrections Corporation, and a host of others, would acquire

---

11. Once the DOC destroyed the self-help concept of the programs they devised their own Orwellian terminology (i.e., Double-speak, coined within the Ministry of Truth, in George Orwell's book: *1984*) for self-help, which meant: dangling good time credits and parole possibility before prisoners to bolster attendance, become the font of useless and inapplicable information to lend to an illusion that something is being accomplished, and to "help" their "self" to State and Federal Funds that escalate every year. Our once free programs were turned into cash cows for the PIC.

the construction monies themselves by underwriting tax-free lease-revenue bonds, which did not need voter approval. Or, they would simply construct the prisons themselves, then charge the state and taxpayers rent for the prisoners caged therein. Frankenstein had arisen!

The success of the lease-revenue bond scheme to construct new prisons in the US without a vote from taxpayers, opened the door for a similar plan to spread the tentacles of the PIC abroad. One of the basic requirements of structural adjustment loans offered by the International Monetary Fund and the World Bank is the privatization of government services. The requirement includes the privatization of prisons. Does Abu Ghraib and Guantanamo Bay ring a bell? The World Trade Organization accepted a proposal from the US in 1999[12] to require international bidding upon the provision of government services, which included the maintenance and operation of privately owned prisons, essentially opening up the international market for the PIC and its shareholders. It is presently estimated that the selling of tax-exempt bonds for prison construction is an annual 2.3 billion dollar industry in and of itself.

The PIC has become a consortium of various business concerns listing over 1,000[13] whose financial wellness and future hinge upon a sizably maintained prisoner population. Corrections Corporation of America (CCA),[14] as of 2013 is the largest owner of for-profit prisons and immigration detention facilities in the United States.[15] It has 15,400 employees, with revenues in excess of $1.7 billion,[16] 100% funded via government contracts.

It is said that you can tell quite a bit about a culture by its public works. If that is indeed the case, then Amerik.k.k.a, due

---

12. Working Group on the WTOIMAI, "A Citizen's Guide to the World Trade Organization," (Washington, DC; Public Citizen, July 1999), pp. 19-30.
13. Corrections Yellow Pages Web site, at <http://www.correctionsyellow.com>; reviewed in 1999 at the Old Colony Correctional Center, Bridgewater, Massachusetts.
14. Corrections Corporation of America, Annual Report/Form 10-K, Feb 27, 2013.
15. Grassroots Leadership, The Dirty Thirty: Nothing to Celebrate About 30 Years of Corrections Corporation of America, organizational report, June 2013.
16. Corrections Corporation of America, Form 10-K, SEC filing, fiscal year ended December 31, 2013.

to its prison expansion and astronomical rate of incarceration, will be partially remembered as the society of imprisonment and institutional slavery—thanks to the PIC, as the past two decades has been dominated by the construction of hurricane fences and razor-wire enclosed structures penning human beings.

c. Profit sharing and propaganda.

> "You . . . telling me the things
> you're gonna do for me—
> I ain't blind,
> and I don't like what I think I see."[17]

When the Berlin Wall fell, signaling the end of the cold war, there was a decline in military spending. Even though the military-industrial complex received resuscitation with the Bush war in Iraq, the growth of the PIC was an interim scheme for numerous corporations once involved in military hardware sales to cash in. Companies like Westinghouse lobbied in Washington, DC, for their share of the law enforcement market. Night vision goggles once used by the military during the Gulf War, electronic fencing, handcuffs, electronic listening devices, protective (knife proof) vests, metal detector chairs, and an assortment of other high-tech toys and hardware deemed "security devices" has shifted from the military complex into an industry geared toward prisons, as well as toward border patrols.

A maintenance and construction industry, a tentacle of the PIC, has also arisen as big business in similar fashion to the arms industry of the Armed Forces. Corrections Corporation of America is under contract with both federal and State governments charging a fixed amount per prisoner, in an effort to maximize profit. By cutting corners in diet, health care, guard training, and standard living accommodations, owners of private prisons are profiting in the billions of dollars.[18]

Telephone and communications companies such as AT&T, Sprint, MCI, and Global Tel Link, profit by price gouging—

---

17. 1974 rock song lyrics by Michael McDonald and The Doobie Brothers, "Takin' it to the Streets."
18. Judith Green, "Bailing Out Private Jails," *The American Prospect 12*, No. 6 (September 10, 2001).

charging prisoners and their families exorbitant fees, and sometimes up to six times the normal long-distance charge for telephone calls made by the average citizen in the free outside community. Corrections Communications Corporation operates solely in prisons, as does Global Tel Link, and provides surveillance services to prison administrations.

Within the past two and a half decades, pure punishment, and the warehousing of humans like cattle, have replaced any semblance of rehabilitation in prison. As any notion of rehabilitative and vocational training programs have virtually disappeared within the prison environs of Mississippi, to include prisoner-owned advocational businesses, guards' salaries have increased along with the skyrocketing costs of incarceration in general foisted upon the taxpaying public.

Today, Amerik.k.k.a has over ten million children that have either one or both of their parents imprisoned.[19] This mass incarceration has come not only as permanent damage to individuals, but also to their respective communities. As the children of imprisoned parents, they are five times more likely to be arrested as juvenile offenders,[20] and face a high probability of death before they reach twenty years of age, due to extreme incidences of urban violence against the most vulnerable in society.

The previously covert acts of racial discrimination in liberal Mississippi have found open display in public policy, under the guise of not wanting to appear soft on crime and the media-induced hardening of the public attitude toward the criminalized population. Over the past twenty years numerous Acts and provisions have been passed to exclude the criminalized class from economical, political, and social participation in society. Persons with felony records have been excluded from the job market, via Criminal Offender Record Information (CORI) policy and practices, and are often left without the means to support themselves—other than to resort back into the criminal

---

19. Charlene Wear Simmons, "Children of Incarcerated Parents," 7(2) California Research Bureau, Note 2 (March 2000).
20. Women's Prison Association and Home, In., *Family To Family: Partnerships between Corrections And Child Welfare*, (New York: Women's Prison Association And Home, 1998).

behavior that led them to prison in the first instance. The media-glorified "one strike" eviction policies in public housing have singled out parents convicted of drug felonies, making them ineligible for public housing.

This policy has also now spread, surreptitiously, to those convicted of sex crimes, and, I suspect, will eventually spread to all persons once convicted of a felony. The United States Supreme Court ruled in 2001 that whole families can be evicted from public housing as the result of the actions of one family member. Grandmothers have been reported in the news as losing their subsidized homes, as the result of unknown activities of a grandchild, because that child may live at or frequent the home of the grandparent. A direct result of this "one strike" policy is that an estimated 50 percent of urban parolees have found themselves homeless and desperate.

The US Citizenship and Immigration Service (USCIS), part of the Department of Homeland Security, has also expanded its participation in the "war on crime" by embracing the "war on terror." Practices of racial profiling (that is; police stops for driving while black or brown), once denied by law enforcement, have now been expanded and legitimized as public policy, including a requirement that Arab men from over twenty-five nations register and submit to United States Immigration and Naturalization Service (INS) interrogation.[21] These men have been detained and held incommunicado. Although widespread resistance resulted in a temporary halt to registration procedures, Arab Americans and those assumed to be Muslim continue to be profiled, both by law enforcement and a terrified general public encouraged by the news media to be extra vigilant in search of terrorist suspects.

When these enforcement efforts did not fill ample enough prison and jail space, the USCIS sent its Immigration and Naturalization Service (ICE) agents upon a pogrom to raid job sites, to arrest and detain those arbitrarily deemed "illegal" immigrants based upon their skin color and native language. These ICE agents were often

---

21. US Department of Justice, Fact Sheet: National Security Entry-Exit Registration System, (Washington, DC; Department of Justice, June 6,2002).

viewed on television news separating screaming children from the arms of their arrested mothers.[22] These arrests only served to boost the corporate dividends of PIC shareholders, as more incarcerated bodies meant enhanced bank accounts.

The militarization of the US borders initiated in the 1990s has also been enhanced by the so-called wars on crime and terror. At the same time, State border enforcement has been supplemented by white supremacist vigilantes, on the Mexican border, who hunt down[23] undocumented immigrants, uninhibited and often encouraged by border patrol agents.[24] The fact of being an economic refugee has been criminalized, for the sake of arrest and detention.

"Free trade" has also had a significant impact upon the criminalization of immigrants in the United States. North American Free Trade Agreement (NAFTA) regulations have drastically increased imports of food produced by US agribusiness, destroying traditional agriculture throughout Mexico. Millions of peasant farmers have been driven off their lands into the slums of Mexico City, making them fodder for crime—forcing them into a lifestyle of victimization, imprisonment, and death. They are refugees within their own country, victimized by US policies of "free trade" enforced by the World Trade Organization. Mexico's economic policies are directly controlled by the US-dominated International Monetary Fund and the World Bank, as is the PIC, making sovereignty an illusion.

Without actually reducing crime or "illegal" immigration, recent policies within the past decade have subjected immigrants

---

22. See; Donna Wyant Howell, *The Partings*, "I Was A Slave: True Life Stories Dictated By Former American Slaves In The 1930s, Book 6: Slave Auctions," (Washington, DC; American Legacy Books, 2004), p. 33; compare: "Stearlin Arnwine: 'I seed the women and little chillun cryin' and beggin' not to be separated, but it didn' do no good. They had to go'"; also, "Samuel Boulware: 'I'se seen de slave speculator cut de little nigguh chillun with keen leather whips 'cause they's cry and run after de wagon dat was takin' their mammies away after they was sold.'"
23. See; John Hope Franklin and Loren Schweninger, *Runaway Slaves: Rebels on the Plantation*, (New York: Oxford University Press, 1999, pp. 154-155. Patrolers ("patty rollers") were vigilantes who typically had legal sanction to hunt down escaped slaves, who were in actuality undocumented immigrants to America.
24. Border Action Network, "Hate or Heroism: Vigilantes on the Arizona-Mexico Border," (Tucson Border Action Network, 2002).

and people of color to struggle, suffering, and indignity entrenching existing racial, ethnic, and national stereotypes and hierarchies.

The shared profits from all of these endeavors appear within diversified stock portfolios, IRA accounts, and market shares, as AmeriKlan corporations have invested their shareholders within the lucrative business of human bondage, by way of the PIC.

Even during this 2008-09 national and state economic crisis, Governor Duval Patrick of Massachusetts has earmarked half a billion dollars of the fiscal budget to prison expansion via the proposed construction of new prisons and jails,[25] where all other line items in the State budget pertaining to the social welfare of the citizens of the Commonwealth have been stricken with massive cuts.

Today, one in every thirty-one males in America finds himself within the clutches of the AmeriKlan correctional "shitstem" (one in eleven black adults versus one in twenty-seven Hispanic adults versus one in forty-five white adults . . . one in eighteen men versus one in eighty-nine women). "Black adults are four times as likely as whites and nearly 2.5 times as likely as Hispanics to be under correctional control."[26]

Mississippi's incarceration and correctional control rates rank fifth in the United States, according to the March 2009 PEW Center on the States' report, controlling 1 in every 24, or 4.10 percent of its adult males—a staggering 420 percent control growth between 1982 to 2007.

In tandem with Governor Patrick's call for one half of a billion dollars to construct and expand Mississippi prisons is his request for trial judges to enforce mandatory minimum sentences—in an effort to fill his prospected new prison cells and to bolster the percentage ranks of those incarcerated. It is my guess that with his slumping voter approval rating in the state, he is attempting to rely upon the tried and true practice of appearing to be "tough on crime" to spearhead his bid for reelection in 2010.

This political parlay will come as a detriment to taxpayers

---

25. Section 2D of Chapter 304 of the Acts of 2008.
26. The PEW Center on the States, 901 E Street, NW, 10th Floor, Washington, DC 20004, "One in 31: The Long Reach of American Corrections," p. 5, (March 2009)

as well as the targeted class of poor, to the advancement of PIC deteriorating stock market shares in which he is in all likelihood invested. For over three hundred years, slavery, in its many semantically disguised forms, has remained the bedrock of the Massachusetts economy.

Until there is a movement of the people, directed at their political representatives in the U.S. House and Senate, set in motion to ratify the exemption to slavery in the Thirteenth Amendment to the United States Constitution, profiteering from human bondage will never cease to exist in American society.

Lesson 7

Preferences and Percentages in Mississippi Parole.

a. Attachment to the leash and lash.

The Mississippi Parole Board consists of seven voting members, and they are considered a "full Board" pursuant to Massachusetts General Law, chapter 27, section 4.

It is my recollection that throughout the 1970s, the Parole Board never sat more than one African American member at one time in its fullness, and never sat a Hispanic member. The Parole Board, as with all State and county agencies and departments, was always dominated by Irish Americans, so that what they decided in the way of granting certificates of parole—as an ethnic bloc—could never be overridden. The Board had complete discretion under the law (as it does today), and their decisions could not be vetoed. All appeals pertaining to what they decided went back to them for determination. In the overwhelming majority of cases where there was a white victim and a black perpetrator, the Board emphasized the fact to the black prisoner during the course of the parole hearing when they denied the request for parole. The Parole Board always catered to the political whim, or flavor, of the day.

Somewhere in the 1970s, the Parole Board was removed from under the auspices of the Department of Human Services and placed under the jurisdiction of the Department of Public Safety, by the governor. The prisoners of the state relinquished their convict-human status distinction then and were relegated back to being mere objects—i.e., statistics. This change of agency venue afforded county prosecutors of criminal cases greater influence (beyond the stage of conviction) upon parole granting decisions. If you were not an informant for the prosecutor's office and did not aid in the conviction of your codefendant(s), then they would encourage the Parole Board not to grant parole. Where the victim was white and the perpetrator black, the county District Attorney found racist and sadistic pleasure in retrying the case before the Board (or writing a letter summing up the particulars, in an extrajudicial manner), and sharing in the denial, especially in decades old cases, expressed like it was yesterday.

My first encounter with the members of the Mississippi Parole Board happened around September/October 1973, just four years after my initial imprisonment. In those days, the Board held two or three member hearings in a small conference room behind the main visiting room that had two egress points—one through the visiting room itself where the Board members accessed, and the other off the main corridor of Walpole Prison—utilized by the prisoners.

In a few years, due to a federal lawsuit, this conference room would come to house the prison's first law library. The NPRA and BANTU were still operating as prisoner self-help organizations, and on this particular morning in Autumn, BANTU was seeking support and human resources for its upcoming Kwanzaa celebration in December. The prison administration wanted all proposals detailing requests for upcoming events submitted to them two to three months in advance of the proposed event date.

Efrid Brown (Dini Zulu), an imprisoned member of De Mau Mau,[1] and newly elected chairman of BANTU, and myself (still representing the NPRA) were in a meeting with the Protestant

---

1. De Mau Mau was an organization of black combat Vietnam veterans that was founded within the all black Long Bihn Jail (LBJ) in Vietnam around 1967-68, in an effort to present a united front against the violence and racism that they were encountering in the military. Upon their return to the States their newly awakened black consciousness made them acutely aware of the overt racism in Amerik.k.k.a thought left behind in the military and the jungles of Vietnam, as well as the sundry teeming social ills witnessed within the black urban community. The Mississippi De Mau Mau based an organizational headquarters in Mattapan, which they called a "tee pee," and launched into an attempt to eradicate drugs from the community. Unfortunately, with their membership suffering from one form of PTSD or another due to their war experience abroad and at home, they succumbed to the plague that they initially set out to combat—drug abuse.

Chaplain in his office adjacent to the conference room. We were having the meeting to request the Reverend's assistance in the orientation/screening process of a church choir from Boston that BANTU had received confirmation regarding their performance at the Kwanzaa celebration.

During the course of the meeting, we were continually interrupted by yelling and screaming issuing from the conference room. We heard the word "boy" being bandied about quite often in the adjoining room, which was paramount to calling a black man a "nigger" in 1973; so Zulu and I cut our meeting with the Reverend short, and then we burst through the conference room door to assess what was transpiring therein. If a black prisoner was in trouble, as what we had heard led us to believe, then he might be in need of backup assistance—if he was being physically threatened by either white guards or prisoners.

Zulu and I were both initially taken aback when we saw three civilians seated behind a long conference table and a black prisoner (James "Jimmy" Pina) standing in front of them—his head bowed, with his hands clasped in front of him. There was a white man and woman, as well as a black man seated behind the table. I recognized the black man as being Reverend Michael Haynes of the Mississippi Parole Board; and he confirmed it by getting to his feet and informing both Zulu and myself that we were interrupting a parole hearing.

I was livid and admonished Reverend Haynes for allowing the white Board members to call a black man "boy," without his saying anything to stop it. His response was "How do you know that it wasn't me?" I told him that I could distinguish a black person's voice, and that it was not him doing the yelling. I also said that I would not be surprised if he would have idly sat by if one of his fellow Board members called the black prisoner a "nigger," obviously being a "house nigger" himself.

The two white Board members remained seated and red faced with stunned expressions. Reverend Haynes appeared angry from my statement but did not respond. The black prisoner did not even turn around to look at Zulu or myself but remained standing with his head bowed. When no one else spoke, Zulu queried the Board by asking if they were truly the Parole Board or the Klan, then looked at Reverend Haynes, and said, ". . . with one Klansman obviously wearing black face." I proceeded to tell Reverend Haynes that I would not have expected the acquiescence of racist remarks from him, to which Zulu chimed in that he would expect it.

The end result of this encounter was that Zulu and I grabbed the prisoner by the arms and pulled him out of the room, all the while telling him that he did not have to take that racist shit from the Parole Board. The black prisoner complained that Zulu and I had ruined his chances for a parole, and that he didn't care what they called him—as long as they let him out of the front door. Zulu kept trying to console him, while I stomped away in disgust.

Later that evening, while Zulu and I were having a discussion on the Kwanzaa and other BANTU business in the cellblock A3 game room, the black prisoner, who we pulled out of his parole hearing that morning, rushed over to us to inform us that the Board had granted him immediate parole release.

We were all surprised, because it was rare for a black prisoner to receive a parole from Walpole Prison in those days, and rarer still for the two most infamous radical black militants in the prison's history to have disrupted a parole hearing, only for that action to garner a beneficial outcome. I do not know for certain if the parole was granted because Zulu and I exposed the Board's racism, and they were concerned that we would somehow use it against them through our contacts with community leaders, because the parolee had only one year left to complete his sentence, and the Parole Board simply wanted to put a leash on him, or that the tongue lashing we gave Reverend Haynes spurred him to request a favor of the remaining two Board members on behalf of the black prisoner, because of his reputation being called into question.

This was my first experience with the leash and the lash, and I harbored a dread of having to face a parole board myself in the years to come, because I did not know how I would respond to a full seven-member Board under similar racist circumstances i.e., if I would throw their racism back into their faces.

My second encounter with the Parole Board, and its racist

practices, happened years after the first episode, a year or so before I was to appear before them after having served thirty years on my second-degree life sentence—pursuant to Massachusetts General Law, chapter 127, section 133A. In this instance, I would come to assist another black prisoner, Robert Aldridge, prepare information requests to supplement a reconsideration petition he would submit as a consequence of his parole hearing decision.

Aldridge, and eight other prisoners, had appeared before a three-member parole hearing panel (members: Doyle, Murphy, and Dewey) for their annual parole consideration hearing. There were three black candidates for parole, three whites, and three Hispanics, interviewed by the Board at the Old Colony Correctional Center in Bridgewater, Mississippi. The all-white, all-Irish, parole granting panel afforded parole release in all nine cases, with the exception that the three black prisoners received stipulations. They alone, out of the nine, had to first be transferred from medium security to a minimum security facility and spend six months there, then be transferred again from minimum security to a prerelease facility and spend six months there before a parole certificate would be afforded to them. Their paroles would be in "open reserve" status pending the date of their meeting the stipulations, or rescinded if a year had passed, and the requirements were not fulfilled.

After the year had passed and the prisoners had not made their way to completing six months in pre-release, then a second Board would be convened to review their cases again. The critical aspect in understanding this parole decision resides in the fact that prisoners have no say in when, or where, they will be transferred to a lower security level—that decision rests within the sole discretion of the Commissioner of Corrections.

The Parole Board panel, in granting this type of stipulated parole, was well aware of this fact. Parole Board member Doyle was so bold as to tell Institutional Parole Officer GN that the panel afforded the black prisoners the stipulated paroles because they knew that the prisoners could not meet the requirements. GN then told Aldridge what Doyle had said, and stressed how he thought that it wasn't right.

About a week or two later, a staff attorney for the Parole Board visited Aldridge on an unrelated legal matter pending in the court against the Board. During the visit, Robert told the lawyer what the Institutional Parole Officer had said to him regarding the stipulations attached to his parole release. The lawyer asked Aldridge to wait in the visiting room while he went to the office of the Institutional Parole Officer to inquire into what Aldridge had told him. When the lawyer returned to the visiting room, he instructed Robert to file a reconsideration petition, and that he would support it before the Full Board.

Robert and I drafted his petition for reconsideration, which the Full Board granted—affording him a forthwith parole certificate. I believe that they did so not because of some obscure sense of justice and fair play, but because they knew that both Aldridge and myself had no qualms about taking them to court, with two parole board employees as witnesses, and that we were not going to let the issue lie.

I was to feel the brunt of the Board's duplicity and racism first hand, at my March 1999 parole eligibility hearing.

b. Quotas and the race factor.

When Robert Aldridge and I queried the Parole Board about affording us statistics on parole granting according to race, ethnicity, and gender, they responded by stating that they did not keep such statistics. But they did so in 2006. At the time that I was helping Robert Aldridge, I found the Board's lack of statistics odd since race is noted upon the original booking sheet at the police station upon arrest, on court documents, on prison intake forms, as well as within the paperwork released to the community parole officer by the Parole Board when a prisoner is paroled. How could race not be a statistic?

Be that as it may, in 2007, the Parole Board released its newly promulgated annual statistical report.[2] On page 34 of said report it reveals that whites received 60 percent of paroles granted in 2006, blacks received 21 percent, and Hispanics received 16 percent from a total of 4952 cases. Those discharged

---

2. Massachusetts Parole Board, 2007 Annual Statistical Report, 12 Mercer Road, Natick, MA 01760.

from supervision, page 43 of the report, were 62 percent white, 20 percent black, and 15 percent Hispanic from a total of 4247 cases.

The two aforementioned sets of percentages are too close in resemblance to one another to be random; therefore, they prove to be a purposeful quota. It is interesting to note that blacks comprise only 3 percent of the total population of Mississippi; yet in both 2006 and 2007, they make up 27 percent of the overall prisoner population[3] in the state. I utilize these statistics to highlight the point that if blacks are receiving 21 percent of all paroles granted now in 2007 and 2008, one can rest assured that they were receiving fewer paroles in the 1970s, since the number of imprisoned blacks was much less than 27 percent then. It is my recollection that we were 9 percent of the prison population in 1973, based upon what I remember of the NPRA compiled statistics and media accounts from the era.

Over the past forty years, I have come to learn that if you are white in Mississippi . . . if you are Irish . . . if you are an indentured-servant (prisoner) of the state, then your chances of regaining your physical freedom are great no matter what the nature of your crime may be—albeit, attached to the leash. If a state prisoner fits any, and especially all, of the above listed criteria, the prisoner can:

- be convicted to serve a second-degree life sentence for the wanton killing of a police officer;
- be initially convicted for armed robbery, and receive a subsequent sentence/conviction for possessing a gun in a medium security prison and shooting two unarmed correctional staff;
- be sentenced to serve a second-degree life sentence for murdering a black man by throwing him off a South Boston housing project building roof, be implicated in several murders during incarceration, and beat another prisoner in the head with a pipe just ten months prior to

---

3. See; January 1, 2007 Inmate Statistics, Massachusetts Department of Correction Research and Planning Division, MCI-Concord, SFU Building, P.O. Box 9125, Concord, MA 01742.

appearing before the Full Parole Board;
- be sentenced to second-degree life for a double murder;
- be serving second-degree life for murder, escape from custody and shoot a bank guard during an armed robbery in Canada where you fled on escape, be convicted in Canada, and serve a sentence for armed assault and robbery in a Canadian prison, then be extradited back to Mississippi to complete fifteen years to serve upon your initial life sentence;
- be sentenced to serve a second-degree life sentence for cutting off the head of your roommate, then using her head as a soccer ball; and,
- be convicted for twenty-two counts of child molestation, and never undergo one day of sex offender treatment while incarcerated;

... pay a $65 a month manumission fee (which can be waived) and a parole permit will be granted you back to the community.

However, I am one of African descent[4] and received a second-degree life sentence for "intent" in the 1960s, have served over forty years on this first offense, and no amount of manumittance payments will afford me my physical freedom from the penal—plantation as a slave, because the Parole Board is predominantly white, the victims of my crime are white, and the Board has to all intents and purposes sworn to uphold the racist legacy of their ethnic forebearers.[5]

---

4. "[d]uring the post Civil War period, the percentages of black convicts in relation to whites was often higher than 90 percent"; Fierce, "Slavery Revisited," Ibid., p. 88. Today, this practice has spread north, and throughout the US, as the PIC use of the just-us system plays a critical role in creating the new social status for former prisoners: acknowledging a citizenship status for ex-slaves specifically in order to deny it.

5. "We ought to be locking up folks we are afraid of not folks that we're mad at," Commissioner of Correction Harold W. Clarke, *Sunday Boston Herald*, 12 October 2008, p. 6. Essex County has a history of torturing black people via its institution of just-us, based upon a hallucinogenic view of reality propelled by political gain—as well as the means to vent their fear, frustration, and anger. Significantly, in 1692, a black female slave named Tituba was one of the first women accused of witchcraft in Salem Village, as a catalyst for the ensuing infamous witch trials. See; Sharon Harley, *The Timetables of African American History*, Ibid., p. 18.

Being black, with a white victim of crime, also poses a particular problem when the original District Attorney in the criminal case retires and his namesake replaces him, then later becomes a high ranking secretary on the governor's staff and the overseer of the Parole Board. It doesn't help either when the Assistant District Attorney who tried my case utilizes my conviction as the jewel in his prosecutorial crown before the judicial nomination committee, and thereby becomes a superior court justice.

Nepotism, and the calling-in of favors, runs rampant within Mississippi politricks, which aids in the repression of people of color, keeps proverbial skeletons in the closet, and prevents any truth from appearing in the light of day. Lesson learned: the torch of white supremacy burns brightly and is never dropped, nor extinguished, it is merely rekindled and passed on to their future generations.

In recent years, the Mississippi Parole Board, or more accurately the governor through his Secretary of Public Safety, has been compelled by community pressure to compose the Board to reflect the diversity of the communities that it is alleged to serve. Toward that end, the Board presently has what it touts to be two black members and one Hispanic member. The remaining four positions, and thus the visible majority (for full board voting purposes), is of course comprised of Irish members.

In regard to the two so-called black members of the Board, the tendency has been to either place Cape Verdeans, first generation nationalized immigrants from Africa and the Caribbean, or fully indoctrinated Africa Americans into those positions; especially lawyers or ones with law enforcement (police) backgrounds. Why? Because the overwhelming number of Cape Verdeans and nationalized immigrants in Mississippi who hold state and county law enforcement positions have been programmed to shun their conquered African (black) ancestry, and to clearly identify and depend upon the conqueror Portuguese (white) side of their genealogy.[6] They conveniently develop amnesia when it comes to recalling the history of racism in Mississippi, especially in reference to the criminal just-us shitstem.

---

6. Read; Fanon, *Black Skin, White Masks*, chapter 4.

The same can be said of the light-skinned African American. So, in essence, the Parole Board remains with six white, or European-minded members, and one Hispanic (minority group) voting member. She may vote in reflection of her knowledge of her culture and the plight of the poor and disenfranchised in general, when it comes to granting a certificate of parole to a minority group prisoner, but she is only one vote out of seven, even in the face of the fact that she may be the only credentialed, and thereby qualified, criminal psychologist.

The Parole Board utilizes such published factors for parole granting as:

1. Accepts responsibility,
2. Expresses remorse,
3. Understands causative factors of criminal behavior,
4. Truthfulness,
5. Nature of the offense,
6. Minimal disciplinary reports,
7. Ability to abide by prison rules,
8. Amenability to treatment and supervision,
9. Juvenile at the time of crime,
10. Family and community support,
11. Solid parole plan,
12. Health issues, and
13. To immigration.

However, if the prisoner is black, understands the true history and condition of his confinement, has educated himself while incarcerated, has somehow maintained strong family and community support throughout the course of his imprisonment, and was in fact a juvenile at the time of his offense, all of these factors work to his detriment, and he is deemed a threat to society with a high risk to re-offend, parole is thereby denied, with a maximum five-year review if he is serving a second-degree life sentence based upon the nature of the offense (which never changes), and/or a refusal to accept responsibility for the crime.

The true social, environmental, and political causative factors underlying his conviction cannot be stressed during the parole hearing by the prisoner, because that would be the truth, and he will then be determined to lack remorse for the crime (even if he is innocent). The irony of this prestidigitation is that a prisoner can complete his sentence without a parole (if not serving a second-degree life sentence), leave the walled environment as a sociopath or borderline psychopath due to his "treatment" while incarcerated, and thereby fulfill the desired effect of his imprisonment without a mention of public safety.

As more people of color enter the prison, the percentage of parole granting have decreased. In 2007, the overall approval rate for parole was 28.5 percent, the lowest in five years, and it is rapidly declining—a testament to the economics of institutionalized slavery in Mississippi. Yet, even with the decline in parole-granting, whites still receive 60 percent of all parole permits.

c. Designed to failure.

Soon after the Revolutionary War in this country, Mississippi began in earnest its perverse campaign of race hatred. Legally "free" in the Baystate simply meant that blacks be transformed into nonpersons.[7] It is telling that some of the restrictions upon the lives of black people that passed as town ordinances in 1777 still impact upon the lives of blacks today. Of the eleven major ordinances, at least four have found full effect within Mississippi public policy, and regulations, in 2008. These four passed on ordinances are as follows:

1. Blacks were compelled in 1777 to "bind out" all of their children between the ages of four and twenty-one years to an English master [today, the English master has been supplanted via the Thirteenth Amendment to be a teacher to the age of sixteen-then replaced at seventeen, more often than not, by a probation officer or parole officer who instills domination and subservience through a policy and procedure of graduated sanctions[8]];

---

7. See; a detailed account of this issue; Joanne Pope Melish, "Disowning Slavery," (New York: Cornell University Press, 1998), specifically, chapters 4 and 5.
8. See; Massachusetts Parole Board, Policies And Procedures, 120 PAR 600, Graduated Sanctions, 10/31/06, Commonwealth of Massachusetts Parole Board, 12 Mercer Road, Natick, MA 01760.

2. Blacks could be whipped, or banished, or reenslaved for life, or "shipped off beyond sea" for minor offenses [herein lies the promise of the state's parole system, as well as the Board's immigration/deportation policy which almost exclusively affects prisoners of color,[9] and reveals the underpinnings of my life sentence];
3. A black person's testimony meant nothing in Mississippi courts of law [nothing has changed in this regard since 1777, with the possible exception that a black person's testimony accounts for nothing even in quasi-judicial proceedings—especially when posed against the word of a white person[10]];
4. Blacks were restricted in the distance they could travel beyond the town limits without permission [this particular ordinance also finds itself unchanged within the state's parole regulations[11]].

More evidence of the Parole Board's design to have paroles fail lies within the practice of affording prisoners "paper paroles." A paper parole is an illusory parole granted to a prisoner by the Board, but the prisoner never actually receives it.

The parole shows up on "paper" (i.e., within Parole Board statistics), and is thereby recorded as a parole granted. It gives the illusion that the Parole Board is actually performing its statutorily mandated task: deliberating and affording state prisoners supervised release from prison, as opposed to allowing prisoners to complete their sentences in prison and then be released back into the community without supervision.

There are two applied methods that I know of by which the practice of paper-paroling is exercised. In the first method, the

---

9. See; Massachusetts Parole Board, 2007 Annual Statistical Report, Figure 29, pp. 97 and 98.
10. I have brought black Boston City Council members, black State Senators, black ex-correctional officers, and written evaluations from black and white licensed therapists to bear at my parole eligibility hearings, but all to no avail; confounded by the all Irish Parole Board and District Attorneys of Essex County.
11. 120 PAR 600,600.02, D.; 600.6, High 5; to include the introduction of technology and the GPS monitoring system. Attachment to the leash has currently found itself anchored to the near reaches of space via the Global Positioning Satellite (GPS). Slavery has gone high tech, as well as galactic!

prisoner in question has less than a year left on his sentence before his completion (wrap-up) date, and the parole panel affords him an uncertified parole based upon his meeting all of the prior-to-release requirements of housing, job, counseling services, etc., to the satisfaction of the Institutional Parole Officer (IPO)—a satisfaction that is actually dictated by the Parole Board itself. By the time that the prisoner meets the requirements to the Board's satisfaction, after months have passed going back and forth with the IPO, the parole has become physically meaningless to the prisoner as his sentence is now statutorily completed, and he walks out of the prison gates a free man. In the Parole Board's statistics, however, this gray area only expresses that a parole was granted months earlier.

The second method of paper-paroling is similar to the one outlined within the previously mentioned Robert Aldridge situation, where a parole is granted to a prisoner with over a year to serve before completing his sentence again, with prior-to-release on parole stipulations, as stated above. After a year has passed and the stipulations have not been met because the prisoner cannot effect his own transfer to lower security unless approved by the DOC, the prisoner is summoned before a subsequent parole granting panel, the previous parole is thereby rescinded, and a second parole may be granted carrying the same un-met stipulations as the first parole, or something equally impossible to fulfill.

In this respect, the Parole Board is statistically credited with having granted two paroles, but no one is released from prison. These two practices are more often than not employed against black and Hispanic prisoners, as the racial composition of the Board, as well as its interdepartmental mandate, all but guarantees. White prisoners, on the average, receive stipulation-free prerequisites for parole release. In my estimation, they always have and they always will.

The next designed proof of failure that I will mention is contained within the DOC's two "flagship" programs that all but lose their volunteer status once the Parole Board coerces prisoners to attend them as a prerequisite for any legitimate parole consideration. This type of coerced prerequisite for a parole affects the prisoner who is serving a second-degree life sentence more so than a prisoner serving an indeterminate sentence, because the latter can relinquish his parole privilege and opt to wrap-up his sentence—never stepping foot in one of the DOC's programs.

On the other hand, the prisoner serving a second-degree life sentence has no wrap-up or completion date, so his only release from prison rests upon the discretion of the Parole Board. A request to a prisoner with an indeterminate sentence to undergo a treatment program by the Board is simply that—a request. The same request to a prisoner serving a second-degree life sentence becomes a mandate, a veiled threat, coercion, for he really has no other choice, other than through the Board, to obtain his freedom.

The two DOC programs mentioned above are:

1. The Corrections Recovery Academy (CRA).
2. The Sex Offender Treatment Program (SOTP).

The underlying premise for both programs is to alter the deemed aberrant behavior of the offender, and to bring him into direct contact with the root cause of his offending. Both programs borrow heavily from the drug and alcohol abuse programs of the 1970s (i.e., Alcoholics Anonymous, Narcotics Anonymous, and Inside/Out Inc.).

When attending to the root cause of crime or deviancy, however, these programs turn a blind eye to the fact that the criminalization process works so well because of the cloaked logic of racism and fear, which cuts both ways. Persons who have come from poor communities where there is high unemployment (possibly due to the manufacturing jobs having been outsourced to foreign markets, due to cheaper labor and the lack of unions) find themselves without an economic base in their respective neighborhoods. Combined with a failed educational and social welfare system they are easy prey for the drug trade. This makes them a perfect candidate for prison, following the caste tracking system deployed in this country.

Also, the media-produced fear of black people, be that economically or sexually rooted, create an expressed conclusion of the criminality of black people, which fosters high instances of imprisonment amongst blacks, and lengthier prison sentences. The prisoners attending the DOC treatment programs are not informed that they are simply fuel or fodder for the criminalization industry. Instead, it is reinforced psychologically, through a Freudian system of rote behavior modification, that everything wrong within their lives is of their own making and choosing.

Neither of these programs rely upon, encourage, or give credence to the individual's creativity in an honest manner; and because of this fact, the programs are designed for manifest failure.

What the taxpaying public fails to recognize in the use of these behavior modification (brainwashing) programs or systems by the DOC and the Parole Board, is the nature of the human being to rebel against the alien intrusion upon their psyche. Both state agencies have become "masters" at utilizing statistics, even though the utilized statistics are founded upon a lie. The prisoners will answer the questions, that the statistics are built upon, in line with what they have come to know their captors want to hear, to facilitate relief; for, historically, it is the first line of defense of the oppressed to lie to the oppressor.

If the statistical premise is false, then the entire project will bear witness to it. On paper, it appears that some aberrant behaviors have been programmatically altered for the good. However, the possibility of changing a person's behavior by force has been historically, and clinically, proven not to happen. So, the real purpose of these programs is to afford the general public the belief that the government is working hard to protect them from violence and violent offenders—a true impossibility as proven by nightly news accounts televised into homes across the State—as well as to garner State and federal tax dollars to fuel the PIC, at a cost to the public's welfare.

The facilitators of both the CRA and the SOTP are comprised of predominantly white women. Why white women? For the same psychological purpose used by organized religion and the government through missions and spy networking in the Third World: to invoke the natural law of attracting opposites . . . to lure black and brown skinned men. These facilitators are often referred to as "therapists," but in actuality they are teachers—most possessing Master degrees in education. In the mind of most prisoners who attend these programs, resides the belief that a particular facilitator either "likes" them or "wants" them as a mate, and are thereby enticed to be subjected to the same type of failed brainwashing that they first encountered, and rejected, in secondary and high schools. The DOC cannot afford to pay real full-time therapists to (wo)man their programs, because the hourly rate for professionals would be astronomical.

So they often rely upon hiring graduate students in sociology, psychology, and education from local colleges who are completing field study work for a Master or doctoral thesis. Also, if real therapists were to be employed by the DOC, it would defeat the true purpose of the programs—to perpetuate the cycle of institutional slavery, and to secure a sound economic future for the few over the many.[12]

During the course of the principal programming of the prisoner, when he has been sufficiently brainwashed by the facilitators to where he can regurgitate the program's language[13] and philosophy at the proverbial drop of a hat, the program brings in Board and Commission members to evaluate the program's effectiveness and progress through a series of interviews with the selected prisoner.

The prisoner, for his part, parrots what he knows that they want to hear—under the watchful eyes and ears of a facilitator. He hopes that his cooperation will place him in good standing with his primary facilitator, ease his way through the remainder of his program toward graduation, and ultimately assist him in obtaining a good "write up" for parole. If the prisoner graduates,

---

12. Former Governor of Mass-is-sippi William Weld once remarked, after he was questioned by the media concerning his position against higher education programs for State prisoners, that an educated prisoner was a dangerous prisoner . . . that he plans ahead for a better future; he wanted his prisoners (slaves) to exist from day to day without hope for the future.

13. Here, the old adage: "The truth will set you free" does not apply. Because when the slave masters the "new" language and realizes the truth sustaining his condition of slavery, he formulates the audacity to lend a voice to his newfound beliefs that exposes those truths, and thereby incurs the slavemasters's fear and contempt, as well as wears the brand: "Not Suitable For Parole."

he does so as a master manipulator. The fact that his lies and cooperation aid and abet his perpetual slavery to the PIC, as well as fuel the incentive to enslave his peer generation and future generations due to his faked compliance, does not register upon his cycling mind. His paramount concern has been to "work his program" toward pseudo-manumission.

In league with the DOC and the Parole Board is the Criminal Offender Record Information (CORI) system. In its present day application in Mississippi, the system contains an after effect—the law as it stands is being utilized by prospective employers to deny ex-offenders jobs. So without a legitimate means to support themselves, parolees and ex-offenders risk a high likelihood to re-offend, meaning that they often "cycle" back into a criminal lifestyle, which leads them back to prison.

The SOTP offers a reentry assistance program[14] that looks good on the DOC website, but in reality it affords prisoners obsolete information about resources and support systems in the community, forcing them to potentially fend for themselves upon release. The parole system also often exacerbates the problem by continually interfering with prospective home or housing environments for the parolee. Thus, the newly paroled prisoner is forced out of necessity to seek refuge in a shelter (or, if he has wrapped-up his sentence, he can become homeless), bottoming out an already low level of self-esteem. Through these applied methods, the ex-offender or parolee is kept within a cycle of high risk to reoffend, with the inevitable return to prison in his immediate future. Recidivism makes "good economics"[15] and good sense for those making a living off the public tithe.

Today, parole fees ($65 per month, and escalating), GPS

---

14. Other so-called reentry programs have reportedly prevented ex-offenders from securing housing by phoning prospective landlords and terrorizing them not to lease to ex-cons; thereby forcing the ex-offender into a shelter, or into a state of homelessness.
15. US Supreme Court recently ruled within Graham v. Florida, (2010), that juvenile offenders who committed their crimes under the age of 18 should not be sentenced to life imprisonment without the possibility of parole for non-capital offences, the Mississippi Parole Board has zeroed in on the words "possibility of parole" contained within the court's Decision as the method by which to impose extrajudicial death sentences upon those minority group juvenile offenders who have grown up in prison to become men of conviction and conscience. The Board's new methodology is to utilize the statutorily mandated parole eligibility hearing for second-degree life

installation and monitoring fees (over $300 per month), offender polygraph testing ($500 per test), counseling fees ($25-$100 per month), attached to the cost of housing, food and clothing, utilities and services, transportation, and miscellaneous costs of survival, coupled with CORI inhibitions preventing the securing of a job, have lashed the parolee into a state of perpetual economic slavery from which he is hard pressed to find relief.

On April 20, 2000, three PhDs working for Corrections Research in Canada (another tentacle of the PIC), released "Coding Rules for the Static-99." Doctors Amy Phenix, Karl Hanson, and David Thornton claimed that

> "the Static-99 is a brief actuarial instrument designed to estimate the probability of sexual and violent recidivism among adult males."[16]

This "actuarial instrument" is based upon information forwarded by the oppressed as a defensive measure, as well as arrest records of past offenses. Static-99 is just what it implies—a never changing, rigid statistic. No amount of personal rehabilitation, advanced educational achievements, factors of maturity, nor advancement through correctional programs, can alter the initial findings of the coding system, which bases itself upon the following four items:

1. whether the victim is male or female;
2. is the victim related or unrelated;
3. was the victim a stranger; and,
4. did the offender have a two-year live-in relationship with a woman prior to offending.

These four reference points fix a prisoner's status to re-offend in time. These statistical results are also pure hocus pocus.

(cont) sentences (fifteen years), to repeatedly deny parole to the offender and impose five year annual reviews ad infinitum, and thereby insure that the said offender dies in prison . . . inflicting a lifetime of slavery to the State from childhood.

16. Amy Phenix, Karl Hanson, David Thornton, "Coding Rules For Static-99," (Corrections Research, Department of the Solicitor General of Canada, 340 Laurier Avenue, West, Ottawa, Canada, KIA OP8, 2000), p. 2.

Lesson 7: Preferences and Percentages in Mississippi Parole.

Both the DOC and the Parole Board rely upon Static-99 to classify, and often penalize, those prisoners that are singled out for extreme application, although both corresponding agencies will claim that their Canadian-built tool is applied equally across the spectrum. For example, I was convicted for a crime that occurred in 1968—when I was seventeen years of age. Static-99 recommends that it not be applied to adolescents less than eighteen years old, yet it has been detrimentally applied to me with a conclusion that I am a medium-high risk to re-offend.

Keep in mind that I had not acquired an adult criminal record until my first offense conviction in June 1969. According to Static-99 and the DOC's SOTP, if I had raped all five of my sisters and been convicted for the crime, I would pose a low risk to reoffend. An alleged[17] "intent" to rape a stranger makes me a medium-high probability, coupled with the fact that I did not share a two-year live-in relationship with a woman by the age of seventeen.

The lack of a two-year live-in relationship adds a crucial point to my base score. However, realistically speaking, how many children of fifteen years of age or younger can boast a live-in commingling relationship with a female by the age of seventeen? The very concept of an adolescent in a sexual relationship with a female over the age of eighteen lasting two months, two days, two hours, or two minutes is a violation of Massachusetts General Laws;[18] yet, I have been penalized via Static-99 for *not* violating the law while an adolescent. Mississippi sleight of hand.

It is both a known and a proven fact that the high incidents of child molestation and rape within this country are perpetrated by a family member, and occur mainly within white families. Static-99 is designed to protect family member molesters and rapists, by floating illusory statistics with the obvious intent to forever penalize (criminalize) the first offender prisoner

---

17. I use the word "alleged" based upon my stance regarding my conviction.
18. See; Massachusetts General Law, chapter 265, section 23—Rape and Abuse of a Child; Massachusetts General Law, chapter 265, section 24B—Assault of a Child With Intent to Commit Rape; Massachusetts General Law, chapter 272, section 35A—Unnatural and Lascivious Acts with a Child Under 16; and, Massachusetts General Law, chapter 272, section 2—Enticing Away a Person for Prostitution or Sexual Intercourse.

convicted of adult sexual assaults upon a stranger, i.e., the statistically targeted black offender. "The black man is fixated at the genital level, or rather he has been fixated there," therefore, "whoever says rape says black man";[19] Static-99 thereby becomes overtly racist in its intent and application.

In 2002, Static-99 was supplemented with another statistical evaluation for recidivism based upon age. It claimed that as the offender ages his chances to re-offend decrease. For instance, by the time that the offender reaches fifty-six to sixty years of age, his risk for recidivism become zero. This supplemental statistic is designed to lower the calculated static base score.

However, Mississippi in its ultimate wisdom, possibly based upon manifest destiny, has altered this new factor to the detriment of the targeted aging prisoner population. The DOC programs, as well as Parole Board decisions, apply it in a backwards manner by claiming that it is designed as a means not to add points to the base score—as opposed to subtracting from it. The Parole Board has gone as far as affording the least amount of paroles to the statistically proven lowest risks to reoffend—the prisoner over fifty-one years of age. A review of the Board's 2007 statistical report reveals that they afforded paroles to the aforementioned age group at a 5% ratio[20] for those serving indeterminate sentences, and at a 0% ratio for those prisoners facing a lifetime of parole supervision[21]—those with an eternal leash, and above all the least likely to reoffend.

---

19. Fanon, *Black Skin, White Masks*, page 143; also, read page 142.
20. Massachusetts Parole Board, 2007 Annual Statistical Report, Ibid, p.34.
21. Ibid. p. 35. Also, traditionally, prisoners serving second-degree life sentences that carry a statutorily mandated parole eligibility after the completion of fifteen years service, who have received successive and arbitrary denials for parole release to where they have served over thirty years in prison, are confronted by yet another form of age discrimination. The Parole Board being the ones responsible for repeatedly denying him parole for a decade or more (for no truthful reason other than they can), come to the capricious conclusion that the "window of opportunity" for granting him a parole has passed him by. He is thereby declared "institutionalized," and unfit for supervised release from prison. This form of arbitrary and malicious abuse of discretion and authority is primarily reserved for those prisoners that the Board is "mad at," although their Decision may rest upon the standard catch-all phrase criteria of: nature of the offense, disciplinary history, lack of remorse, not in touch with causative factors underlying criminal behavior, etc.

Mississippi paroles more young offenders based upon the premise that they are more susceptible to change, even though they represent the highest percentage of recidivists. If the Parole Board's assumption regarding the young offender's ability to change were true, then how are they applying Static-99 which is structurally based upon the premise of stagnation? Herein lies a question of age discrimination, doubly offensive when coupled with overt manifestations of racism.

If, according to Static-99, the younger offender has been proven to be more prone to recidivate, and more younger offenders are apt to receive paroles in this state (especially if they are not black or Hispanic), then it is obvious to me that the parole system is designed to fail given this, and previously outlined, factors.

Michael Foucault, the author of *Discipline and Punish: The Birth of the Prison*,[22] after visiting Attica Prison in New York in 1972, in an interview with John K. Simon in 1991 regarding his tour of Attica after the rebellion, remarked that prisons "produced nothing." He went on to state that they were:

> ". . . a great sleight of hand, a curious mechanism of circular elimination: society eliminates by sending to prison people whom prison breaks up, crushes, physically eliminates; the prison eliminates them by "freeing" them and sending them back to society; . . . the state in which they come out insures that society will eliminate them once again, sending them to prison."[23]

Herein lies the state of Mississippi's prison and parole system designed to release broken and crushed individuals, only for them to be recycled back to prison.

> "They tell me of the pie up in the sky
> waiting for me when I die.
> But between the day you're born and when you die,
> they never seem to hear even your cry.

---

22. Michel Foucault, *Discipline and Punish: The Birth of the Prison*, (New York: Vintage, 1979).
23. John K. Simon, "Michel Foucault on Attica: An Interview," Social Justice, 18 (3) (Fall 1991), p. 27.

So, as sure as the sun will shine,
I'm going to get my share now of what's mine.
And, then the harder they come,
the harder they'll fall—
                        one and all."[24]

---

24. Jimmy Cliff, lyrics from his reggae song "The Harder They Come," 1965.

LESSON 8

Rude Awakenings (The Recapitulation).

a. Another peek under the cowl.

The United States of Amerikkka is responsible for founding four unique shitstems of incarceration, according to Angela Y. Davis, and they are:

1. The Native-American reservation system (emulated by South Africa in 1976, with the creation of the Transkei[1]);
2. chattel slavery (imposed upon kidnapped Africans in 1641);
3. the mission system (imposed upon Mexicans and Native Americans alike);
4. the interment camps of World War II (imposed upon Japanese-Americans).

By way of these four systems of incarceration, people have been confined and tortured (both physically and psychologically) for no other reason than because of the color of their skin. This country has also lent its selective expertise to another system, and that is the penal shitstem.

In all four of Amerikkka's shitstems of incarceration, it was the white supremacist notion that the cultures of the enslaved and imprisoned were inferior, which was the belief utilized to condone their being tortured. Recent examples of this ideology

---

1. "There is thunder in the Transkei, watch the little children run—for shelter from the storming of a lethal, smoking, gun."; excerpted from poem: "Thunder In The Transkei," by Ralph C. Hamm, 1974.

have been demonstrated in both Abu Ghraib and Guantanamo, where the use of torture was acquiesced (bypassing the mandates of the Geneva Convention) based upon the racist notion that the torturers could learn everything they sought about the tortured through their culture.

The methods of torture used in these two examples were performed and perfected over centuries of abuse in the four shitstems given by Ms. Davis and reached their zenith in the latter shitstem—the prison. The prevailing ideology of cultural dominance gave us the CRA, SOTP, and Static-99, to name a few examples of the supremacist notions exercised within the prison setting, to dominate the culture deemed inferior by the torturer, derived from the four European-American methods of conquest: white supremacy, manifest destiny, eminent domain, and the discovery doctrine. They have been used and abused to dispossess people of color of their lives, and land, here and everywhere around the world.

By way of the study of AmeriKlan his-story, as well as via studying the histories of the ethnic groups that make up the thoroughly immigrant populace of this country, I was able to relate the past to the present. I was brought into the realization that a dominant civilization was one that expressed how people were organized, what values and ideals they entertained, and how they visualized themselves in conjunction with the world around them. I was rudely awakened to the fact that if we, as prisoners—the considered dregs of society—were to evolve into men of conscience and conviction, then we had to cease being passive coconspirators in our own torture (criminality). Only then could we become active influences upon our consciousness revolution.

In education, the foundation of BANTU, and ultimately the NPRA, I came to the realization that we could not resolve the issues of our slavery to the shitstem with the same manner of thought process that produced it. But, within the sea of chaos that was Walpole Prison in 1972-73, that was initially what we were attempting to do. We found ourselves trying to combat racism, criminality, poverty, cultural and ethnic conflict, and drug abuse, utilizing the same methods and means that aided in producing the problems in the first instance—i.e., relying upon an ignorance instilled and perpetuated by a rote system of dominance. We were forced out of necessity to refocus our attention upon the creativity inherent within each individual, and their innate desire to contribute to their own upliftment. We, therefore, attempted to sever the aorta that supplied the justification and economic life force to the heart of institutional slavery—frustration, hopelessness, fear, and ceaseless/senseless violence. Those were the turbines that cycled our criminality.

I shared the vision of my fellow board members (board of directors) that we were at the crossroads of prison reform, and that it had become our task to reroute the accumulated steam within the compressor that had become our daily existence, and proverbially blow the covers off the cyclic culture of our imprisonment. We were to either take the quantum step beyond reform to the abolition of prison, or sink within the mire of criminality with its attendant reinstitutionalization and servitude to the state, as was the promise made to the profiteers of slavery, within the language of the Thirteenth Amendment to the US Constitution.

b. Revelations.

In the Spring of 1974, I had once again been released from segregation in Block 10 of Walpole Prison, back into the general prisoner population. Fred "Red" Williams offered me a paid position ($50 per month) as the Orientation Director for Inside/Out Incorporated drug rehabilitation program, that he and outside community Program Director Debra Sayre had convinced the LEAA to fund via a two-year operational grant.

This was an agreed upon opportunity for me to utilize Inside/Out's DOC-approved format to educate newly arrived prisoners to the goals of BANTU and the NPRA reform and abolition efforts. It was the pledge of all BANTU/NPRA members to make newcomers to our extended family aware of our continuing protracted struggle against repression and institutional slavery, even though our political education seminars had been banned above ground (so to speak).

It was still the popular assumption in society then that blacks were intellectually inferior to whites, and I used this ill-founded belief to my advantage whenever I could; especially when I took on the role of the Inside/Out Orientation Director. My job as cofounder of BANTU was to demonstrate to prospective BANTU members that black people were capable of the same level of achievement as whites, and much more.

Through my creative, educational, and leadership efforts, I exemplified to my fellow black prisoners what could be accomplished when one's mind was set to the task. I expressed that our fear of success was a by-product of chattel slavery, rather than any genetic or racial abnormality, and that it was this old slavery-induced mentality which bred ignorance and self-hatred within the psyche of African Americans today. I stressed that we, as a united front, had to break the cycle of oppression imposed upon us by the slavemaster and his children, in order to evolve our consciousness. The shackles that encircled our minds to psychological imprisonment were not only a belief in white supremacy and dominance passed on through the educational system and organized religion, but was also maintained by what we took in through daily viewing of television and movies. Yet, we could endeavor to break the chains (the code) now, and thereby hopefully free the future of the children.

Bobby Dellelo was either still on escape or interred within the federal prison system, so it was left upon the shoulders of John Kerrigan and myself to keep progressive thought and unity alive within the prison population. Paolo Freire, had educated me to the fact that

> ". . . organization is not only directly linked to unity, but is a natural development of that unity. Accordingly, the leader's pursuit of unity is necessarily also an attempt to organize the people, requiring witness to the fact that the struggle for liberation is a common task."[2]

So, it came to pass that every Tuesday and Thursday afternoon I would walk out to the prison's industrial area in

---

2. Paola Freire, Pedagogy of the Oppressed, page 176,

the main yard. Armed with notebooks containing history and political lessons under my arm, I took advantage of the empty garage space between the license plate shop and the warehouse (allotted for a future automotive class), to orientate newly arrived prisoners under the umbrella of Inside/Out, Inc. I was afforded the use of a double-sided blackboard upon which a twelve-step recovery process (similar to AA) was written on one side, and the Prisoners' Bill of Rights was inscribed upon the other.

If a prison staff member was seen coming our way by the posted lookout, I would be signaled to flip the board over, and I would begin speaking on the points to recovery until the threat passed. This is not to say that drug addiction was taken lightly, because the true nature of the program was facilitated and addressed by individuals within Inside/Out that were more qualified than myself to speak on the issues of drug abuse.

My secondary duty to Inside/Out was to draft correspondence to the courts and other agencies on behalf of the prisoner-clients, and to provide any other serious writing service required by the program.

It was during my brief tenure with Inside/Out that I came to realize the toll that 1972 and 1973 had taken upon my sensibilities. In many ways I found myself to be suffering from environmental disorientation turmoil similar to that of Vietnam combat veterans who struggled through bouts of PTSD, except my symptoms had a double impact due to post-traumatic slavery disorder[3] I had survived a two-year tour of duty in the combat zone that was Walpole Prison, as well as over twenty years in Amerik.k.k.a, which left me prone to fits of rage and vulnerable to being baited by my environment into verbal confrontations with the prison staff when I perceived them to be infringing upon my human rights (which they always did), or the humanity of a fellow prisoner. I viewed every encounter as an encroachment upon my personal space, which in all actuality is exactly what prison is about; but at various times it was a difficult pill for me to swallow, and I considered each infraction as an overt act of racism.

---

3. Read: Omar Reid, "Post Traumatic Slavery Disorder: Definition, Diagnosis and Treatment," passim; and, Joy Leary, "Post Traumatic Slave Syndrome: America's Legacy Of Enduring Injury and Healing," passim.

These points of view may have been true, but they had to be confronted behind a non-committal mask of complacency, or the result would be a stint in departmental segregation or isolation. So, I was frequently being escorted to Block 10 segregation—remaining therein for extensive periods of time, which lent to an image of disruptiveness that the prison administration was creating for me. My residence in segregation created the side effect of forwarding a non-orientated prisoner population through the prison shitstem.

Once housed within segregation, away from the eyes of other prisoners and possible witnesses, it was easy for the prison administration to step up isolated attacks upon me, as well as upon other NPRA members thus confined. These attacks came in the form of character assassination (i.e., guards yelling down the tier that I was caged upon, referring to the nature of my conviction), systematic withholding of my mail, failing to process my visitors for entry into the prison, placing foreign material into my food, turning off the water to my cell, then flooding it, as well as physical assaults.

Everywhere that I traveled outside of my designated cage in segregation, I went cuffed and shackled. So physical assaults could easily be conducted this way. In a few instances, my responses to being physically assaulted by guards resulted in my being brought into the Norfolk County Superior Court on assault charges.

The Norfolk County District Attorney was a well-published adversary of the NPRA.[4] Under the circumstances, I was left with no other defensive posture than a last desperate act of defiance, screaming in open court the words of my childhood: "You have to bring some ass to get some ass!" Thereby reminding the court that I was not a graduate of the Martin Luther King school of self-defense, where one is required to roll up into a ball to allow the patty rollers to kick me until they grew tired—you kick me, and I kick you back. Needless to say, I was always found guilty.

These episodes of guard assault charges brought against me afforded me the analogy of a black man returning home from

---

4. Bissonette, *When the Prisoners Ran Walpole*, Ibid., pp. 34, 152-153, 167, 170, 184-185, 188.

work to find his house on fire, his wife raped and murdered, his only son naked, gelded, and hanging from a nearby tree, and three bloodied Klansmen sitting upon his front lawn watching the fire, laughing, drunk from their blood lust and his beer. The black man finds a way to subdue the three and delivers them to the nearest police station where he is subsequently arrested and charged with assault with intent to murder the three Klansmen. He appears before a judge and attempts to explain the circumstances to him, but it is an experience similar to trying to complain about racially motivated attacks to the Grand Wizard of the Ku Klux Klan and expecting relief therefrom.

My study of the history underlying and surrounding the *Dred Scott v. John Sandford* case had convinced me that, indeed, I had no lawful rights or Constitutional protections that whites were bound to respect. I viewed my ventures into the Norfolk County Superior Court through the lens of the 1960s Civil Rights era, where blacks were attacked by white patty rollers and their dogs, then charged with assault themselves, especially if the white man or the dog were hurt during the course of the administered beating.

With respect to my world view, I arrived at the realization that African Americans may never gain the respect of other nations (including those in Africa) because we did not take up arms and fight for our freedom, in the traditional sense of the word. Frantz Fanon explains this perception, wherein he says:

> "As master, the white man told the black man: 'you are now free.' But the black man does not know the price of freedom because he has never fought for it. From time to time he fights for liberty and justice, but it is always for a white liberty and a white justice, in other words, for values secreted by his masters. The former slave, who has no memory of the struggle for freedom or that anguish of liberty . . . draws a blank when confronted with this young white man singing and dancing on the tightrope of existence."[5]

Ours was, and has been, an abstract struggle for freedom.

---

5. Frantz Fanon, *Black Skin, White Masks*, pages 195-96,

Mississippi liberals have consistently attempted to persuade me over the years that it was white people of the north who led the movement to abolish slavery and thereby brought about the emancipation of the slaves. Truth being the point (elaborated within Lessons 1 and 2 of this book) that it was white people of the north who had a deliberate hand in the initial kidnapping and enslaving of Africans (affording its justification as a sound economic base), which is where Mississippi's most prominent families obtained their vast fortunes.

The liberals have refused to discuss these historic truisms; rather, they have tried to wave me off with the declaration that I am living in the past and that they personally had nothing to do with slavery. They personally had nothing to do with abolition either, but that has never stopped them from throwing that into my face.

My response to them is this: if you pay your taxes, if your stock portfolio contains investitures within any of the over 1,000 corporations that make up the PIC, if your IRA account draws stock dividends for your retirement from any of the corporations listed within the Correctional Yellow Pages, then you support, and economically benefit from, the human bondage of people of color here and abroad. I will always refuse to accept the liberal worldview, nor will I ever stoop to kiss their asses simply to get along with them.

c. Fading back and forth to black.

Back in 1973, BANTU took it upon itself to resuscitate the comatose consciousness of black prisoners. It was a quest seeking unified cooperation, in an effort to stimulate a struggle of liberation from over four hundred years of spiritual, cultural, psychological, and physical violence at the hands of our historical oppressors and their children/grandchildren. To our surprise, we found that consciousness of spiritual and psychological freedom resided within all of the prisoners held as slaves-to-the-State, behind the electrical barbed-wire twenty-foot walls that surrounded our prison-plantation. I came into the understanding that universal consciousness was actually color blind.

Based upon this knowledge, BANTU extended the concept of family to a larger body—one that encompassed 75% of Walpole Prison's prisoner population; which included prisoner wives, girlfriends, children, mothers, fathers, grandparents, nieces, nephews, and cousins. We involved every ethnic group that had come together in the prison for a common purpose and goal, defining the true essence of the word Bantu.

This is what we accomplished, even if only for a brief moment in history, and this is precisely what the shitstem feared the most. Once the shitstem came to fully comprehend the depths and scope of this phenomenon, they set about to destroy it with every means at their disposal.

Comprehension was soon followed by multiple lock downs, mass classifications, and transfers to other state and federal facilities, the creation and expansion of Inner Perimeter Security (IPS), ever changing classification systems, prisoner identification cards, harassment of outside community supporters of self-help programs and regular visitors, destruction of prisoner advocational businesses, recruitment and deployment of greater numbers of informants and agent provocateurs to sow seeds of distrust and racial animosity, greater use of electronic surveillance,[6] defamation of the character of prisoner leaders, curtailment of higher education beyond high school equivalency and the process by which to acquire books from outside stores, and the eventual destruction of the prisoner self-help concept. The effort of the shitstem was designed to disrupt, dehumanize, and suppress creativity in the name of security.

BANTU's organizational ability to provide *food* for consumption and thought, afford *clothing* to those left naked to both social and economical elements, and to *shelter* the helpless and the lonely with an extended family are the three basic needs of humanity, which family units are designed through culture and history to provide. They are services that have been usurped and drastically modified by the forces of government (state) repression, in an

---

[6]. "Punishment can be seen more as a consequence of racialized surveillance. Increased punishment is often a result of increased surveillance. Those communities that are subject to police surveillance are much more likely to produce bodies for the punishment industry," Davis, *Abolition Democracy*, Ibid., p. 40.

effort to coerce allegiance and control.

The greatest threat manifested by the Black Panther Party to the government was not armed resistance and militancy, but rather it was the Party's ability to provide free *food* to school children via its school breakfast program.[7] The MOVE organization in Philadelphia displayed a threat to the government because they claimed squatters' rights upon abandoned houses and buildings, then turned them into homes—*shelter* for the poor and homeless.[8] UHURU SASA SHULE in Brooklyn was a threat to the powers-that-be not only because they taught the truth to black children via an alternative education program, but because it also provided the children with clothing. Both state and federal governments shared responsibility in the curtailment and destruction of the aforementioned grassroots community efforts; so it would be naive to believe that BANTU would be applauded and spared, as we too provided a thorn in the side of white supremacy.

The penal shitstem today, as the system of chattel slavery yesterday, is successful because it is based upon the concept of control (often referred to these days as "security"), which creates divisions amongst the prisoner population. Class, ethnicity, educational level, material acquisition (prison canteen or store), age, and nature of the crime are the illusions utilized to disunite, fostered by the Eurocentric method of mind control.

It has been said that approximately 85 percent of the black population of this country are unconscious to the fact that all of their actions and behaviors find their root in yesterday's chattel slavery system. BANTU undertook an effort to break the controls, and to excavate the roots. We dug up everyone's roots— be they black, white, or Hispanic.

As previously stated, the success of BANTU (and consequently the NPRA) did not reside within our program development and

---

7. In 1966, the Black Panthers also sponsored free medical care, free clothing, and free legal advice.
8. In 1985 Mayor Wilson Goode ordered the MOVE organization to be bombed by state police helicopters, killing 11 members—four of which were children. 300 people were homeless as a result of the bombing and its ensuing fires that spread through the black neighborhood.

organizing; rather, it was anchored upon our belief that we were one extended family unit. This ability to view ourselves as one in unit-y was also the cause of our undoing, because it is the destruction of the family unit that perpetuates slavery as an economic system. Family is the mortal enemy of oppression, and domination, for therein resides solace and peace of mind . . . allegiance stronger that any flag or slogan.

It has been the concept of the black family that has been under siege in Amerik.k.k.a since the country was founded by Europeans. It is the bane of this white master-male-dominated society, whose philosophy has always been "cut off the head of the family and the body, the unit-y, dies."

Today, for all of the above mentioned reasons, the black male remains the target of repression.

Angela Y. Davis once articulated an interesting and proven aspect of criminalization and race by expressing the point that almost one-third of young black men find themselves in prison or under some form of direct control of the criminal just-us shitstem. Most people in this country, she postulated, have been involved in some form of delinquent behavior during their lifetimes, but only a small faction of the overall criminal activities find their way to the criminal shitstem.

There resides a stark implication to this scenario of the increasing number of blacks who are entering the ranks of the imprisoned: there is a greater chance of someone going to jail or prison if black, than it is for someone who is actually a lawbreaker. She continued to explain that while most black men may be imprisoned for breaking the law, ". . . it is the fact that they are young black men rather than that they are lawbreakers which brings them into contact with the criminal justice system." Through trial and error, I have learned that it is the economics of black male incarceration, combined with the illusion of liberation for the black female, which propels the evolution of the methodology behind slavery. We have been de-evolved from our original nature, and divided from ourselves, which is the true essence of domination, as a divided family cannot stand, and a family is truly home.

> "So, you want to build a home.
> Is your foundation set upon stone?
> Because if life doesn't settle
> the way that it should
> time will find a tinderbox
> where a family once stood—
>> gone,
>> gone
>> house of wood."[9]

By heeding the voices of black scholars and era poets, I have come to the realization that black consciousness is simply—that it does not have to seek the universal, because there is no relative probability inside of itself. Black consciousness cannot appear to be less, because it is all. It merges with itself as the state of everything.

The key to the door of black consciousness, to manumission, is love.

> "Because love is an act of courage, not of fear, love is commitment to others. No matter where the oppressed are found, the act of love is commitment to their cause-the cause of liberation."[10]

It is a creative power, and as everything develops from within outward, or from the invisible to the visible, when love dominates the heart of man, the creative faculties of mind and body will be quickened and the evolution of the human race will proceed by leaps and bounds.

---

9. Verses from the poem: "The Tinderbox," by Ralph C. Hamm, 1979. Reissued by Little Red Tree Publishing, 2013.

10. Freire, *Pedagogy of the Oppressed*, Ibid., p. 89.

Epilogue

On Becoming BANTU

"Ban-tu (ban'too), n., pl. -tus, (especially collectively) -tu, adj., -n. 1. A member of any several Negroid peoples forming a linguistically and in some respects culturally interrelated family . . ."[1]

In the beginning there was isolation . . .

In August of 1963, at the age of 12, I was declared a "stubborn child" by the Essex County Court system and was sentenced by the juvenile court to Essex County Training School, where I was to remain until I reached the age of 16. I was declared a "stubborn child" due to my truancy from junior high school, and having run away from home between the months of June, and July of the same year.

My first experience in isolation/segregation happened while I resided in the training school. I had failed to return to the school from a Memorial Day furlough home in 1964. I was 13 years old at the time. My mother located me after a couple of days on the run, through the help of my so-called friends in the neighborhood (Lynn), whereby she returned me to the school. After being chided by the headmaster, and beaten (punched repeatedly and kicked) by the adult male counselors, I was placed within a room containing only a mattress. This room was located to the left of the entrance of the school's so-called "Wing" dormitory. There were two entry points to the room—one was a thick wooden door that led to the corridor one walked down to enter the dormitory, and the other was also a wooden door

---

1. Webster's *Encyclopedic Unabridged Dictionary of the English Language*, Deluxe Edition, (Random House Value Publishing, Inc., 2001), p. 165.

but with a heavily wire-meshed window cut into it that faced the dorm-proper. The other window in the room was also heavily wire-meshed, and looked out upon the wall of the school's second dormitory ("Bates").

During the daytime hours, between 7 A.M. to 8:30 P.M., the dorms were out-of-bounds and there was not a soul around. The boys in the school were forbidden to approach the room or speak with its inhabitant, or face dire consequences. It was a 24 hour a day lock up for me, clad only in my underwear. No reading material, letters from home, radio, nor anything else was allowed into the room. The three meals a day were delivered by a counselor who would throw it at me if I did not move fast enough to accept it from him. There where no showers, or any other personal hygiene products present. I spent two weeks in this room upon this first occasion. I cried, I laughed at nothing in particular, and I talked to the flies (my only companions). I often amused myself by imagining that I could physically beat down the counselors with my hands or a hammer. I contemplated thoughts of revenge when I grew up. If I was somewhat of a loner before I entered isolation, I was learning how being alone helped to protect me, and entertained thoughts of how no one loved me . . . how no one cared if I were alive or dead . . . how I hated everyone as much as they hated me. I found myself awakening from daymares and nightmares where I was trapped underground amongst pipes, and although I kept running . . . crawling forward I could never escape. I'd wake to find that I was indeed trapped, but in a cage. During the day I would pace up and down the small area talking to myself, until I got dizzy. I would scream to myself, and anyone else who might hear me . . . kicking on the wooden doors until I was exhausted, or a counselor or two rushed into the room and beat me into submission.

No one ever asked me why I ran away from home in 1963, nor why I ran away from the school. No one seemed to want me, and my mother had twice turned me over to the State. I resented her for the betrayal. It appeared to me that all that anyone was concerned with was punishing me, both psychologically and physically. I began to trust no one, as I believed that everyone was out to hurt me.

Upon my release from isolation/segregation in 1964, I sat

off by myself away from the other boys in the school. I sullenly responded to orders from the counselors, until I got slapped or punched in the back of the head. When I ate in the dining room with the rest of the school I ate in silence. I did my chores in silence. I ignored those who tried to communicate with me. I wrote no letters home during the letter writing period. After about a week or two I began to open up and blend with the rest of the boys. I tried to forget what had happened to me in isolation, until I ran away again . . . and again . . . and again. My stints in isolation began to build a seething repressed anger within me, transforming me into a pressure cooker of suppressed emotions.

After leaving the Training School in 1966, my next experience in isolation/segregation occurred between January and June of 1969, while I was awaiting trial in the Essex County Jail in Lawrence, Massachusetts. My court-appointed attorney (Bruce N. Sachar) had conspired with his friend (Essex County Assistant District Attorney, Peter Brady) to convince the Master of the jail to segregate me away from the rest of the jail population (including my two codefendants), as the means to psychologically soften me up for my pending trial in June. I was placed on an unoccupied wing of the jail that faced the side of my old high school (Central Catholic). There were three tiers to this wing, with five cells on each, and I was placed within the middle cell of the top tier. Although I was allowed to read, there was no contact with others. A guard served me my food, which often had spit and other foreign objects in it, that I refused to eat. I lived off of potato chips, candy bars, and ice cream that could be purchased twice a week from an outside of the jail community store. I had a weekly chaperoned excursion to the shower when the jail was locked down for the night. I received no attorney visits, but my mother visited every Sunday during the allotted period. I learned of the threatening phone calls she and my sisters were receiving, as well as the threats my sisters received when they went to school. I was deeply troubled and concerned for them. My awareness of racism and revenge steeped during this time in segregation, and gnawed at me. My lawyer refused to answer my letters, and would send messages laced with lies to me through my mother. I would wile away the hours steeped in self pity . . . concern for my family's well-being . . . worry over the condition of the victims . . . hatred for my lawyer . . . paranoia, anxiety, stress, and plans for revenge. The nightmares of being trapped underground that arose during my stints in isolation while I was in the Training School began to reoccur, and I would awaken in a cold sweat—only to find, once again, that I was indeed trapped. The sound of jangling keys, laughter, or noises in the distance began to startle me. I sang aloud to myself . . . cried . . . screamed aloud for no apparent reason. I could not pace the cell because it was too small. I recall awakening one night delirious—believing that I could see the shadows of National Guardsmen, cops, and police dogs on the wall outside of my cell; as they made their way down the tier below as if searching for me. I was so afraid to eat that I lost 25 pounds awaiting trial, and at 6 feet 6 inches in height I went to trial weighing 160 pounds. I was emotionally, physically, and psychologically exhausted; and by the time my trial began I did not care what happened to me, just as long as my ordeal in segregation ended and my family was safe due to my conviction.

I was convicted in June of 1969, and taken to Walpole State Prison straight from segregation/isolation. I was then 18 years old, as the non capital offense for which I was convicted had occurred when I was 17 years of age. I was the first of three criminal defendants convicted, and therefore bore the brunt of the white backlash from the criminal episode. I entered the Walpole Prison population believing that everyone was out to get me. From Training School the counselors, the jailers, and now the prison guards were all white and both the jail and prison populations were predominantly white. I believed that everyone was talking about me . . . looking at me . . . and I jumped at the slightest noise or movement around me. For weeks, sleep was out of the question and I relied upon short naps in order to rest.

Isolation/segregation in Walpole opened up an entirely new experience for me, where isolation was in a dark cell behind a solid steel door. The only light came from a low watt bulb, that one could choose to have on or off for 24 hour durations, controlled by a switch outside of the cell accessed by a special key that only the guards possessed. The only other available option came from the sliver of light that emanated from under the door via the tier windows. I received one meal a day of my choosing (morning, noon, evening) I wore only my underwear, could receive no mail, no visits, no exercise outside of the cell, and for 15 day periods I could not receive a shower or have personal hygiene products. My one meal a day was served to me by a guard through a locking slot in the steel door. The only reading material that was allowed was a Bible. The first time that I was placed in isolation it was for 30 days (15 days in, one day out, 15 more days in) for some mediocre disciplinary infraction. After about a week into my isolation, in the dark, I began to think that I heard voices muttering to me. Then, I believed that someone/thing touched me on my shoulder, while I prayed to God for help. I can still remember the cold shiver that ran down my spine now 45 years later . . . the hair standing on end upon my arms . . . the unbridled fear, and my gasping for air. I mewled and screamed. The other prisoners who were housed on the tier, not confined behind a steel door, yelled out for the guard—who came down to my cell and opened the steel door. I don't know what I looked like, but he silently stared at me for a moment and walked away . . . leaving the door open for about ten minutes.

After I was returned to population, I harbored an intense feeling of paranoia that someone was out to get me. I believed that loudly played radios at night, running water in the sink and the flushing of toilets in surrounding cells was a conspiracy by my fellow prisoners to annoy me.

After having eventually spent years in segregation, and political/racial confrontations with the guards, I always emerged from those stints with a chip on my shoulder . . . ready to snap at anyone, especially the guards . . . and would harbor thoughts of perpetrating serious bodily harm upon them at the slightest provocation. Eventually, I acted upon these thoughts and have accumulated several assaults upon guards. Today I can understand that all of my past hostility can be retraced to my first experience in isolation while interred within the Training School.

> As I lie here
> (hear?)
> in this solitary prison cell
> I hear

the cries of misery . . .
the cries of frustrated anger . . .
and the ever present sound
of the countless cell doors
clanging
echoing.
I feel the others
before me
who left something behind them
some part of themselves here.
And what of the others
after me
who will hear
(here?)
in this solitary
prison cell?

["Solitary"; excerpted from *Dear Stranger / The Wayfarer*]

Questions from a legal lynching.

The road upon which one must travel in search of a liberated consciousness is cobbled—paved with many questions that serve as obstacles, and require an answer.

Prior to 1984, when I received an Appeals Court decision on my 1980 motion for a new trial, one major question that I harbored that begged to be answered was:

> If the Lawrence, Massachusetts Police Department had all three criminal defendants in custody by November 28, 1968, how did I come to be singled out as the principle assailant of the female victim (Kathleen) in the November 22, 1968 criminal episode?

During the course of my most recent 2014 parole eligibility hearing , the only black and male member of the Massachusetts Parole Board informed me that my asking questions pertaining to my mistreatment in the "Mississippi" criminal just-us system was simply me being argumentative. I responded by telling him that whenever someone says something stupid to me, or gives me information or instructions that I do not understand, I ask questions. My questions concern my life, not his, and he can sleep walk through life as an ignorant yet obedient black man if he so desires.

The search for an answer to the identification question was exhaustive. It took my codefendant Emanuel E. Smith's filing of an affidavit in support of his 1984 motion for a new trial, and my attorney of record at the time receiving a copy of same, for any light to illuminate the subject. I had previously engaged in decades of letter writing to the police department, the District Attorney's office, my trial attorney, and the courts, with little or no results. The police and District Attorney refused to answer my letters, and although I did receive a court order to receive my trial transcripts, no one honored it. All of the documented material in the criminal proceeding was purposefully withheld by the cohorts of the criminal just-us apparatus (the "good old boy" network). This was so, even in spite of superior court Orders to provide me with trial transcripts and other documents related to my arrest, trial, and conviction.

The following are my detailed convictions (beliefs) of the "how" and "why": the questions surrounding my identification, and the suppression of physical evidence at my trial.

The Lawrence police did not have anyone in custody to answer for the November 22, 1968 criminal episode until November 26, 1968. Detectives Sergeant Lannon and Lieutenant Tylus visited all twelve homes in the greater Lawrence and Methuen area where black males resided, and questioned the young men and boys regarding their whereabouts during the early morning hours of November 22, 1968. When the two detectives visited the home of Robert S. Preston on November 22nd, Robert's mother told them that Emanuel E. Smith and myself had been in her house with her son earlier that morning, and that she thought Robert and his companions had travelled to New York to visit Robert's girlfriend. Mrs. Preston readily gave the police a recent photograph of her son, and she also gave them the address of the girlfriend and the name and address of a relative in New York that Robert might visit while he was in the area.

Armed with the addresses, Lannon and Tylus visited me at my mother's house in Methuen, Massachusetts on November 24, 1968. They questioned me concerning the whereabouts of Robert Preston, and asked me if I had been with him at any time during the 22nd of November. I told them that I had not seen him, and they asked to look at the clothing that I was wearing on the night in question. I gave them access to my closet, and pointed out what I had worn. The two detectives left my house. On or about November 26, 1968, Detectives Lannon and Tylus, along with Raymond (the male victim of the November 22nd criminal episode), travelled together by automobile to New York in search of Robert Preston. Upon their arrival in New York the two detectives from Lawrence enlisted the assistance of the New York Police Department in locating the dwellings of Preston's girlfriend and his cousin. The NYPD had determined that Preston's cousin had recently been paroled from Riker's Island prison. The two detectives from Lawrence left Raymond (the male victim) at the local police station, and both the detectives from New York and Lawrence drove to Robert Preston's girlfriend's apartment. The police contingent ruthlessly questioned the girlfriend in regard to Robert's whereabouts, and when she could afford them no answers they terrorized her and ransacked her apartment—slapping her and calling her a "nigger lover," as she was white and Robert was black; while telling her what Robert does to white women, based upon the nature of the crime for which they were hunting him down. When the police finally left her apartment/ they drove to Preston's cousin's place of residence. When the cousin opened the door to his apartment, the police forced their way in. As the detectives questioned the cousin regarding Robert's whereabouts, they punched him and hit him over the head with their guns. When he could not afford them any answers, they forced him to ride with them in the squad car; while they cruised the streets in the vicinity of the girlfriend's apartment searching for Robert Preston. The cousin spotted Preston and Smith, then identified them for the police. The police unceremoniously shoved the cousin out of the squad car, and onto the pavement. Preston and Smith were then cut off by the police car, forced to the ground and searched and kicked, then forced under gun point into the car. Robert Preston and Emanuel Smith were still wearing their blood soaked attire from the early morning of November 22nd.

The following is a quote from the affidavit of Emanuel E. Smith, in support of his 1984 motion for a new trial:

"I was initially arrested in New York City on November 26. I was taken by many police officers from Lawrence, Massachusetts and New York to the home of a friend of my codefendant, Robert Preston. I saw Preston being hit. I was handcuffed and taken into a bathroom. I was threatened that I could be shot if I did not make a statement concerning the November incident. Finally, in complete terror, I told the officer what he wanted to know—that Ralph Hamm had assaulted the female victim."

Why did the police bring Robert Preston and Emanuel Smith to the girlfriend's apartment, as opposed to immediately transporting them to the police station where Raymond (the male victim) was waiting for their return? The police wanted to further terrorize Robert's girlfriend for associating with a "nigger" by beating him in front of her, as well as to impose their own form of interrogation upon Preston and Smith where there would not be any credible witnesses: torture them.

Between the dates November 22-26, 1968 Robert Preston[2] was the primary suspect in the investigation of the November 22nd criminal episode. What changed? It was not until the two Lawrence detectives had crafted a sworn, albeit libellous, statement from a terrorized Emanuel E. Smith that I became the principle suspect.

Why did Emanuel Smith say that I was the defendant who assaulted Kathleen (the female victim) with the stick outside of the automobile where Robert Preston had placed her? Because it was the paramount aspect of the criminal episode that the police appeared to be interested . . . Robert Preston was his cousin, and Smith had met me for the first time on the evening of November 21st . . . he was protecting himself from being "shot" by the police, and/or for being charged with the assault upon Kathleen. Smith must have realized by the manner in which he was being questioned by the police that they did not have a clue

---

2. All three criminal defendants were tried separately, even though the criminal case was philosophically tried as a joint venture. The criminal case was severed to prevent any possible use of exculpatory physical evidence carrying over for any single defendant during a possible joint trial. Robert Preston admitted during testimony in his 1969 trial, which occurred six months after my trial and conviction, that he was the individual who punched and knocked out the screaming Kathleen; and then carried her off into the woods . . . actions that were attributed to me by the prosecution during my June 1969 trial.

as to what happened in the Grove Section of Lawrence on the 22nd, and the female victim did not know either due to trauma. I was not in New York with my two codefendants when they were apprehended and tortured by the police. Rather, I was at home with my mother and five sisters in Methuen, Massachusetts.

I was seventeen years old at the time of the criminal episode, Emanuel Smith was 20 or 21, and Robert Preston was 19 or 20 years of age.

If I had been the prime suspect of the Lawrence Police on November 22, 1968 Detectives Lannon and Tylus would have immediately taken me to the Lawrence police station for questioning and identification by Raymond (the male victim). All of this would have taken place prior to the three of them (2 detectives and Raymond) venturing all the way to New York City in search of Robert Preston. I would have been the first suspect to be terrorized by the police, but on November 24, 1968.

Raymond identified Preston and Smith at the police station in New York City, when Lannon and Tylus eventually decided to bring them in. Raymond testified during my trial this was his initial identification of Robert and Emanuel, although there being a close resemblance in a photo that he was shown in the Lawrence police station by Lieutenant Tylus (given to him by Preston's mother on November 22nd) before they left for New York. Although Raymond continually described Preston as the initial principle, Detectives Lannon and Tylus returned to Lawrence with Preston and Smith in tow, and arrested me in Methuen on November 28, 1968, as Kathleen's assailant. Emanuel E. Smith had become the Prosecution's "cooperating"[3] witness to the criminal episode.

To this day in 2015 I believe that Kathleen was too traumatized by the attack upon her that she could not readily identify anyone,[4] until she was prompted by the police and prosecutor to identify

---

3. Emanuel Smith's trial attorney had arranged a sentencing deal for his client (that was undisclosed during my trial when the trial judge asked Smith) where he would not receive a life sentence for a guilty plea, and if he became a cooperating witness for the Commonwealth. This information came to light when I received a copy of Smith's affidavit in support of a new trial in 1984. Emanuel was released from prison in 1986, as a direct result of his "secret" sentencing deal.
4. The annals of criminal law are rife with the vagaries of eyewitness and victim identification.

me (in conformity with Smith's statement to the police in New York). During my June 1969 trial Kathleen testified to falling in and out of consciousness,[5] and placed me on the back seat of the 1965 Ford Mustang fastback automobile assaulting her as she screamed at me. Yet, no one else involved in the criminal episode (to include Raymond) placed me in the automobile, but testified that I was distanced outside fighting Raymond when she was screaming.

By 2009 I had read three different police report accounts pertaining to crimes committed on November 22, 1968; which the Massachusetts Parole Board has determined that I must acquiesce as fact before they will honestly consider me for parole release from prison. A legal lynching stacks all of the proverbial cards against the person being lynched, to the degree where it is almost impossible to unravel the rope around one's neck. The aforementioned police reports declare that Kathleen identified me by a ring that I was to have worn on the night of the criminal episode, which was also on my person on November 28, 1968 when I was arrested.[6] However, Kathleen testified during my jury waived trial to have identified me by way of a suggestive photo array that my trial attorney never questioned. No ring was ever mentioned, or entered into evidence, during any court proceeding.

The 2014 Parole Board determined in their 2015 <u>Decision</u> on

---

5. Kathleen testified during my trial that I was kneeling over her upon the backseat of Raymond's 1965 Ford Mustang Fastback automobile. It was there that she testified that I removed her underwear . . . she screamed at me . . . someone said "Did you fuck her yet?", and I replied "Not yet." . . . and I then punched her into unconsciousness. Further, she testified to waking from unconsciousness to find me straddling her upon the ground in the woods . . . she told me to kill her . . . I said "I am." . . . she felt a tearing between her legs and lost consciousness. I could not fit upon the back seat of the automobile alone, and surely not be able to kneel upon the seat over anyone else. At the time of the criminal episode I was 6' 6" in height, Preston was approximately 5' 9", and Smith was around 5' 6". I was never in the automobile, yet I received a life sentence for "intent" to rape. When the criminal defendant is black and the victim is white, physical evidence can be withheld from trial and takes a diminished role to victim testimony in Massachusetts jurisprudence. The laws of physics and geometry cease to apply, and the proverbial square peg easily fits into a round hole.

6. The Lawrence police reports contain exaggerations that would not be found credible within any court of law, but have been declared the "official version" of the 1968 criminal episode. In spite of court evidence to the contrary, the reports are utilized extrajudicially to keep me imprisoned. There is no defense.

my request for a parole that I lack "candor" in my explanation of my role in the criminal undertaking, because I refuse to accept the 1968 Lawrence Police Department reports as "official version" of the crimes. Because I have the audacity as a black criminal with white victims to have convictions (beliefs) that run contrary to the government, I should "die in prison" for non capital first offenses. There exist no statistics nor evidence to support a conclusion that denial of culpability in a criminal episode makes the convicted individual more susceptible to recidivate or reoffend. My acceptance of the police reports as "official version" of the crimes would absolve the Commonwealth of duplicity and racism.

By Massachusetts criminal just-us standards: I was an easy, fast, and inexpensive conviction; once a "cooperating witness" was established, victims were coerced, physical evidence was withheld or suppressed, the defense was in league with the prosecution based upon race and the nature of the crimes, and any notion of due process and equal protection of the law was subverted.

When Detectives Lannon and Tylus both testified during my trial to have found hand and fingerprints, as well as blood[7] throughout the interior of the automobile, and the owner of the prints and blood was never confirmed or identified, due process was subverted. When the attested to assault with intent to rape (for which I was sentenced to life in prison) was to have taken place upon the backseat of the 1965 Ford Mustang fastback automobile and returned to the male victim (Raymond, the owner) two weeks prior to my trial without the backseat area dimensions being measured and presented to the court, due process was subverted. The physical evidence was exculpatory, and a detail best determined by an independent fact-finder: a jury; but the physical evidence was undermined so as not to contradict the prosecution's constructed testimonial trial evidence. The question as to why trial counsel coerced a waiver of trial by jury is answered: for due process and equal protection

---

7. Robert S. Preston was bleeding profusely from a knife wound over his eye, accidently inflicted upon him by his knife wielding cousin and codefendant Emanuel E. Smith, which Preston testified to during his trial. My trial counsel never requested Robert S. Preston to take the witness stand in my defense during my trial.

of the law to be subverted in favor of the prosecution. Was the allowance of physical evidence in favor of the defense at trial to be withheld or destroyed by the prosecution, and a coerced waiver of trial by jury, a "reasonable" defense strategy as concluded by the 1984 Appeals Court? Or, rather a "legal but not factual" lynching tool similar to a noose, acquiesced by the Massachusetts court system; designed to usurp a young and naive criminal defendant's constitutional protections to a fair trial, because "Hamm is black and his victims white"?[8]

It is clear that equal justice in "amerik.k.k.a" is cloaked beneath an enduring legacy of manifest destiny and white supremacy. This particularly holds true in the birthplace of that enduring legacy: "Mississippi," and its criminal just-us system.[9]

Why is it then that when a black child may have a psychological breakdown and commit vicious crimes (a probable backlash due to centuries of physical and psychological trauma visited upon him by the dominant culture in mainstream society[10]), the child is rejected and labelled a "monster", in spite of evidence to the contrary? Why is it that when a white child may exhibit the same violent behavior, or worse, that child is usually determined by the culture to be: "full of youthful angst," "misunderstood," "a product of a bad social environment," "ingesting too much sugar" (the "Twinkie" defense), or "under the influence of violent video games"; and is redeemable? If a black child in the above scenario

---

8. Commonwealth v. Ralph C. Hamm, 471 N.E. 2d 416, 421 (1984).
9. In Massachusetts, the question of white privilege affords an organized crime hit man for the Whitey Bulger's "Winter Hill Gang" to be convicted for racketeering and serve 12 years in a federal prison . . . admit to murdering 18 people . . . receive a parole, without serving one minute for mass murder . . . upon release on parole, receive a $20,000.00 check from the federal government . . . receive $60,000.00 from a Boston newspaper columnist to help him write a book on the "Winter Hill Gang" . . . and receive $120,000.00 from a film production company as a consultant to the movie "Black Mass." White privilege also affords a brother who aided his sibling in the murder of the sibling's wife for insurance money, the ability to abet by hiding/disposing critical physical evidence of the murder; yet not be charged as an accessory to the murder, due to some obscure reading of the Magna Carta. And, white privilege allows a man convicted by a jury of his peers to deny 22 counts of child molestation; yet receive a parole without having to attend a sex offender treatment program or a rating in the Sex Offender Registry Board (SORB). As a black man, when I refute any aspect of my convictions I am declared to "lack candor." White privilege recognizes and accepts the difference in the criminal just-us system.
10. Dr. Joy Degruy Leary, *Post Traumatic Slave Syndrome: America's Legacy of Enduring Injury and Healing*.

is a "monster," is white mainstream society Dr. Frankenstein's laboratory? Is repression one of the culprits? However those questions may be answered, it is a fact that constant unrelenting pressure can create a rough diamond—if one were to only look without prejudice.

From out of the darkness . . .

In 1972, I was empowered through my study of the works of Frantz Fanon (1925-1961), as he spoke for me more than any other person or author, in a singular voice:

> So here we have the negro rehabilitated, "standing at the helm," governing the world with his intuition, rediscovered, reappropriated, in demand, accepted; and it's not a negro, oh, no, but the negro, alerting the prolific antennae of the world, standing in the spotlight of the world, spraying the world with his poetical power, "porous to every breath in the world." I embrace the world! I am the world! The white man has never understood this magical substitution. The white man wants the world; he wants it for himself. He discovers he is the predestined master of the world. He enslaves it. His relationship with the world is one of appropriation. But there are values that can be served only with my sauce. As a magician I stole from the white man a "certain world"; lost to him and his kind. When that happened the white man must have felt an aftershock he was unable to identify, being unused to such reactions. The reason was that above the objective world of plantations [prisons, cotton, cane] and banana and rubber trees, I had subtly established the real world. The essence of the world was my property. Between the world and me there was a relation of coexistence. I had discovered the Primordial One. My "speaking hands" tore at the hysterical throat of the world. The white man had the uncomfortable feeling that I was slipping away and taking something with me. He searched my pockets, probed the least delineated of my convolutions. There was nothing new. Obviously, I must have a secret. They interrogated me.[11]

And, not satisfied with my answers (or non answers), they began to systematically torture me.

I turned away from my tormentors, fading to black with an impervious air of mystery, and swore:

---

11. Fanon, *Black Skin, White Masks*, pp. 106-107.

"Although the strain
may bend me,
  twist me,
  deform me,
I will shoulder
twice my burden,
  laden
  heavily.
There's no choice
in opting sorrows,
  torments,
  miseries,
for I'm shackled
to youth futures
  pioneer
  nowadays.³

Waiting for the light.

And then came a shocking illumination, momentarily blinding me. November 4, 2008, approximately 11:07 p.m., WHAT THE HELL JUST HAPPENED!? Others had prayed for it, but I never believed that I would survive to see it. It would appear as if the oppressor-oppressed contradiction has been unexpectedly superseded by the humanization of the people, brought about by post-Civil Rights generations and college-educated young white people. The Amerik.k.k.a that I had grown to loathe is miraculously being transmuted into the promised land,⁴ envisioned by the late Dr. Martin Luther King Jr. An unjust reality has been transformed. A prophetic black man has become President-elect of the United States of America! And my final lesson, imparted upon me by Paolo Freire, has become the will of the collective consciousness of the world, it would seem . . . .

I cried, for he told me that in order for our struggle to have significance, we must not, in the effort to regain our humanity, become the oppressors of the oppressor; rather, we had to become the restorers of the humanity of ourselves and the oppressor

---

3. Poem: "The Pledge," by Ralph C. Hamm.
4. Is this apparent transformation of Amerik.k.k.a the harbinger of another Civil War in this country; or is it simply a dream to be deferred—much like the promise held out for Blacks in the 1865 Reconstruction Era?

as well.⁵ I had arrived at the proverbial mountain top, but the true struggle for manumission continues for me. And, if there is only one truism that wielding the tool of history has taught me, it would be to always beware of Europeans bearing gifts . . . especially if that gift bears the label: "MADE IN AMERIK.K.K.A"⁶

> Consciousness
> is a matter of feeling . . . feeling
> is a matter of faith . . . faith is
> the very substance of things hoped for,
> and is the element
> out of which they are made.

---

5. On November 6, 2008—two days after the election of Barack Obama as the 44th President of the United States, a Cape Verdean prison guard at the Massachusetts Treatment Center in Bridgewater, Massachusetts allowed me to read a blog that had apparently been circulating on the internet since November 4th, and it read:

> "Rosa sat so that Martin could walk,
> Martin walked so that Obama could run,
> Obama ran so that children could fly."

6. The fanatical right wing, white rabble rousing, drug addicted, talk radio show host Rush Limbaugh utilized the radio airwaves to stir up divisiveness (what made him a millionaire) by declaring that the presidential election was rigged against John McCain, that the millions of votes cast by the white middle class, suburbia, college students, ethnic minorities, was a ruse created by the "liberal" news media (although said news media is owned by conservative corporate America) . . . fanatical white Christian fundamentalists, most of whom submerged themselves beneath religious dogma and fervor (unable to determine what socks to wear upon their own volition) have declared Barack Obama to be the anti-Christ . . . and the American Nazi Party, as well as the functionally illiterate rank-and-file of the Skin Heads, have declared Obama a terrorist, based upon Republican Party propaganda, thereby forwarding the premise that Adolf Hitler was a misunderstood saint.

APPENDIX A

COINTELPRO (Revisited)

Spying and Disruption FBI Domestic Intelligence Activities

In black and white: the FBI Papers

Following are transcripts of official FBI COINTELPRO documents obtained under the Freedom of Information Act. The March 4, 1968 communique was sent out by J. Edgar Hoover himself just one month before the assassination of Martin Luther King Jr. It specifically identified Elijah Muhammed and the Nation of Islam as primary targets of COINTELPRO, as well as Rev. King's Southern Christian Leadership Conference. Other released FBI documents show the Bureau had infiltrators within Malcolm X's Muslim Mosque, Inc. Still others prove the FBI had undercover agents in the very room when he was assassinated; one such agent actually administered mouth-to-mouth to the dying man.

Note: in the originally released documents, most of the names of COINTELPRO targets are censored. However, the names which are included here exactly fit the spaces marked out by the FBI. It is also now known that all of these individuals were in fact targeted for "neutralization" by the FBI.
[Some emphases added by the editor.]

SAC, Albany August 25, 1967
PERSONAL ATTENTION TO ALL OFFICES

[From] Director, FBI

COUNTERINTELLIGENCE PROGRAM
BLACK NATIONALIST-HATE GROUPS
INTERNAL SECURITY

[. . .] The purpose of this new counterintelligence endeavor is to expose, disrupt, misdirect, discredit, or OTHERWISE NEUTRALIZE *[emphasis added]* the activities of black nationalist hate-type organizations and groupings, their leadership, spokesmen, membership, and supporters, and to counter their propensity for violence and civil disorder. The activities of all such groups of intelligence interest to the Bureau must be followed on a continuous basis so we will be in a position to promptly take advantage of all opportunities for counterintelligence and inspire action in instances where circumstances warrant. The pernicious background of such groups, their duplicity, and devious maneuvers must be exposed to public scrutiny where such publicity will have a neutralizing effect. Efforts of the various groups to consolidate their forces or to recruit new or youthful adherents must be frustrated. NO OPPORTUNITY SHOULD BE MISSED TO EXPLOIT THROUGH COUNTER INTELLIGENCE TECHNIQUES THE ORGANIZATIONAL AND PERSONAL CONFLICTS OF THE LEADERSHIPS OF THE GROUPS AND WHERE POSSIBLE AN EFFORT SHOULD BE MADE TO CAPITALIZE UPON EXISTING CONFLICTS BETWEEN COMPETING BLACK NATIONALIST ORGANIZATIONS. *[emphasis added]* When an opportunity is apparent to disrupt or NEUTRALIZE *[emphasis added]* black nationalist, hate-type organizations through the cooperation of established local news media contacts or through such contact with sources available to the Seat of Government [Hoover's office],[1] in every instance

---

1. "Seat of Government" (SOG) is an official designation created by J.. Edgar

careful attention must be given to the proposal to insure the targeted group is disrupted, ridiculed, or discredited through the publicity and not merely publicized . . .

You are also cautioned that the nature of this new endeavor is such that UNDER NO CIRCUMSTANCES SHOULD THE EXISTENCE OF THE PROGRAM BE MADE KNOWN OUTSIDE THE BUREAU *[emphasis added]* and appropriate within office security should be afforded to sensitive operations and techniques considered under the program.

No counterintelligence action under this program may be initiated by the field without specific prior Bureau authorization. [Emphasis in orig.]

COUNTERINTELLIGENCE PROGRAM
BLACK NATIONALIST-HATE GROUPS
RACIAL INTELLIGENCE   3/4/68

GOALS

For maximum effectiveness of the Counterintelligence Program, and to prevent wasted effort, long-range goals are being set.

1. Prevent the COALITION of militant black nationalist groups. In unity there is strength; a truism that is no less valid for all its triteness. An effective coalition of black nationalist groups might be the first step toward a real "Mau Mau" [black revolutionary army] in America, the beginning of a true black revolution.
2. Prevent the RISE OF A "MESSIAH" who could unify, and electrify, the militant black nationalist movement. Malcolm X might have been such a "messiah;" he is the martyr of the movement today. Martin Luther King, Stokely Carmichael and Elijah Muhammed all aspire to

---

Hoover to refer to his own office. Hoover was director of the FBI for some forty years, even receiving a special exemption from compulsory retirement by President Ford. The "SOG" appellation is indicative of his egotistical view of his power, which saw presidents come and go.

this position. Elijah Muhammed is less of a threat because of his age. King could be a very real contender for this position should he abandon his supposed "obedience" to "white, liberal doctrines" (nonviolence) and embrace black nationalism. Carmichael has the necessary charisma to be a real threat in this way.
3. Prevent VIOLENCE on the part of black nationalist groups. This is of primary importance, and is, of course, a goal of our investigative activity; it should also be a goal of the Counterintelligence Program to pinpoint potential troublemakers and neutralize them before they exercise their potential for violence.
4. Prevent militant black nationalist groups and leaders from gaining RESPECTABILITY, by discrediting them to three separate segments of the community. The goal of discrediting black nationalists must be handled tactically in three ways. You must discredit those groups and individuals to, first, the responsible Negro community. Second, they must be discredited to the white community, both the responsible community and to "liberals" who have vestiges of sympathy for militant black nationalist [sic] simply because they are Negroes. Third, these groups must be discredited in the eyes of Negro radicals, the followers of the movement. This last area requires entirely different tactics from the first two. Publicity about violent tendencies and radical statements merely enhances black nationalists to the last group; it adds "respectability" in a different way.
5. A final goal should be to prevent the long-range GROWTH of militant black organizations, especially among youth. Specific tactics to prevent these groups from converting young people must be developed. [...]

TARGETS

Primary targets of the Counterintelligence Program, Black Nationalist Hate Groups, should be the most violent and radical groups and their leaders. We should emphasize those leaders and organizations that are nationwide in scope and are most capable of disrupting this country. These targets, members, and followers of the:

> Student Nonviolent Coordinating Committee (SNCC)
> Southern Christian Leadership Conference (SCLC)
> Revolutionary Action Movement (RAM)
> NATION OF ISLAM (NOI) *[emphasis added]*

Offices handling these cases and those of Stokely Carmichael of SNCC, H. Rap Brown of SNCC, Martin Luther King of SCLC, Maxwell Stanford of RAM, and Elijah Muhammed of NOI, should be alert for counterintelligence suggestions. [...][2]

---

2. Source: Brian Glick, *The War At Home: Covert Action Against U.S. Activists And What We Can Do About It* (Boston: South End Press, 1989) ISBN: 0-89608-349-7.

Appendix B

Opening Statement at my September 15, 2009 Parole Hearing.

Greetings Mr. Chairman, Ladies and Gentleman of the Parole Board. My name is Ralph Hamm the Third, and I am entering into the completion of my 42nd year of imprisonment upon the crimes charged against me. I have been appearing before varying auspices of the parole board for over the past ten years requesting a supervised release from prison, but to no avail; and through the course of these past ten years members of my immediate family and community supporters have passed away due to illness. My crimes were committed when I was 17 years of age, in the company of two codefendants: one who was 21 years old, and the other 20; and both of whom have been released from prison many years ago.

Prior to both my 1999 and 2004 parole eligibility hearings, I was informed by the life parole liaison Anne King that the Board does not retry criminal cases. Yet, during both hearings I faced retrial as well as questioning surrounding my race and the race of the victims of the crime. In neither instance was there any discussion or open consideration upon the obvious impact that race played upon my sentence structure.

When I entered Walpole Prison in June of 1969 from the Essex County Superior Court, no prisoner in the correctional system of memory or recent history had ever been sentenced to life imprisonment for a first offense intent to rape conviction except myself. This was prior to the 1969 sentencing of my codefendant Robert Preston. The concept of sentencing someone to life imprisonment for "intent" was determined to be so draconian in nature that, I believe in 1972, the state legislature amended Mass. Gen. Law Ch. 265 §24 to where "life" was no longer a penalty for a violation of the statute.

So, in 2009, I remain the only prisoner in Massachusetts to ever receive and still be incarcerated under a life sentence for intent to rape. Secondly, no one incarcerated had been sentenced to serve life in prison for a first offense unmasked armed robbery, where a life was not forfeited during the commission of a crime, except Robert Preston and myself. These sentences were predicated upon race.

In 1984, the Massachusetts Appeals Court determined that skin color was a "reasonable" means by which to coerce an unknowing and unintelligent waiver of my constitutional protections during my 1969 trial, and thereby upheld the superior court denial of my 1980 motion for a new trial.

The court's resolve obviously impacted upon my sentence in prison, as skin color has effectively been used against me throughout the procedural history of my conviction. Whenever I question the implication of institutional racism upon my conviction and sentence, those deemed in authority who field the question accuse me of "playing the race card," as their method to avoid the issue and not answer the question.

I am also accused of sounding angry. Blame is thereby shifted back onto me. The "race card" response comes from those individuals and institutions that have historically utilized the entire 52-card race deck against me throughout my lifetime. Some continue to do so.

Today, I am before a new board whose members I hope will view my case with a broader and clearer vision. I want to make it perfectly clear now that the events of which I am about to speak upon do not reflect upon any individual sitting before me. I will be talking about my arduous history within the Massachusetts criminal justice system, as well as certain actions made by the predecessors of this particular board.

I am here today confronting the probability of another 5 year review for parole consideration, which will then place me at the age of 64—the statistically proven life expectancy for black men in this country. The possible full development of prostate cancer looms in my immediate future; and with prison health care being what it is, or what it is not, I have decided to take the opportunity this afternoon to say what I feel needs to be said about my case. Life may not afford me a second chance.

I am not the 1970s Norfolk State Prison inmate who shot prison guards, nor am I the 1980s Middle Eastern bomber and mass murderer who both received clemency due to illness. I am simply a black man before you with nothing to loose, and nothing else left to give.

During my 2004 parole eligibility hearing the Assistant District Attorney expressed that the Lawrence community was still traumatized by the 1968 crimes. I expect that we will hear a similar reference today. It is my recollection that in 1968 Lawrence was a predominately European-American community with less than 15 African-American families throughout, and only 3 to 5 Hispanic families residing therein. Today, it is almost entirely Hispanic. I would find it extremely incredible for the three to five Hispanic families of 1968 to have passed on the nature of our charged offenses to their descendants, and to newcomers to the neighborhood to where the entire community is traumatized still. If that were so, then my codefendant Robert Preston would not likely be residing there with his sister Linda today.

Most of today's Lawrence residents were not even born, nor living within this country when these crimes were committed; and those adults then living have no doubt either passed away or moved out. We are considering four decades, not four years, four months, or four days. For those community members who may still remember and suffer from the memory, all that I can do is offer my sincerest apologies for my codefendants and myself: for aside from having the entire criminal episode foisted upon me, I have nothing left to give save my death.

As in 2004, the Essex County Assistant District Attorney will undoubtedly attempt to mislead the parole board today into accepting the fallacy that I was the principal assailant in the crimes against both Kathleen McGrath and Raymond Gagnon. This is not true. As previously stated, I have two co-defendants—Emanuel Smith and Robert Preston—who are related to one another as first cousins. Emanuel Smith, the eldest, was the only state witness to testify that he witnessed me stomp Kathleen McGrath and then shove a tree branch into her vagina. He testified after first being threatened at gunpoint then coerced by the Lawrence police upon his arrest in New York. His court-appointed trial counsel also offered him a sentencing deal. He was not convicted of assaults upon Kathleen McGrath, as he pled guilty to other charges; which led to his testimony against me as her principal assailant.

This secret sentencing deal was the subject of his motion for a new trial, through which he was ordered released from prison on probation in 1984. The Assistant District Attorney complained to the 2004 parole board about my audacity to file an appeal in court on these matters.

In 1999 I came before the parole board with a psychological/risk Assessment rendered by the late doctor Theoharris Seghorn of New England Forensic Associates. The Parole Board rejected his Assessment because it was favorable to me, as they were seeking something more adverse. I asked the board at that time if they wanted me to undergo the Department of Correction' Sex Offender Treatment Program (SOTP). If so, then I suggested that they order me to do so. Board member Pomerole adamantly stressed to me that the Parole Board did not order prisoners to do anything as a prerequisite to parole release, and I received a flat denial upon my request for parole that year.

In 2004 I appeared before the parole board again, accompanied by several of my community supporters. During this hearing the Essex County Assistant District Attorney made a first appearance, and spent most of the afternoon circulating photographs around the hearing room that depicted the facial injuries sustained by the female victim, Kathleen McGrath. Not once was it mentioned that her injuries were inflicted upon her by my codefendant Robert Preston by his own admission during his trial, as well as within a recent Affidavit that he rendered to my attorney.

During the course of the 2004 hearing, Chairperson Maureen Walsh informed me that I had been punished enough, which afforded me hope after having served over 35 years in prison. However, on May 6th, the day after the hearing, the same parole board panel that had recently afforded Gerald Amerault a parole without his having to undergo the SOTP for his conviction of sexual abuse against twenty-two child victims at the Fells Acres Day Care Center, determined that I should complete the SOTP even though the Chairperson told me during the course of the hearing that I probably would not be able to complete Phase Four of said program.

The only possible-way for me to undergo the DOC's SOTP was to lie and accept the "official version" of my crimes as fact, in its depiction of me being the principal assailant of Kathleen McGrath. After being coerced by the parole board's decision for me to complete the SOTP as a prerequisite to parole consideration, I accepted the "official version" under duress to comply as being the only way to regain my freedom from prison, and the sole method by which to be transferred by the DOC from OCCC to MCI Norfolk to begin phase one of the treatment program.

I arrived at MCI Norfolk in September and by October 2004 I began the SOTP. By March 2005 I had completed two of the three phases, marking time in phase three through 2006 while awaiting my answer from the parole board on a submitted petition for reconsideration. I had asked the Board if I could pursue the completion of the treatment program while on a parole at NEFA, having arrived at the full realization of what Chairperson Walsh meant when she acknowledged my inability to complete phase four.

My petition for reconsideration was ultimately denied, and I was told in the decision to complete the SOTP before I could receive parole consideration. I found myself trapped within a proverbial "Catch-22," and consequently made the decision to be transferred to the treatment center in Bridgewater for what I believed would be the beginning of treatment in the phase four aspect of the Program.

Upon my arrival at the treatment center, I spoke to several prisoners concerning the FHS assessment, and had the opportunity to read several of them, to determine precisely what the assessors would be expecting from me. In my effort to acquiesce the mandate of the parole board, as well as attempt to be accepted in the Phase Four core program, I admitted to every lie attributed to me in the "official version" during my FHS assessment; as well as concocted other embellishments to create a convincing story—a SOTP accredited fairy tale that depicted me assaulting Kathleen McGrath while in a drunken rage. The 2006 assessment concluded that I was a medium high risk to reoffend based upon one assessment point formulated in their assessment tool "Static-99."

The specific point in question was reached upon the fact that at the age of 17, when my crimes were committed, I did not have experience in a 2-year cohabitating relationship with an adult female in my background. Such a sexual relationship would have had to begin for me at the age of 15 or younger, and placed my female partner in violation of: MGL Ch. 265, ß 23—rape & abuse of a child; MGL Ch. 265, ß 24—assault of a child with intent to commit rape; MGL, Ch. 272, ß 2—enticing away a person for prostitution or sexual intercourse; and, MGL Ch. 272, ß 35—unnatural & lascivious acts with a child under 16.

"Static-99" was thereby used to my detriment in spite of my objections to the assessor and two FHS directors, as well as in spite of its own implied recommendation not to be applied to anyone under the age of 18. Therefore, the 2006 FHS assessment is totally invalid; yet adverse enough to receive the previous parole board's OV acceptance, and is precisely what the DA's office requires to utilize against me.

My FHS assessment did, however, yield one positive aspect. It made me aware of the existence of a January 1969 Lawrence Police Department report. The report, or rather Kathleen McGrath's initial statement to the police on the night of the crime contained therein, substantiated my then 38-year proclamation that I was not her assailant. My proclamation was not only clarified by the police report, but also supported by testimony rendered by Raymond Gagnon and by my codefendant Robert Preston during his severed jury trial, as well as within a recent affidavit that Preston afforded my attorney.

After the assessment by FHS was finalized, I underwent and completed the clinical transition phase of the SOTP. Yet FHS staff prevented me from entering phase Four by informing me that: (1) I was not clinically ready, (2) that the three beds allotted to prisoners serving life sentences were occupied, (3) that I was a "fighter" and a possible threat to the core Program, and (4) had to accept still another version of the "official version" of the crime: notwithstanding the fact that the annals of criminal law are rife with the vagaries of eyewitness and victim identification of perpetrators during the commission of crimes.

In January 2007 I wrote a letter to FHS director Dr. Perrou recanting my assessment based upon all of the aforementioned reasons that I was denied access to the core program, as well as detailing how and why I concocted my story in an effort to comply with the SOTP parameters and to receive supervised release from prison. I also decried the improper use of "Static 99" to my situation and assessment. I never received a reply.

In January 2009 I terminated myself from the SOTP based upon what I considered to be an invalid 2006 FHS assessment. The reasons are: the misapplication of "Static-99" to determine my risk assessment; my inability to be accepted in the core program; and the fact that I will not be able to complete or truly benefit from the core program if my cooperation with the facilitators is based upon lies. I was unwilling to accept yet another "official version" of my crime as true. In addition to this, my appeal was pending. I terminated myself after giving the program a four-and-a-half year commitment and effort toward completion. I am presently awaiting my requested and approved transfer back to Norfolk Prison.

I claim not to be directly responsible for every criminal act charged against me. Yet, there is both a moral and a social responsibility that I lost sight of in 1968 when these crimes were committed; but I have come to clearly recognize, appreciate, and accept. The moral responsibility rests within my knowledge then of right from wrong, which was instilled within me by way of my parents and the church at an early age—a knowing that my ingesting of excessive amounts of alcohol may have disinhibited, and thereby assisted me to violate.

Then there is my social responsibility, a sacred trust bestowed upon me to live in harmony with, and abide by the rules of the greater community; which I wantonly squandered, as a willing participant in the criminal episode. This was my folly—a teenager's attempt to be accepted by his peers, at a cost of everything else. Although I could not have been in all places at once, as the official version would like the reader to believe, I cared more for acceptance from my wounded codefendant than I did for the welfare of the victims of the crimes.

This lack of compassion for others, and loyalty toward my comrade, may have been instilled within me as a sign of the times in which I was then living, or somewhat by way of my military training as I was home on military leave for a scheduled tour of duty in Vietnam. But still, I should have known better, and it serves as no excuse. This lack of compassion and inability to act in a responsible manner haunts me still, and serves as my greatest regret. It can be said that at the time that these crimes were committed I was only 17 years old—sleepwalking through life with a limited life experience, relying upon brain stem activity without the benefit of rationalization. I simply had a fight or flight impulse which was firing off simultaneously. I was undeveloped in that area, much like all adolescents of my age group, and as a result I have spent my entire adult life incarcerated.

I am an offender who has served over 40 years in prison, whose older codefendants have received a second opportunity at life over a decade ago; as I remain the sole codefendant designated as the proverbial scapegoat for a charged intended sexual assault upon Kathleen McGrath. I am here before you under the assumption that true parole consideration has already been foreclosed, based upon the decision rendered within the 2006 denial of my petition for reconsideration.

As I look upon my prison sentence today, referring to crimes committed in the 1960s when I was still a juvenile, I see that for all intent and purpose, taking into account over ten years of parole denials, my prison sentence continues to be altered. First, in 1982, by way of the 1977 Henschel Policy used to aggregate my sentence to circumvent affording me a statutorily mandated parole eligibility hearing in 1983 on my concurrent second-degree life sentences. If I had been paroled then to begin serving an aggregated 27-40 years indeterminate consecutive sentence, I would have been able to apply all of my statutory and earned good time credits to complete said sentence, thereby probably obtaining release from prison on life parole years ago.

Then in 1999, 2004, and 2006, parole board decisions, and the retroactive application of 103 Doc 446 to nullify my 1975 assessment by the Department of Mental Health as not being sexually dangerous, have forced the evolution of my overall sentence into one without the possibility of true parole consideration on non-capital first offenses.

Dr. Dou Dou Diene, the United Nation's special rapporteur on contemporary forms of racism, racial discrimination, xenophobia and related intolerance, presented his final report to the United Nations on June 16, 2009 in Geneva, Switzerland. The report came after a yearlong tour of American cities to research the problem of racism and its negative impact. One of the points stressed within his report came as a call to the United States Congress to pass legislation that would end the sentencing of juveniles to life in prison without the possibility of parole.

As I am currently serving life without the possibility of true parole consideration, with my health failing, I have reached the conclusion that the criminal justice system in Massachusetts has intentionally altered my sentence to be a slow death in prison. This conclusion will undoubtedly be supported by the position taken today by the Essex County District Attorney's Office, as a request to the Board that parole not be granted in my case.

This tortuous death sentence was foreseen at the time of my 1969 trial not to be much unlike the lynching of black men throughout the 1900s, at the hands of white southern mobs. In 1969 Massachusetts was subtler in its approach for the reckless eyeballing or fantasy rapes of white women, and could rely upon its criminal justice agencies to facilitate the lynching, as opposed to simply attaching me to a tree. The public spectacle remained the same by way of the courtroom and the media, with the crowd satisfaction of watching me dangle in agony more prolonged and repeatedly enjoyed day after day and year after year stretching into the decades that I remain alive in prison.

Rational thinking and common sense have not been applied in my case, but only the raw emotion of hatred. This was impressed upon me during my 1999 parole eligibility hearing. Chairperson Sheila Hubbard and board member Mary Ellen

Doyle made it perfectly clear to me that they did not believe the material facts presented at my hearing to be contained and withheld within my criminal case; but rather believed, or accepted as true, the fables that they heard from their unnamed source. This proclivity toward accepting fiction over fact is the typical, emotional mentality of the lynch mob—a mentality that more often than not reaches the frenzied conclusion to hang the wrongly accused.

So, here we are in 2009, forty years after my crimes were committed.

I will be 59 years old in November. I am here today searching for a new beginning with a new parole board, consisting of people who have not heard from me before this afternoon. Nothing in anything I've said is meant to detract from the severely horrendous nature of the offenses charged against my codefendants and me. Nor has it been said to lessen the pain and suffering inflicted upon Ms. McGrath and Mr. Gagnon.

I can only imagine the horror that they had to endure at the hands of my codefendants and myself on that November morning in 1968: Mr. Gagnon being stabbed and dragged from his automobile, then relentlessly beaten into unconsciousness by strangers, hearing his girlfriend's screams before losing consciousness—Ms. McGrath trying desperately to ward off her assailant, assuming that she is about to be raped, and screaming for help in the darkness where no one can hear her, then praying for death to come.

It is a scenario from which horror movies are made, and I've lived my entire adult life with the agony of knowing that I was one of the perpetrators of their horror. I cannot speak too much upon what my codefendants may or may not have done during the course of this criminal episode, I can only speak upon my actions and inaction.

No matter how difficult my incarceration has been, I seriously doubt that anything that I had to go through can compare to the lifetime of torment that the victims of my crime have been forced to endure as a result of the nightmare that my codefendants and I visited upon them on the early morning of November 23, 1968. Whatever my experiences may have been are a result of a chain of events that I helped to set into motion over forty years ago, and I have no one to blame but myself

I am here before you today seeking a favorable resolution to the underlying questions of: When is enough punishment truly enough? Does my involvement in these crimes as a juvenile warrant that I should spend my entire life in prison? Are my crimes more heinous than that of one who takes the life of a police officer, or any other human being? Do I deserve a second opportunity to live the remainder of my life in a free society, under reasonable prerequisites and stipulations?

I have requested that my attorney be present at this hearing as a representative, and to address any legal matters that may arise. Otherwise, I will be speaking for myself and personally answering queries posed by the members of the board. There are also members of my community support team present; to include my friend and spiritual advisor for over 30 years, prospective employers, and members of my extended family. All can be called upon to speak in regard to the support that they can provide me in my transition back into society, if parole is actually still available to me. They are also here to answer any questions that the parole board may wish to ask them in regard to their support.

Thank you.

Ralph C. Hamm III

[The Parole Board decision was issued on September 29, 2009, stating that I was not a suitable candidate for parole. Parole was denied with a review in 5 years. I immediately launch into an appeal, see Appendix D.]

Appendix C

Appeal and Reconsideration of the September 29, 2009 Parole Decision

TO: The Commonwealth of Massachusetts
Parole Board
12 Mercer Road
Natick, MA

FROM: Ralph C. Hamm III (W32301)
M.C.I. Norfolk
P.O. Box 43
Norfolk, MA

DATE: January 7, 2010

RE: Appeal and Reconsideration of the September 29, 2009 Decision

On December 11, 2009 I received the September 29, 2009 Decision of the Parole Board request for a parole, as a result of the September 15, 2009 parole hearing.

I am hereby appealing that Decision and seek reconsideration pursuant to 120 CMR 304.02, (3), (b), (d), as well as 304.03, (d); thereby exhausting the afforded available remedy.

Paramount to my appeal and request for reconsideration is my contention that the Parole Board should not rely upon a police version of my charged crimes, masquerading as the "official version," which is a misleading report as pertains to the exact evidence and facts presented and determined in my trial.

1. One of the grounds determined by the Board to deny my request for parole rested upon my viewed failure to address the "factors" of my past criminal behavior, as well as 30 year old disciplinary infractions. Forty years of program and rehabilitation material contained within my case file, submitted to the parole board over the past ten years, states otherwise. I contend that the true reasoning underlying the Board's denial of parole rests upon a collective inability or refusal to separate and distinguish a view of Corrections in Massachusetts today from what it was yesterday.

The Board is in denial, as it is unable to accept the reality of my existence within Walpole Prison between the years 1969 to 1984, where I was thrust by the court as an 18 year old first time adult offender—a Black male having been convicted of a vicious assault upon a white couple, in a prison population of approximately 465 that held only 48 Black prisoners. I was repeatedly set up, set upon, and physically assaulted by both white guards and prisoners alike—forcing me to fight for my survival, at a time in history when Walpole Prison (with its 20 murders in one year) was touted as worst prison in the country.

The initial years of my existence in Walpole Prison was similar to torture that defrocked pedophile priest John Gagon underwent, with the exception that I was much younger than he and capable of defending myself. His torture is well documented within an official investigative report, compiled as a result of his murder in Sousa/Baronowski Prison. Our disciplinary histories are quite similar, especially during my early years of incarceration. It appears to me that many in State employ are angry with me because I had the audacity to survive 1970s Walpole Prison relatively intact, which is probably the reasoning behind Parole Board Chairman Mark Conrad's several quips asking me if I were a man of my conviction then why don't I die in prison. I further contend that such a query, viewed in light of the Board's Decision, is an abuse of discretion.

2. The Parole Board contended once again during my hearing that they do not retry criminal cases. I beg to differ. For example; Gerald Amerault was tried by a jury of his peers and convicted

of sexual assault upon 22 children at the Fells Acres Day Care Center. He adamantly and publicly professed his innocence, and refused to even consider undergoing the Department of Correction's Sex Offender Treatment Program (SOTP) to address the "causative factors" underlying his criminal behavior, yet he received a parole nonetheless.

I find it interesting how the Parole Board can determine 22 victims as wrong in accusing a white man of sexual assault, in spite of a jury's finding of guilt; yet, cannot see one victim's mistaken identification in accusing a Black teenager of intent, in spite of a coerced jury-waived trial determination. I contend that I was denied equity and/or equal protection/treatment, thereby discriminated against in not being afforded the same consideration as Gerald Amerault in 2004. Especially where I underwent the SOTP for four years—a program that didn't come into existence until 1997.

3. I find it quite interesting how the Board cited an altercation between Correctional Officer Hutton and myself in the 1970's as an example of my violent behavior upon incarceration. The Board should have cited the entire story of the incident. C.O. Hutton was a member of Walpole Prison's notorious "goon squad" a gang of prison guards who relished in beating prisoners for entertainment, often crippling them. As a member of the "goon squad," he professed to be a card-carrying member of the Ku Klux Klan. Hutton was the C.O. assigned to cellblock A3, in the minimum section of the prison, and was responsible for planting a knife in a lamp in my cell during an alleged routine cell search. The knife was utilized as justification to transfer me to segregation Block 10.

C.O. Hutton was later reassigned to cellblock B5 in the maximum section of the prison. It wasn't long after my release from segregation for the planted knife and I was placed within cellblock B7, that Black prisoner Robert Kines' cell was firebombed by white prisoners on Hutton's shift in cellblock B5, and a mini race riot ensued. During the course of the violence, C.O. Hutton grabbed Black prisoner Curtis Earltop around the neck and placed him in a choke hold. C.O. Hutton was observed holding a buck knife in his right hand.

Upon my arrival at the scene, prisoner William Johnson and myself both attempted to persuade C.O. Hutton to release his hold from around Earltop's neck. Hutton grinned at us, and refused. I feared for Earltop's life. William Johnson dumped a bucket of water upon Hurton's head, and I picked up the mop wringer and hit him over the head with it, and knocked him out, thereby releasing his grip from around Earltop's throat. If the story must be told, then tell the entire story.

It is illuminating how throughout the annals of Mississippi history the Klansmen are always portrayed as the victims of their prey when the prey fight back. In comparison, there is the story of State prisoner William Royce, who shot two Norfolk prison guards in the 1970s—the same decade that the Parole Board refers to in order to justify my denials for parole. We, the Black prisoners in Walpole prison, were fighting for our lives, whereas Mr. Royce shot the guards for recreational purposes. William Royce was afforded a parole just prior to my 1999 parole eligibility hearing without his having to address the "causative factors" underlying his criminal behavior and acts of violence upon correctional personnel via existing Department of Correction programs at the time, albeit limited in their scope.[1]

4. Discrimination is apparent where prisoners serving a second degree life sentence for murder can receive repeated paroles without serving forty years in prison, and I cannot receive one because I have not taken a life during the commission of my crimes; which astonishingly has made me a threat to public safety and thereby less likely to be considered a "suitable candidate" for parole.

Twice convicted murderer GH was determined not to be a threat to public safety and a "suitable candidate" for parole by this Board, yet he committed another series of violent felonies only 42 days after his parole release from prison. Did he address the "causative factors" of his criminal behavior? I sincerely doubt it. Or, if so, does that mean that the Correction's Recovery Academy

---

1. Since my arrival at Norfolk Prison on October 29, 2009, I unsuccessfully attempted to be admitted into both the CRA and Alternative to Violence Programs, based upon my aggregated life sentence; which aids in facilitating parole release denials.

(CRA) program is truly a farce? There exists a double standard for those serving second-degree life sentences for murder, and those serving life sentences for non-capital offenses.

It appears upon the surface that the Parole Board is intentionally seeding the community with convicted killers. Does that make the Parole Board, and its decisions, a threat to public safety? What if my name was VF, and I obtained a furlough from prison to be sworn in as a member of the New England Mafia—a swearing-in ceremony that was recorded by the Federal Bureau of Investigation. I would then receive a parole. Would I not be a threat to public safety as a sworn member of a crime family?

5. The facts relied upon during the course of my September 15, 2009 parole eligibility hearing and the subsequent September 29, 2009 Decision are not the true facts of my case at all. Rather, they are a summation of assumptions derived from the police version of the crime. Although available at the time of the parole eligibility hearing, I believe that the panel members did not read the Bill of Particulars nor the trial transcripts when they unanimously stated during my hearing that they read "everything" surrounding my case and determined that I assaulted Kathleen McGrath. Proof in support of my belief is found in the statement made by a panel member: that Kathleen McGrath identified me by a ring that I wore on the night of the crime and upon arrest.

I never wore a ring on the night of the crime, nor was I arrested with one. A ring was never introduced within either my trial as evidence nor within my codefendant Robert Preston's trial. Ms. McGrath testified during my trial that she identified me from a suspect photo array.[2] The statement regarding a ring only appears within the police version of the crime, and never proven as fact within any court of law.

Another example of how I have come to believe that the Board did not read "everything" in my case to draw their conclusion rests within the confirmation, made by the Essex County Assistant District Attorney (citing from transcript testimony), that the sexual assault occurred within the automobile, when I

---

2. Trial transcript testimony submitted to the Parole Board on my behalf in 1999, by my attorney Daniel S. Tarlow.

was purported to have said "not yet" when I was asked by one of my codefendants if I had "fucked her yet." I was never in the automobile with Kathleen McGrath, nor did a conversation regarding having sex with her ever occur. Kathleen testified during both trials that her underwear was removed while she was on the back seat of the automobile.

The insertion of the stick inside of Kathleen McGrath's vagina was submitted in court through indictment as being an assault with intent to murder, and the only evidence submitted during my trial to truly substantiate any resolve by the Board that I shoved the stick into her vagina was forwarded to the court within the coerced testimony of Emanuel Smith, which turned out to be self-serving. Smith was offered a secret sentencing deal through his trial attorney when he became a witness for the Commonwealth,[3] unbeknownst to myself or the trial judge when Smith pled guilty to the charges against him.

He was released from prison on probation by Superior Court Justice Lindscott in 1984, as a result of an affidavit supporting his motion for a new trial. According to that affidavit,[4] Smith identified me as the codefendant who shoved the stick into Ms. McGrath after witnessing his cousin Robert Preston being beaten by the police, and a gun aimed toward himself, upon their arrest in New York where the two had fled after the commission of the crimes.

Smith was one of the "two negroes" who was mentioned by Ms. McGrath in the newly found January 9, 1969 Lawrence Police Department Report to have entered the automobile and attacked her and Raymond Gagnon.[5]

6. My codefendant Robert Preston was afforded a parole after having been on escape for seven years, and without having been

---

[3]. The Commonwealth's star witness Essex County, Emanuel Smith, is presently serving a 40 years sentence in Maryland for his role in a knife attack upon a white couple there, as codefendant to yet another one of his cousins—Turner Burnett. Apparently, Maryland District Attorneys do not play the same bartering games as Massachusetts. Essex County's deals are a threat to public safety.

[4]. The Affidavit of Emanuel Smith in support of his motion for a new trial was submitted within the memorandum submitted to the parole board by my attorney Daniel Tarlow in 1999.

[5]. Trial transcript, *Commonwealth V. Robert Preston*, testimony of Emanuel Smith, [page 70]. See Appendix D, page 165.

held to address the "causative factors" of his criminal behavior. He is the codefendant who admitted to being the individual who physically assaulted Ms. McGrath during his October 1969 jury trial,[6] supported by the testimony rendered by codefendant/State witness Emanuel Smith during my June 1969 jury waived trial.[7] Preston also admitted during his trial that he was the person who removed Kathleen McGrath from the automobile.[8]

Yet, I have been designated by the Parole Board to bear the burden of the entire criminal episode, based upon an accusatory and inaccurate police depiction of the crime; and thereby held to an impossible standard to undergo and complete the Department of Correction's "causative factor" addressing programs. Both of my codefendants never underwent the physical and psychological brutality that I endured as a result of my joint involvement in the crimes of November 23, 1968; yet both were released from prison over 15 years ago.

Smith admittedly removed Raymond Gagnon from the automobile after cutting him with a knife, and Preston admittedly beat Kathleen McGrath and removed her from the automobile. Three of us did not attack both victims, as I never touched Ms. McGrath; nor was I involved in the initial attack upon the automobile.[9]

7. The September 29, 2009 Decision states that I did not have a job. I am assuming that meant a prison job, because several letters were submitted to the Board regarding employment if granted a parole. If the Board is referring to one of the menial

---

6 *Commonwealth V. Robert Preston*, trial transcript, testimony of Robert Preston, [page 250]. See Appendix D, page 166.
7 *Commonwealth V. Robert Preston*, trial transcript, testimony Emanuel Smith, [page 38]. See Appendix D, page 164.
8 *Commonwealth V. Robert Preston*, trial transcript:
[page 257], testimony of Robert Preston; See Appendix D, page 167 & 168.
[Page 103], testimony of Emanuel Smith; See Appendix D, page 167.
[Page 137], Testimony of Raymond Gagnon. See Appendix D, page 163.
9 *Commonwealth V Ralph Hamm*, trial transcript:
[page 136] testimony of Raymond Gagnon. See Appendix D, page 163.
Commonwealth V Robert Preston, trial transcript:
[Page 72], [page 74] & [page 75], testimony of Emanuel Smith. See Appendix D, page 163 & 164.

limited jobs offered by the Department of Correction to its wards, then I was working for three years with the Recreation Department at the Treatment Center as the only prisoner facilitating their newspaper program. I did not work for "good time" credits because my sentence has been restructured to such a state where "good time" credits have no effect upon it, and I did not work for the $1.00 per week pay; rather, I deferred those gratuities to be applied to create another work assignment in the recreational department for a prisoner that was in need of the credits or the money. If asked, any DOC employee on the recreational staff would have verified my employment.

Conclusion

Based upon all of the aforementioned, and the possibility that I have been designated to die in prison for non-capital first offenses as is the Board's stated desire, I refuse to go silently to my grave and therefore appeal.[10]

Submitted by,

Ralph C. Hamm III
W32301

---

10. Hamm III, Ralph C., *Blackberry Juice*, Little Red Tree Publishing, 2015.

APPENDIX D

Transcript Testimonial Statement of the Case

Commonwealth v. Ralph C. Hamm III

The following is extracted from both the trial transcripts of *Commonwealth v. Ralph Hamm* and my codefendant *Commonwealth v. Robert Preston*, as well as the description of the assault afforded by Kathleen McGrath in the newly found January 9, 1969 Lawrence Police Department Report. The Commonwealth made sure that there were no Grand Jury minutes or testimony afforded the defense in 1969, nor ever upon post-conviction appeals.

In the January 9, 1969 Lawrence Police Department Report, Kathleen McGrath is recorded as having said:

> "I saw two negroes come into the car [. . .] Ray and started beating him. At this point one of the negroes [dragged me out] of the car. He started punching me in the face. [. . .] he was straddling me and punching me in the face with both [hands]. I noticed a big ring on one of his hands. This lasted for [. . .] minutes. Then he picked me up and put me in the back seat. [He took] off my underclothes and tried to assault me and I screamed [stop]. This seemed to enrage him and he started to punch me in the face again. The next thing I knew I was on the ground on the driver's side on my back and he was straddling

me across my middle with his hands around my throat, strangling me. I heard someone say we have [to wipe the] fingerprints off the car. I asked my assailant to kill me. He said I am. I started praying. I then played dead. My eyes were closed. I felt a tearing between [my legs]. I heard one of them say don't worry about the other guy, he's [dead]. At this point they left."

I will not dwell too much upon what was testified to during my trial, in my trial transcripts, but will mostly refer to my codefendant Robert Preston's trial transcripts. As he was tried four months after me, therein resides testimonial evidence unheard during my June 27, 1969 trial, nor during my November 12, 1980 motion for a new trial evidentiary hearing. Preston was on escape from a MCI-Norfolk furlough during the filing of my motion for a new trial and the ensuing evidentiary hearing, and I did not have the opportunity of reviewing a copy of his trial transcripts until years later when he was captured in California and returned to MCI-Walpole where I was then housed.

Commonwealth v. Robert Preston; Testimony of male victim Raymond Gagnon:

[Page 134] Q *Then what happened?*
A *The driver's side door opened.*
Q *Your side?*
[Page 135] A *Yes. And a Negro fellow came in with a knife raised.*
Q *A knife raised?*
A *Yes.*
Q *Sir, do you know who that, you say Negro fellow, was, that person who came into your car originally with a knife in his hand?*
A *Yes, I do.*
Q *Is he in this courtroom at the present time?*
A *Yes, he is.*
Q *Where is he?*
A *Sitting right there [pointing].*

	Q	*Are you referring to the defendant?*
	A	Yes.
	Q	*Mr. Preston?*
	A	Yes.
[Page 136]	Q	*Did you see somebody else?*
	A	Yes, there were two other fellows standing outside the driver's side door.
	Q	*How far away were they?*
	A	There was one right near the door and one in the background.
[Page 137]	Q	*Who was outside of the car?*
	A	Mr. Hamm and a Mr. Smith.
	Q	*Prior to being hit in the back of the head outside of the car, could you hear Kathleen saying or doing anything?*
	A	Yes, she was screaming.

Commonwealth v. Robert Preston; Testimony of Emanuel Smith:

[Page 72]	Q	*He was knocked out?*
	A	Yeah.
	Q	*Who had done that? Mr. Preston, or you, or Mr. Hamm, or a couple of you?*
	A	Just me and Hamm.
	Q	*Just you and Hamm?*
	A	Yes.
	Q	*Where was Preston when you were knocking out Gagnon?*
	A	He was still over by the car.
[Page 74]	Q	*Was he in the car?*
	A	Well, when I, when we started to turn back, you know, from fighting Gagnon, he was coming out of the car.
	Q	*So when you turned back from the Gagnon escapade, if I can use that word, you saw Preston getting out of the car. Is that a fair state? Is that what you just said?*
	A	Yes.

	Q	*You knew there was a girl in the car; didn't you, sir?*
	A	Yes, I saw a glimpse of her, yes.
[Page 75]	Q	*When you got back, did you look in the car?*
	A	Yeah.
	Q	*Where did you see the girl, if you saw the girl?*
	A	She was in the back seat.
	Q	*She was in the back seat?*
	A	Yeah.

Commonwealth v. Ralph Hamm; Testimony of Emanuel Smith (Smith begins to suffer from memory loss or ignorance during Preston's trial, when testifying against his cousin, so I must refer to *Commonwealth v. Ralph Hamm*, regarding the beating of Kathleen McGrath.)

[Page 38]	Q	*Where was—by the way, did you hear—*
	A	Excuse me—anyways, the girl, you know, like, she started to scream something.
	Q	*The girl screamed?*
	A	And so Preston was still, you know, by the car, and so he had, you know, hit her, knocked her down.
	Q	*Preston hit her?*
	A	Yes.
	Q	*How did, he hit her?*
	A	Hit her with his fist, with his hand.

✶ ✶ ✶ ✶ ✶

[Page 136]	Q	*Where was Mr. Hamm?*
	A	He was standing off by the tree.
	Q	*By the tree. He wasn't by the car door?*
	A	No, sir.
	Q	*Then what happened?*
	A	Anyways, after when I cut him, you know, I pulled him out of the car, you know—
	Q	*You pulled who?*
	A	The man out of the car. And so when he hit the ground, he jumped up, and that's when he started to running.

Q Who started to run?
A The man. So then he ran to Ralph, and he went to grab him like that, around the throat, and Ralph hit him.
Q Ralph hit him?
A Yes.

Commonwealth v. Robert Preston; Testimony of Emanuel Smith.

[Page 70] Q What happened after Preston went in the car?
A I told you, then there was a scuffle. Him and the man.
Q *Could you describe the scuffle in more detail?*
A There was, he opened the door and the man says, he said, I think it was hello or come in or something like that. Anyway, so when Preston—
Q *Speak loud for the jury to hear you.*
A When Preston went to step in the car, the man hit him, right, and so Preston whirled, you know; whirled around like that, I came running in the car and I grabbed the man.
Q *You had a knife in your hand, didn't you, sir?*
A Yes.

[Page 71] Q *Didn't you knife the man?*
A Yes, I did.
Q *And that is the man you later found out is Mr. Gagnon?*
A Yes.
Q *And, sir, you knifed him in the face; is that right, the nose?*
A Yes.
Q *And, sir, while you were knifing the man, did something happen in relation to the man and Mr. Hamm? Did you see Mr. Hamm do something to him?*
A That's when I pulled him out of the car. I yanked him out of the car.
Q *That's when you pulled Mr. Gagnon out of the car?*
A Yes.

Q Then Mr. Hamm did something to him?
A He got up and when he got to his feet, he had hit Hamm.

Commonwealth v. Robert Preston; Testimony of Robert Preston:

[Pages 247-248]
Q *Now what happened after that? Step by step, Robert, and go slowly and speak loudly so the jury and I and all can hear you.*
A I went in, he pulled me in, and he started hitting me, and then Emanuel came up behind me and -
THE COURT: *Who came up behind you?*
THE WITNESS: Smith, and he came in and he had his knife raised.

[Page 250] Q *Did this young lady do something with reference to you?*
A She was hollering and hitting me.
Q *Did you know at that time that it was a young lady that was hitting you?*
A No, I didn't,
Q *All right. What did you do in response to that?*
A I turned and hit back.

Commonwealth v. Robert Preston; Testimony of Emanuel Smith:

[Page 104] Q *And do you remember Mr. Brady saying: Then you went over to the car?*
[Page 105] A Yes.
Q *And you said yes? And then Mr. Brady said: Who was at the car? And you said: That's when Preston put her in the back seat because I was getting in the car to start it. Do you remember that? Mr. Brady said to you: Who was at the car? And your answer was: That's when Preston put her in the back seat because I was getting in the car to start it. Do you remember that?*

	A	I—
	Q	*Do you agree that this was your testimony back in June?*
	A	Yes.
[Page 103]	Q	*And did someone try to take Miss McGrath out of the car?*
	A	Well, Preston took her out. He was on the other side of me, you know.
	Q	*Where was she at this time?*
	A	She was in the back seat.
	Q	*In the back seat?*
	A	Yes.
	Q	*Now at some time did Ralph Hamm get in the back seat with Miss McGrath?*
	A	No.
	Q	*Now you are saying that Ralph Hamm did not get into the back seat with her?*
	A	No.
[Page 104]	Q	*Was never in the back seat with her?*
	A	Not to my knowledge.

Commonwealth v. Robert Preston; Testimony of Robert Preston:

[Page 257]	Q	*Who took the girl out of the car?*
	A	I did.
	Q	*You did?*
	A	Yes.
	Q	*And what manner did you take her, by the arms?*
	A	Under the armpits.
	Q	*Where was Smith and Hamm at this time while you were taking Miss McGrath out?*
	A	Hamm came around to the driver's side of the car.
	Q	*All right.*
	A	And Emanuel was standing there holding the back seat, and Ralph was standing next to him.
	Q	*Did you take Miss McGrath out and put her somewhere?*
	A	Yes.
	Q	*In what condition was she at the time with reference*

    to consciousness or unconsciousness?
   A She was still unconscious.
   Q *All right. You took her out?*
   A Yes.
[Page 266] Q *What were you doing at that time?*
   A We watched Emanuel while he wiped the car down and we started walking.
   Q *And you and Hamm started walking?*
   A Yes.
   Q *At some time later on, did Mr. Smith catch up with you?*
   A Yes.

Dated: [March 6, 2008]
Signed: [Ralph C. Hamm III]

APPENDIX E

The "Cooperating Witness"

During the course of liberating my consciousness over the past 46+ years of enslavement to the State of "Mississippi," I posed many questions to the relatives of Emanuel E. Smith. I came to learn that he was one of the children who gathered at the Sixteenth Street Baptist Church on May 2, 1963 for a march through the city of Birmingham, Alabama. He, along with scores of other black children were firehosed and had attack dogs set upon them by Sheriff Bull Connor and his men . . . then herded upon school buses, and arrested. Dr. Martin Luther King, Jr. had just recently been released from the Birmingham Jail, for his participation in an antisegregation protest earlier that year.

I question the significance of the May 2nd March, the September 15, 1963 bombing of the Sixteenth Street Baptist Church,[1] and Emanuel's leadership role in the November 22, 1968 attack upon a white couple in the Grove section of Lawrence, Massachusetts.

Emanuel E. Smith is the only individual who can speak on the psychological and emotional trauma that he has endured since the age of fifteen, via his role in the struggle for human rights in 1960s Birmingham.

It would be naive for me to believe that the traumatic events that Emanuel was forced to endure as a child did not impact upon the violence that he set into motion in Massachusetts in the early morning hours of November 22, 1968 as a young

---

1. Addie Mae Collins, Denise McNair, Carole Robertson, and Cynthia Wesley were murdered by white supremacists when the church was firebombed.

adult. The psychological and emotional scarring allowed him to be susceptible to coercion by the police in New York City on November 26, 1968, (see below) as well as to blame me as the principle assailant of Kathleen, thereby, inducing him to become the "coooperating witness" for the Commonwealth during my June 1969 trial.

The "Mississippi" criminal just-us apparatus promotes the standard practice of making deals with the devil to barter the souls of the innocent, as the means of forwarding the careers of the minion of the "beast."

COMMONWEALTH OF MASSACHUSETTS

Superior Court
Criminal Nos. 63055,
63056, 63057, 63058,
63062

COMMONWEALTH OF MASSACHUSETTS

V.

EMANUEL E. SMITH

AFFIDAVIT IN SUPPORT OF DEFENDANT'S MOTION FOR A NEW TRIAL

I, Emanuel E. Smith, on oath depose and state:

1. I am 34 years old, having been born on January 13, 1948, in Lowell, Massachusetts. At the present time, I am housed at M.C.I. Norfolk.

2. My childhood was spent in Massachusetts. I was the eight of nine children. My parents died, and I moved to Birmingham, Alabama to be with an aunt, and I graduated from an all black high school there.

In 1968, after my schooling, I returned to the Boston area to live with other members of my family.

3. As a youth, I had no involvement with the criminal justice system except for a 1964 juvenile matter for breaking and entering. The matter was suspended and eventually dismissed. I had no court supervision at this time. My arrest for these cases was my first offense.

4. On or about November 16, 1968, I was arrested for various offenses which occurred on or about November 23, 1968, in Lawrence, Massachusetts.

5. On june 25, 1969, at the age of 21, I pleaded guilty to Indictment 63055 (Armed Robbery), 63056 (Armed Robbery), 63057 (Mayhem), 63058 (Malicious Injury to Personal Property), 63057 (Mayhem), 63058 (Malicious Injury to Personal Property), and 63062 (Assault and Battery by Means of a Dangerous Weapon). On July 1, 1969, I was sentenced to concurrent terms of 30-40 years at M.C.I. Walpole on the armed robbery charges with lesser concurrent terms on the others. I have been incarcerated since the date of my arrest.

6. I was initially arrested in New York City on November 26. I was taken by many police officers from Lawrence, Massachusetts and New York to the home of a friend of my co-defendant, Robert Preston. I saw Preston being hit. I was handcuffed and taken into a bathroom. I was threatened that I could be shot if I did not make a statement concerning the November incident. Finally, in complete terror, I told the officer what he wanted to know—that Ralph Hamm had assaulted the female victim.

7. Preston and I were taken to a New York police station. we were locked up and moved to court and locked up again. I have no memory of a line-up taking place, but, I guess, it could have. I have read the Hamm and Preston transcripts to this effect.

8. I was returned to Lawrence, Massachusetts and was placed in a 24-hour lockup.

9. I remember being brought to Court and being sent to Bridgewater for observation in February, 1969. I was in general population at Bridgewater and was frightened. I do not remember seeing any doctors or receiving any treatment or evaluation until the day before I returned to court. The doctor asked if I wanted to leave and return to the Lawrence House of Correction. Bridgewater was so hideous at the time that, of course, I said "yes."

10. In Lawrence, I had the same lawyer as Preston, a Mr. Lewis. He eventually told me that he could not represent both of us. Then, Mr. Dever was assigned to represent me.

11. I received only three jail visits from Mr. Dever. I do not believe that he did any significant preparation or investigation. At least, he did not make me aware of any.

12. I do not believe that Mr. Dever ever filed any important motions in my case, especially Motions to Suppress identification and statements. (After many years of being incarcerated and having learned about the law, I now understand that these Motions were crucial in a case like mine.)

13. Mr. Dever was always talking to me about the possible death of the victims. He made me think that I would be charged with murder. He made me believe that if I went to trail, that worse charges could be brought. Even on the day of my change of plea, I still had no idea what condition the victims were in. I never saw the victims at court before I entered my plea.

14. Mr. Dever always told me that I had no choice but to plead guilty. He told me that I did not have any defense and therefore, I had no choice. He told me that my statement to the police in New York ended any chances I might have had.

15. Mr Dever told me that the penalty for some of the offenses was life imprisonment. He said that if I pleaded guilty I would not get a life sentence. I thought life imprisonment meant natural life, no parole. He never explained anything about the parole system to me. He told me that he would ask the court for 10-20 years if I pleaded guilty. He said I would never have to serve more than ten years upon a plea, even if the District Attorney were to recommend 30-40 years, which he did.

16. Now I understand that when the Commonwealth recommended 30-40 years that the parole eligibility is 20 years, or 5 years longer than the eligibility of a life sentence. Mr Dever never said one world about these things.

17. At the time of my pleas, I knew nothing about the court system, let alone how to properly prepare a defense. I knew nothing about sentencing. I was terrified and confused; Mr. Dever did not do anything to lessen these feelings. He kept telling me about life sentences and worse charges. In fear and confusion, I pleaded guilty. I surely never understood the nature and consequences of my pleas. My lawyer told me what to say "to satisfy the court" and assure the court that I was "aware of the proceedings" and "knew what I was doing." I responded to the inquiries of the Court because I was told to; I had no real understanding. Out of ignorance, I believed that my attorney was acting in my best interests. I went along with his instructions without knowing or understanding what was taking place.

18. I believe that my plea was not voluntary and that I was denied effective assistance of counsel.

Signed under the pains and penalties of perjury this 23rd day of August, 1982.

Emanuel E. Smith.

APPENDIX F

"Mississippi"

I provide this Appendix as a concise and understandable reason why I call Massachusetts "Mississippi," aside from my obvious experience of being legally lynched by the southern-style just-us meted out in the state judiciary (aptly outlined throughout the pages of this book), and the word "Mississippi" simply being a euphemism derived from combining Massachusetts with Mississippi.

Up South.

The puritan colony of Massachusetts was the greatest slave trading community in America during the 17th and 18th centuries. Astronomical fortunes arose within this slave-driven economy (much like today, with the expansion of the prison-industrial complex), allowing John Hancock to become one of Boston's prominent slave traders. The tall ships docked in Massachusetts ports to unload their unholy human cargo, for delivery to southern plantation states for sale.

Down South.

The abolition of slavery in 1865 ushered in the passage of the Thirteenth, Fourteenth, and Fifteenth Amendments to the United states Constitution; which afforded civil rights to the newly emancipated slaves. Abolition of slavery did not come without a price: white backlash. In 1875, Mississippians convened a Constitutional Convention, and therein drafted the

"Mississippi Plan": an effort to disenfranchise blacks from their recently acquired rights, and to regain the supremacy thought lost during the era of Reconstruction. The "Mississippi Plan" gave rise to the enactment of "Jim Crow Laws," which extended to Massachusetts until the passage of the Voting Rights Act of 1970.

I first heard the term "Mississippi" spoken by a prisoner named James (Jimmy) Pina during the tumultuous 1970s, when we were both interred within Walpole State Prison in South Walpole, Massachusetts. The term conjured up images in my mind of cross burnings, white mob violence and police brutality toward blacks, and legal lynching; comparative to what I had heretofore learned about Mississippi from textbooks and television news during the 1960s civil/human rights era in America. I took from this imagery and information a connection to my lived experience in Massachusetts during my brief lifespan.

A few comparative historical examples

Example 1.

- In Mississippi, whites unconscionably utilized violence, election fraud, and intimidation to undermine the 14th and 15th Amendment civil rights gains by blacks, with the enactment of "Jim Crow Laws" supported by the exception to slavery held within the language of the 13th Amendment.

Compared to:

- In Massachusetts, jailers were deemed "Masters" by General Law, and "Jim Crow Laws" were utilized by way of literacy tests to hinder blacks in casting their vote. This practice ended only with the passage of the Voting Rights Act of 1970, extending the coverage laws to include Massachusetts.

Example 2.

- On July 11, 1954 the White Citizens' Council [after 1956 known as Citizens' Council of America] was formed espousing white supremacy through economic coercion, in Indianola, Mississippi.

Compared to:

- In Cambridge, Massachusetts the Knights of the Ku Klux Klan and their counterpart the Knights of the White Camelia established themselves in 1921; while in the 1960s Andover, Massachusetts saw the rise of the John Birch Society.

Example 3.

- Emmitt Till was murdered by whites for allegedly speaking to a white woman in Money, Mississippi.

Compared to:

- William Atkins was murdered by a gang of white males in 1982 at the Savin Hill subway station in Dorchester, Massachusetts, allegedly for a similar offense, or simply for being black.

Example 4.

- On April 24, 1960, 125 blacks staged a wade-in on a public beach in Biloxi, Mississippi. A mob of whites attacked them with baseball bats, chains, pipes, clubs, and pool sticks.

Compared to:

- 1975 in Massachusetts, where several black Bible salesmen were attacked by a mob of whites with bottles, bricks, and sticks, while sunning themselves on Carson Beach (now Castle Island) in South Boston.

Example 5.

- In 1961 Freedom Riders were arrested in Jackson, Mississippi for "inflaming the public" by their mere presence.

Compared to:

- Thanksgiving Day 1997, in Plymouth, Massachusetts. The Day of Mourning. United American Indians of New England inflame the public by marching through the center of town during the Thanksgiving celebration. Over 50 police officers block their path and tear gas them.

Example 6.

- In 1875 Mississippi, with the advent of "Jim Crow Laws," came the concept of convict leasing via an interpretation of the exception to slavery language held within the Thirteenth Amendment, and former slaves once held in personal ownership became the property of the State—due to their incarceration. The black men, duly convicted in "kangaroo courts," found themselves legally held in bondage worse than chattel slavery.

Compared to:

- In 2016 Massachusetts, the exception to slavery held within the Thirteenth Amendment allows the state institution of penal slavery to hold black juveniles in bondage (often imprisoning them for their natural lives), even for non-homicide offenses; and thereby undermine the Eighth and Fourteenth Amendments to the United States Constitution.

Selected Bibliography

Bissonette, J. *When the Prisoners Ran Walpole: A True Story in the Movement for Prison Abolition.* Cambridge, MA: South End Press, 2008.

Cambell, S. W. *The Slave Catchers.* Chapel Hill: University of North Carolina, 1973.

Cullop, F. G. *The Constitution of the United States: An Introduction.* New York: New American Library, Penguin Group, 1999.

Daniels, J. *In Freedom's Birthplace: A Study of the Boston Negroes.* New York: Arno Press, 1969.

Davis, A. Y. *Abolition Democracy: Beyond Empire, Prisons, and Torture.* New York: Seven Stories Press, 2005.

Denzinger, S. R. (ed.). *The Real War on Crime: The Report of the National Criminal Justice Commission.* New York: Harper Perennial, 1996.

Dertz, J. *The Times of Their Lives: Life, Love, and Death in Plymouth Colony.* New York: WHF, 2000.

Douglass, F. *Douglass Autobiographies.* New York: Library of America, 1994.

Fanon, F. *Black Skin, White Masks.* New York: Grove Press, 2008.

Fehrenbacher, D. E. *Slavery, Law, and Politics: The Dred Scott Case in Historical Perspective*. New York: Oxford University Press, 1981.

Fierce, M. *Slavery Revisited: Blacks and the Southern Convict Lease System, 1865-1933*. New York: Brooklyn College, CUNY, African Studies Research Center, 1994.

Foner, P. *The Life and Writings of Frederick Douglass*. New York: International Publishers, 1955.

Foucault, M. *Discipline and Punish: The Birth of the Prison*. New York: Vintage, 1979.

Freire, P. *Pedagogy of the Oppressed*, 1970 reprint. New York: Continuum International Publishing Group, Inc., 2007.

Giovanni, N. *The Collected Poetry of Nikki Giovanni 1968-1998*. New York: Harper Perennial, 2007.

Glick, B. *The War at Home: Covert Action against U. S. Activist and What We Can Do About It*. Boston: South End Press, 1989.

Glick, W (ed.). *The Reform Papers*. Princeton, NJ: Princeton University Press, 1973.

Hegel, GWF. *The Phenomenology of Mind*, J. B. Baillie, trans. 2nd ed. revised. London: Allen and Unwin, 1949.

Jones, L. and Neal, L. (eds.). *Black Fire, An Anthology of Afro-American Writing*. New York: William Morrow & Company, Inc., 1968.

Loury, G. C. *Race, Incarceration, and American Values* Cambridge, MA: The MIT Press, 2008.

Miller, J. G. *Hobbling a Generation: Young African American Males in the Criminal Justice System of American Cities*.

Baltimore: National Center on Institutions and Alternatives, 1992.

Quarles, B. *Black Abolitionists*. New York: Oxford University Press, 1969.

Ryan, D. P. *Beyond the Ballot Box: A Social History of the Boston Irish, 1845-1917*. East Brunswick, NJ: Associated University Presses, 1983.

Slaughter, T. P. *Bloody Dawn: The Christiana Riot and Racial Violence in the Antebellum North*. New York: Oxford University Press, 1991.

Strangis, J. *Lewis Hayden and the War Against Slavery*. New Haven, Connecticut: Linnet Books, 1999.

Thurston, L. (ed.), *A Call to Action: An Analysis and Overview of the United States Criminal Justice System*. Chicago: Third World Press, 1993.

Williams, Chancellor. *The Destruction of Black Civilization: Great Issues of a Race from 4500 BC to AD 2000*. Chicago: Third World Press, 2000.

Index

A

Aaron, Lucious, xv.
ABE (Adult Basic Education), x, 22, 57-59, 67, 68.
Abolitionism, 25, 26.
Abolitionists, xviii, 11-13, 15, 19, 21-22, 24-25, 28, 38, 75, 85.
Abolition of Slavery, The, 11, 24, 27, 187.
Abu Ghraib, 90, 120.
Adams, President John, 3.
Adult Correctional Institution, 7.
Alexander, "Miami Lou," xv.
Aldridge, Robert, 101-102, 109.
Ambers, Harry, xiv.
Amerik.k.k.a, iii, 84-87, 91-92, 98, 123, 129, 143, 145-146.
"AMERIKlan JUST-US" (Hamm), iii, xx, 49, 72, 84, 95, 120.
Anarchy. *See chaos theory*
Anti-abolitionism, 25-26.
Anti-abolitionist, 27, 29, 30.
Aptheker, Herbert, 30, 75.
Arujo, Frank, 22, 65.
Ashanti, Dr. Kwaben Faheen, vii.
Atkins, William, 38, 189.
AVIP (American Veterans In Prison), 21, 22.

B

Bakunin, Mikhail, 68, 72.
Baldwin, James, 61.
Banion, Doug, xv.
BANTU (Black African Nations Toward Unity), iii, xvii, xviii, xx, 15-18, 21, 22, 25-30, 34-36, 45, 49, 57,-62, 64-68, 77-81, 88, 89, 98-100, 120-122, 126-127, 131.
Baptiste, Richard, xv.
Barnicle, Mike, 39.
Beacon Hill. 17.
Bell Curve, 41.
Bennett, William, 8, 39, 40.
"Big Brother" Program, 80.
Bissonette, Jamie, xiv, 196.
Black Codes. (See Slave Codes), 4, 85.
Black Consciousness, xvii, xx.
   Movement, iii, 43, 83.
Black Panther Party, xxiii, 46, 47, 66(n), 79(n), 84, 86, 128.
Black Skin, White Masks (See Fanon)
Blake, Albert, xv, 66.
Boone, John O., xxi-xxiii, 24, 26.
Bond, Stanely, xiv.
Bonds, Robert, xv.
Boston Globe, 24-25(n), 39.
Boston Herald, The, 23-24, 36, 39.
Boston Pilot, The, 23, 24.
Boston Transcript, The, 23.
Boston University, 36.
Boyd, Bradford, xv.
Bradford, Governor William, 2.
Bradford, William "Broadway," xv.
Brewer, Lamont "Legs," xv.
Bridgewater Departmental Segregation Unit, xxi, 183.
Bridgewater State Hospital, 49,

146(n5), 157
Brighton, Ms. Pamela, 22.
Brown, Dee, 41.
Brown, Efrid. (See Zulu, Dini).
Brown, John, 98.
Brown, Solomon, xvii, 57.
Brown, Thomas, xv.
Bush, George, 8(n), 91.
Burnett, Lawrence "Buddy," xv.
Burns, Bo, xv.
Butler, Benny, xiv.

C

Cambell, Alvin, xiv.
CARCAP (Citizens And Relatives Concerned About Prisons), 47.
Carter, Vernon, 35.
Casseso, Ronald, xiv.
CCA (Corrections Corporation of America), 90.
Chaos theory, 68.
Christiana, in Pennsylvania, 19-21.
CIA (Central Intelligence Agency), 86.
CIS (US Citizenship and Immigration Service), 93.
Civil Rights Act of 1866, 74-75.
Civil Rights Act of 1875, 75.
Civil War, 4-5, 41, 45, 85, 104 (n4), 145 (n4),
Clinkscales, John, 22.
"C-Note," xv.
Cochise, John, xv.
"Coding Rules for the Static-99," 114-117, 120, 158, 159.
COINTELPRO, 66(n9), 77(n12), 79, 86, 147.
Colemand, Frank, xv.
Coleman, Ronnie, xv.
Columbian Sentinel, 23.
Commonwealth v. Ralph C. Hamm, 15(n4), 73(n6), 143(n8), 171(n9), 173, 176.
Connor, James "The Whale," xiv.
Convention of Colored Men, 7.

convict-lease system, 4-6.
CORI (Criminal Offender Record Information), 92, 113-114.
Corrections Communications Corporation, 92.
Corriea, Joseph, xiv.
Courier, The, 23.
CRA (Corrections Recovery Academy), 110-111, 120, 168(n1), 169.
Cribbs, Henry, xvii, xxiii, 69.
Curry College, viii.

D

Dance, David, xviii, xxiii, 11, 56, 69.
Davis, Angela Y., 8(n16), 86, 127(n6), 119, 120, 129.
Declaration of Human Rights, 75.
Declaration of Independence, 74.
Deer Island House of Correction, 37.
Dellelo, Robert, xxi, 22, 26, 29, 66, 75, 122.
De Mau Mau, 79(n14), 98.
De Salvo, Albert, xiv.
Department of Education, 57.
Department of Human Services, 97.
Department of Public Safety, 97.
Department of Youth Services, 80.
Desire, (Ship) 2.
Devlin, Richard, xiv, 66.
Diaz, Eddie, xv.
Dirring, Tiny, xv, 78.
Discipline and Punish: The Birth of the Prison (Foucault), 117.
DLM (Department of Legal Medicine), 22.
DOC (Department of Correction), 22, 67, 80-81, 85, 88-89, 109-113, 115-116, 121, 157, 172.
Douglass, Frederick, 7, 9, 11-12, 15, 20, 21.
Dred Scott v. John Sandford, 69-75, 81, 85, 125.

Duarte, Richard, xv.
Dukakis, Michael, 8, 22.

E

Education, xix.
    banking concept of, 57.
    BANTU-developed template, 58.
Eighth Amendment, 190.
Eisenstadt, Thomas, 35.
Ellison, Ralph
    Invisible Man, 62, 72.
Emancipation Proclamation, 5.
Emerson, Ralph Waldo, 11.
Enos, Peter, xv.
Essex County Training School, 34, 53, 55, 131, 133-135.
Eviction, one-strike policy, 93.

F

"Family Awareness" Program, 80.
Fanon, Frantz, xiii, 14, 25(n23), 30(n29), 47, 49, 50(n10 & 11), 54, 55(n3 & 4), 105(n6), 116(n20), 125.
FBI (Federal Bureau of Investigation), 66(n9), 86, 147-149, 169.
Federated Eastern Indian League, 36.
Fehrenbacher, Don, 70, 73.
Field Order, 5.
Fifteenth Amendment, 5, 75, 187.
Fillmore, Millard, 17.
Flemmi, Vincent "The Bear," xv.
Flynn, Raymond, [Major], 40.
Fourteenth Amendment, 6, 73-75, 187, 190.
Franklin, Benjamin, 13.
Freedom Riders, 190.
Free trade, 94.
Freire, Paolo, viii, 21, 56-58, 62, 122, 145.
Fugitive Slave Law, 12, 17, 19, 21.
Funderberg, Jerry, xiv.
Funderberg, Luman, xv.

G

Gagliardi, Carmen, xiv.
Gagne, Arthur, xv.
Gallo, James, xiv.
Garrison, William Lloyd, 11, 25.
Garrity, Walter A., 37.
Gauthier, Arthur, xv.
Gawel-Cambridge, Richard, viii, xi.
Geneva Convention, 72, 120.
Gens, Joshua, xv.
Germanotta, Dante, viii, 67.
Giovanni, Nikki, 32(n31), 67(n11), 82.
Gleason, Joe, xiv.
Gonsalez, Robert "Gonk," xv.
Goon squad, xxi, 47-48, 167.
Gorsuch, Edward, 19-20
Grace, Frank "Parky," xiv, 66.
Gray, John, xiv.
Greco, Leo, xv.
Great Depression, 46.
Guppy, Richard, xiv.

H

Haley, James, 22.
Hall, James, xvii.
Ham (Noah's son), 13.
Hamilton, Floyd, 22, 60
Hamm, Margaret Elizabeth, 5, 49, 53.
Hamm, Ralph C., III
    Ralph, vi, vii, 14-15, 83, 139, 143, 153-163, 165-180, 183, 196.
    "AMERIKlan JUST-US," xx.
    birth of, 53.
    encounters with parole board, 97-102.
    first baseball experience, 33.
    miseducation of, 53-57.
    Poetry, xx, 119, 130.
    polling prisoner population in Walpole, 77-79.
    receiving life sentence, 49.

Hamm, Ralph Conrad, Jr., 33-34, 53.
Hanson, Karl, 114.
Harris, Jack, xvii, 57.
Harvard University, xviii, 41-42.
Hawkins, Charles, xv.
Hayden, Harriet, 11.
Hayden, Lewis, 11-12, 15-18, 21.
Hayes, Bob, 21.
Haynes, Michael, Reverand, 99-100.
Heard, Robert "Big Bob," xiv, xxiii, 24, 47.
Hearst, William "Whitey," xiv.
Heinsohn, Tom, 37.
Henson, Josiah, 13.
Hermstein, Richard, 41.
Hicks, Louise Day, 37.
Higgins, Mike, 34.
Hitler, Adolf, 35, 146(n6).
Holley, Charles, xv.
Hooks, Perry, xv.
Hoover, J. Edgar, 77, 79, 147-149.
Houston, Sam, 71.
Hughes, Langston, 35.
Hunt, Herman, xiv.
Hunt, Sam, xiv.

I

ICE, (U.S. Immigration and Customs Enforcement, 93-94.
Incarceration, 59, 77(n12), 85, 86, 89, 91, 92, 95, 103, 119, 129, 162, 166, 167.
INS, (U.S. Immigration and Naturalization Service), 93.
Inside/Out Incorporated, 22, 110, 121-123.
International Monetary Fund, 90, 94.
Invisible Man (Ellison), 62, 72.
IPO (Institutional Parole Officer, 109.
IPS (Inner Perimeter Security), 127.
IRA, 95. 126.

J

Jackson, Arnold "Butch," xv.
Jackson, Jesse, 48.
Jackson, Maynard, 48.
James, Frank, 36.
Jamestown, 2.
Jefferson, Thomas, 74.
Jenkins, Steve "John Doe," xiv.
Jim Crow Laws, xx, 188, 190.
John Birch Society, 189.
Johnson, President Andrew, 5-6.
Johnson, Curtis, xiv, 64-65.
Johnson, Elmo, xv.
Johnson, Hugh, 21.
Johnson, Vera, viii.
Johnson, William, 21, 168.
Jones, Herbert "Beaver," xiv.
Jones, K.C., 37.
Josepatis, Joseph "J.J.", xv.

K

Kangaroo Courts, 190.
Kelly, James, 37.
Kerrigan, John, xiv, 122.
King, Al, xv.
King Alfred Plan, vii.
King, Martin Luther, Jr., 35, 46, 71, 86, 145, 147, 149, 151, 181.
King, Paul, xv.
Knights of the Golden Circle, 41.
Knights of the Ku Klux Klan, 5, 6, 42(n2), 34, 37, 38, 41-43, 100, 125, 176, 168, 189.
Knights of the White Camelia, 6(n10), 189.
Kozol, Jonathan, 35.
Kwanzaa, 99-100.

L

Ladetto, Louis, 22.
Landsmark, Theodore, 38.
Last Poets, The, iii, xiv, 87.
LEAA (Law Enforcement Assistance

Admin.), 22, 67(n10), 121.
Lebeau, Raymond, xv.
Lecain, Dean, xv.
Lee, Bob, 21.
Lee, Joseph, 35.
Liberator, The, 11, 16(n16).
Lincoln, Abraham, President, 42.
Little, Al, xv.
Long, Lebeau, xv, 64-65.
Longville, Norman, xv.
love, (Key to manumission), 130.
Lynching, 4, 14, 43, 49, 80.
    legally lynched, 5, 136, 141, 143, 161, 187-188.

M

Mandela, Nelson, 40.
Manifest destiny, xx, 42, 71, 116, 120, 143.
Manning, Leroy, xv.
Manumission, vi, vii, xiv, 104, 113, 130, 146.
Massachusetts Department of Correction, xxi.
Mississippi, xx, 11, 14-15, 22, 25-26. 33-34, 38-39, 41, 43, 72-76, 79, 81, 84-85, 87, 92, 95, 97-99, 101, 103-108, 113, 115-117, 126, 136, 143, 168, 187.
Mayflower, 1-2.
Mays, Willie, 34.
McAllister, James, xvii.
McDonald, Charles (2X), xvii, 69.
McGrath, John, 7.
McGrath, Kathleen, 155-158, 160, 162, 169-173, 176, 179.
MCI (Massachusetts Correctional Institution), xvii, 92.
Mean Machine (Last Poets, The), 87(n9).
Media resistance, 23-25.
Merchantile Journal, 23.
Miller, Jerome, 80, 84(n2).
Minkins, Shadrach, 16-17, 23(n18).

Mississippi Plan, 187-188.
Molasses, 3, 85.
Montgomery, Wayne, xv.
Moore, Robert (More Gas), xxi.
Morning Post, The, 23.
Morning Star, The, 20.
Morris, Robert, 11.
Muhammad, Donald, Minister, 40.

N

NAACP (National Association for the Advancement of Colored People), 36.
NAFTA (North American Free Trade Agreement), 94.
Native Americans, 1-2, 76, 83, 119.
Nell, William C., 11.
Nelson, Sam, xvii, 78.
Nelson, Walter, xv.
New Bedford Mercury, 23.
Newburyport Daily Herald, 23.
Nigger Hill, (See Beacon Hill), 17.
Noah, 13.
North American Review, 23.
North Central Correctional Institution, 22.
NPRA (National Prisoners Reform Association), viii, xvii-xviii, xx, 7-8, 16, 18, 21-22, 25, 27-36, 45, 48-49, 58, 62-68, 75, 77-78, 81, 88, 89, 98, 103, 120-124, 128.

O

O'Brien, Marshall, xiv.
Old Colony Correctional Center, Bridgewater, 72, 90(n13), 101.
O'Neil, Thomas "Dapper," 37.
Owens, William, State Senator, 18.

P

Paladino, Pixie, 37.
Parker, Eliza, 19.

Parker, William, 15, 18-21.
Pardiseo, Lenny "The Coahog," xv.
Parole Board, 43(n5), 97-118, 136, 141-142, 153-163, 165-172.
Patrick, Duval, 10, 85
"Peaceful Movement," 26(n24), 65(n8).
Pedagogy of the Oppressed (See Freire, Paolo).
Pelletier, Ronald, xiv.
Penrose, Ronald, xvii, 69.
Phenix, Amy, 114.
PIAC (Walpole Prison Inmate Advisory Council), xxi, xxiii.
PIC (Prison-Industrial Complex), 14, 84, 87, 89-91, 94-96, 104(n4), 111, 113-114, 126.
Pickett, Roosevelt, xv.
Pierce, William, Captain, 2.
Pimental, George, xv.
Pina, James (Jimmy), 188.
Pina, Sebastian, xiv.
Pinckney, Alphonso, xvii.
Pinto, George, xv.
Plymouth Pilgrims, 1, 13, 36.
"Poem for Black Boys" (Giovanni), 82.
Pomerance, Andy, xv.
Preston, James, xiv.
Prison construction, 87-90.
Profiling, racial, 93.
PTSD (post-traumatic stress disorder), 22, 98(n1), 123.
Puritan, xix, 187.

R

Race hatred, ordinance, 107.
Racial Imbalance Bill, 35.
Racial profiling, 93.
Racism, v, vii, xx, 25, 98(n1), 33-41, 45, 72, 75, 100, 102, 105, 110, 117, 120, 123, 133, 142, 154.
Ralph, Michael "Mike," 65.
Reconstruction, 4, 6, 74-75, 145(n4).
Remond, Charles Lenox, 11.
Revere, Paul, 17.

Reddick, Mr., xiv.
Rich, Ray, xv.
Roache, Frank, Police Comm., 40.
Robuchaud, James, xv.
Robinson, Donald "Kela," xiv, xvii.
Robinson, Jackie, 34.
Rodman, Edward, Reverend, xvii, 35, 79, 88(n10).
Rodriguez, Hector, 22.
Rooney, Larry, 18, 21, 66.
Royce, Thomas, xv.
Royce, William, xiv.
Royster, David, xiv.
Rumer, Bruce, xv.
Rushing, Byron, 36.
Russell, Bill, 35(n1), 36-37.
Ruth, Babe, 34.
Ryan, Phyllis, 35.

S

Sanchez, Sonia, iii, 70.
Sandford, John, 69, 70-75, 81, 85, 125.
Sayre, Debra, 121.
Scipio, 13.
Scott, Dred, 69, 70-75, 81, 85, 125.
Selected Black Writer's Collection (Langston), 61.
Separatists, 1.
Sewall, Samuel, 11, 13-14.
Sherman, William T., General, 5.
Shitstem, 87, 95, 105, 119, 120, 124, 127-129.
Silver Shield Athletic Assoc., 39.
Simon, John K., 117.
Sims, Thomas, 23.
Slave Codes, 15, 85.
slavery, v, xix, 1-9, 11-13, 18, 20, 23-27, 31, 36, 43, 46, 48, 54, 57, 59, 70-75, 79-80, 84-86, 91, 96, 107, 112-114, 119-129.
 chattel, xix, 3, 6, 31, 48, 54, 59, 72, 79, 85-86, 119, 122, 128.
 institutional, 1, 4, 71, 84, 91,

112, 121.
    mental, xviii, 26, 48.
    runaway slave, xviii.
    "Slavery in Massachusetts" (Thoreau), 23.
Smith, Charles, xv.
Smith, "Cocaine Smitty," xv.
Smith, Roosevelt, xiv.
Societal turmoil, 46.
Sons of Liberty, 41.
SOTP (Sex Offender Treatment Program), 110, 111, 113, 115, 120, 156-159, 167.
Sousa, Jerry, xiv, 66.
Star, Kenny, xv.
Static-99," 114-117, 120, 158, 159.
Statistics,
    Black and Hispanic imprisonment, 79, 84.
    parole, 101-102, 108-109, 111.
    prison population, 83, 103.
    recidivism, 81.
Stokes, Ronald, xv.
Stowe, Harriet Beecher, 11, 13.
Stuart, Carol, 39-40, 74.
Stuart, Charles, 8, 39-40.
Stuart, Matthew, 40.
Subilowski, Joseph "The Pollack," xiv.
Sun-Ra, iii, 50-51.

T

Taney, Roger B., Chief Justice, 70, 73-74.
Tamileo, Henry, xv.
Thirteenth Amendment, 4-9, 71, 74, 85, 88, 107, 121, 187, 190.
Thomas, David, xv.
Thompson, Robert, xv.
Thoreau, Henry David, 11, 13, 23-24.
Thornton, David, 114.
Trinidad, Miguel, 31.
Truth, Sojourner, 12, 15.
Tubman, Harriet, 12, 15.

U

Uncle Tom's Cabin (Stowe), 13.
Underground Railroad, 11-21, 45, 61, 85.
United American Indians of New England, 41.
US Constitution, xxii, 4, 6, 8, 71, 73, 75, 85, 88, 121.

V

Vigilance Committee, The, 16-17.
Volpe, John, Governor, 35.

W

Walker, David, 11.
Walpole Prison, xxii-xxiv, 11, 15, 17-18, 21-32, 45, 49, 56-62, 66-67, 72, 74, 76-80, 83, 88, 98, 100, 120-123, 127, 134, 153, 166-168.
War on crime, 88-89, 93.
War on terror, 93.
Washington, "Giggie," xiv.
Washington, Richard, xv.
White, Bill, xv, 62-63.
White, Ed, xv, 59, 61-62, 68.
White, Jimmy, xv.
White niggers, 13.
"Whitey" Bulger, 143(n9).
White, Raymond, xvii.
White Citizens' Council [Citizens' Council of America], 198.
White supremacy, xx, 25, 29, 33-41, 71, 105, 120, 122, 128.
Wiggers. (See white niggers)
Williams, Darryl, 38.
Williams, Fred "Red," 22, 29, 121.
Williams, John A., vii.
Williams, Larry, xiv.
Williams, Samuel, 19.
"Willie Lynch Letter," vii,
Winter Hill Gang, 143(n9).

World Bank, 87, 90, 94.
World Trade Organization, 90, 94.
World War II, 5, 47, 84, 119.

Y

Yarmouth Register, 23.
Yawkey, Tom, 34.
Young, Andrew, 48.
"Young Fathers" Program. (See "Big Brother" Program), 80.

Z

Zulu, Dini, 98.

ABOUT THE AUTHOR

Ralph C Hamm III

Ralph, born in 1950, is serving a non-capital first offense life sentence for "intent," stemming from a criminal episode that occurred in 1968—when he was seventeen years old. During his decades of imprisonment he has aided in spearheading Massachusetts' prison reform movement, has earned degrees in liberal arts, divinity, metaphysics, and paralegal; as well as developed into a published poet, playwright, musician, and artist. In 2007 he was acknowledged as a contributor to the book, *When the Prisoners Ran Walpole* by Jamie Bissonette; and is author of *Manumission: The Liberated Consciousness of a Prison(er) Abolitionist* (First Edition). Recently *The Tinderbox* (2013) and *Dear Stranger / The Wayfarer* (New Edition: 2014), *Blackberry Juice* (New Edition: 2015), were published by Little Red Cell Publishing, New London, CT.

www.ingramcontent.com/pod-product-compliance
Lightning Source LLC
LaVergne TN
LVHW051828080426
835512LV00018B/2773